French Music *for* Low Brass Instruments

French Music *for* Low Brass Instruments

AN ANNOTATED BIBLIOGRAPHY

J. MARK THOMPSON
JEFFREY JON LEMKE

INDIANA UNIVERSITY PRESS
Bloomington and Indianapolis

The paper used in this publication meets the minimum requirements of American National Standard for Information Sciences—Permanence of Paper for Printed Library Materials, ANSI Z39.48-1984.

Manufactured in the United States of America

Library of Congress Cataloging-in-Publication Data

Thompson, J. Mark (John Mark)
French music for low brass instruments : an annotated bibliography / J. Mark Thompson, Jeffrey Jon Lemke.
p. cm.
Discography: p.
Includes bibliographical references (p.) and index.
ISBN 0-253-35993-7 (cloth)
1. Brass instrument music—Bibliography. 2. Music—France—Bibliography. 3. Brass instruments—Instruction and study—Bibliography. I. Lemke, Jeffrey Jon. II. Title.
ML128.B73T47 1994
016.7889'0944—dc20

1 2 3 4 5 00 99 98 97 96 95 94

Contents

Foreword by R. Winston Morris vii

Foreword by M. Dee Stewart ix

Abbreviations xi

1. Introduction 1

    Purpose 1
    Limitations 1
    Historical Background 1
    Terminology 2
    Method 3

2. System of Annotation 6

    Descriptive and Dedicatory Information 6
    Analytical Information 11
    General Comments 11
    Sample Entry 12

3. Tenor Trombone: Solos 14

4. Tenor Trombone: Pedagogical Materials 55

5. Bass Trombone, Tuba, and Bass Saxhorn: Solos 77

6. Bass Trombone, Tuba, and Bass Saxhorn: Pedagogical Materials 133

Appendixes

A. Publishers' Codes and Addresses 148

B. Discography 152

C. Listing of Solos by Title 165

Bibliography 175

Foreword by R. Winston Morris

Low brass instrumentalists everywhere owe a huge debt of gratitude to Mark Thompson and Jeff Lemke for their work on this publication. French literature for "low brass" has certainly been one of the great mysteries, at least among American brass artists and teachers, of brass literature. *French Music for Low Brass Instruments* answers many questions that have confounded non-French musicians for decades. Perhaps the confusion has not existed to such a great extent among trombonists as it has among tubists. There is virtually no discernible difference between tenor trombones internationally. There is slightly more variation among bass trombones, but from the tubists' perspective any difference is negligible.

Clifford Bevan in his definitive *The Tuba Family* (Faber and Faber, now out of print) lists approximately six hundred different instruments that belong to the "valved bugle-horn" category of instruments. (See Appendix C, pages 218-234.) This is nothing less than an organological nightmare. These instruments, generically referred to these days as "tuba," represent everything from instruments pitched in "C" (Ut)(one whole step above the B♭ euphonium) to the subcontrabass tuba in BBB♭; anywhere from three to seven (Bimbonifono) valves (piston, rotary, or a combination); and every conceivably shaped instrument from the euphonium-looking French tuba to the helicon/sousaphone configuration. In other words, "tuba" has so many possible connotations internationally and historically as to render the word almost meaningless. With the exception of French-speaking countries, the word "tuba" these days implies a three- to five- (sometimes six-) valved bell-up instrument pitched in F, E♭, CC, or BB♭.

Therefore, music composed for "trombone" should basically be fairly specific. But music composed for "tuba" means what? Music for an instrument the size of a euphonium? Music in bass clef or treble clef? Music that is in concert pitch or transposed? Etc.? Surely no other instrument has to deal with the nomenclatorial problems of the tuba. Thus is the basis of the "mystery," for Americans at any rate, of French music for tuba. It has only been in the past two decades or so that French tubists have begun to accept the larger instruments. One must make an assumption, therefore, that virtually all the music designated as published for "tuba" referred to in Chapters 5 and 6 of this book, was intended for the small "French tuba." This instrument is/was available with up to six valves, thusly accommodating a fairly extensive low register as well as a strong high register due to the pitch of the instrument. The French "Tuba en Ut" is pitched in "C" (a whole step above the B♭ euphonium). This is obviously an octave higher than the much more commonly utilized CC (contrabass) tuba. Most of this music also has a part for the "Saxhorn basse Si♭." This is essentially a "euphonium" part.

At this point we can identify the most common error encountered in dealing with this music by American tubists. The "tuba in Ut" part is in concert pitch. The "saxhorn basse Si♭" is a bass clef transposed part. More than one American tuba student has gone to great lengths to learn a very difficult solo part (in Si♭) only to find that they are playing in a different key from the accompaniment! This writer has heard of performances that were done in this manner. A careful reading of the annotations for the solos in Chapter 5 will indicate that virtually none of this music is bitonal! Always utilize the part in "C" (Tuba en Ut) unless one really knows what one is doing.

Other problems relating to this music are not quite as simple to accommodate. There is the obvious range and tessitura problem for the larger tubas. This music, after all, was conceived for an instrument a fifth to an octave higher than that which most American tubists use. The range for all the solo material is given and each individual player can readily eliminate those pieces that exceed what they might consider a "comfortable" range. Some of this literature has been published in editions with the entire "tuba" part taken down one octave (the Barat *Introduction and Dance,* for example). Other pieces can certainly be adapted if necessary for use on the bigger horns. Generally speaking, "as is," this music has very limited potential for use by most American tuba students. If there is a particular piece that holds great interest, however, the means for facilitating a performance can usually be found.

It is important for the tubist to remember that the annotations were written from the perspective of the trombonist. Due to tessitura and range considerations, a solo that might be considered level 3 or 4 on bass trombone, depending on the key of the tuba, might well be considered 5, 6, or 7 on tuba.

Perhaps one of the more important considerations necessary when evaluating the appropriateness of this literature for the larger instruments is the mass of sound that the composer envisioned. This is the "Bydlo problem." The famous "tuba" solo from the Mussorgsky/Ravel *Pictures at an Exhibition* was intended for the small French tuba. Is it appropriate to perform this "solo" on the larger tuba simply because the player is capable of squeezing (usually) out the notes? This "problem" is much more important taken within the context of orchestral or chamber performance than it is when considering solo literature. Tubists are famous (infamous!) for performing anything because they are so desperate for viable literature.

Thus the main value of this publication to the tubist is that it further identifies and explores a large body of previously unexplored, potentially useful literature.

Actually life would be much simpler if we eliminated all these "trombones" and "tubas," and everyone started playing on six-valved small-bore superbone subcontrabass cimbassos.

Foreword by M. Dee Stewart

Although the quantity of music for low brass performance and pedagogy is not voluminous, it has been difficult for the student or teacher to gain sufficient information regarding individual works to make qualified judgments as to their appropriate value for projects at hand. Few attempts at cataloging and annotating this material have been made. As a teacher and performer of both slide and valve instruments in the low brass family, I am painfully aware of the consternation that this void has caused.

Further, it may be stated that the use of French literature in this genre has not been as extensive as might be imagined from the amount of such writings. This neglect may be due to the difficulty in effectively selecting appropriate music when knowledge is limited to the title and composer.

J. Mark Thompson and Jeffrey Jon Lemke have presented the entire low brass community with an outstanding solution to these predicaments. *French Music for Low Brass Instruments: An Annotated Bibliography* presents to the performer and pedagogue all the information necessary to make knowledgeable decisions regarding the selection and study of works for presentation in the studio and/or on the stage. Encompassing literature from the beginner to the professional levels, the document is assembled in a scholarly manner and yet is very accessible to the casual student. The appendices offer unexpected and valuable references in the "Discography" and the "Listing of Solos by Title." The latter even has a quick method to indicate the works with large ensemble accompaniments.

There must be little argument that this book represents a vital addition to the reference material available to the serious musician. It also represents a passion for study and organization by Drs. Thompson and Lemke. Existing as it does in their field of choice, they might call it a labor of love. Nonetheless, there is no doubt that the result clearly indicates their great care and concern.

Speaking for those of us in the musical community, I can unreservedly state that we are very grateful and extremely appreciative for their contribution to our field.

J. Mark Thompson and Jeffrey Jon Lemke—we all say thank you!

Abbreviations

a	alto
acc	accompaniment
b	bass
bar	baritone
bn	bassoon
cb	contrabass
cbn	contrabassoon
cel	celesta
cl	clarinet
cor	cornet
db	double bass (contrabass viol)
eh	English horn
euph	euphonium
fl	flute
glock	glockenspiel
hn	horn
hp	harp
hpch	harpsichord
inst	instrument
ob	oboe
orch	orchestra
org	organ
perc	percussion
pf	piano
pic	piccolo
saxhn	saxhorn
saxphn	saxophone
strgs	strings
t	tenor
trbn	trombone
trpt	trumpet
tba	tuba
timp	timpani
va	viola
vc	violoncello
vib	vibraphone
vn	violin
xylo	xylophone

1
Introduction

Within the scope of the literature for low brass, the researcher quickly finds that there is a very limited selection of solo literature and pedagogical materials. A particularly noteworthy series of reference works began to emerge in 1963[1] in which prominent brass educators have attempted to keep teachers and students informed of what literature is available for their instruments. Some texts list solos by composer, title, and publisher;[2] others include a simple grading system,[3] an upper range stipulation,[4] or short annotation.[5] Only five texts provide extended annotations to include clefs, full range indications, duration, and additional information concerning mutes, mixed meter, and special performance techniques.[6] While many of these publications are useful, they say little about the French literature for tenor trombone, bass trombone, tuba, and bass saxhorn.

PURPOSE

It is the purpose of this text to present the low brass teacher and student with an evaluation of the body of existing French literature for tenor trombone, bass trombone, tuba, and bass saxhorn. Through the compilation of this bibliography, it is our desire to promote the use of more French solos and pedagogical materials by teachers and performers of low brass instruments.

LIMITATIONS

This study is primarily concerned with developments in low brass literature at the *Conservatoire National Supérieur de Musique de Paris* (hereafter called the Paris Conservatory) and other regional French conservatories. The musical material examined for this study includes French solos and pedagogical materials composed specifically for the tenor trombone, bass trombone, French tuba, or bass saxhorn. Examined works also contain pieces commissioned from non-French composers for use in the annual *concours* [contest] at the Paris Conservatory. Through techniques that will be discussed later, a comprehensive list of solo and study literature has been compiled. Out-of-print materials are listed because they might be found in school or private libraries, the International Trombone Association Resource Library, or occasionally in music stores that stock large inventories.

HISTORICAL BACKGROUND

The Paris Conservatory, the prototype for the modern conservatory, was specifically created at the end of the eighteenth century to raise the standards of French music. It has combined a conservative musical atmosphere, a faculty of artist-teachers, and rigorous requirements into a training program which has received international acclaim.

The trombone was taught there from 1795 until the Conservatory's reorganization in 1822. After a fourteen-year gap, Antoine-Guillaume Dieppo (1808-1878), the most celebrated trombonist of his time, became the first official teacher of trombone in 1836.

An essential part of the Conservatory's training program is the annual instrumental competition held for each instrument. The custom of using a particular work annually has been in practice for the trombone class at the Paris Conservatory since 1842.[7] Commissioned contest solos originated in 1897 with the *Solo de concert, No. 2* by Paul Vidal. Since then, more than fifty composers, most of whom received their training at the Conservatory and are among the most noted French musicians, have been commissioned to write tenor trombone solos as contest pieces.

Because of the efforts of Paul Bernard, the Paris Conservatory created an unofficial class for bass trombone, French tuba, and bass saxhorn in 1944, and it was later made official in 1955. About 1960, larger tubas in F' and C' began to become the standard orchestral instruments in France, but the regulations of the Conservatory still required tubists to perform on the *petit tuba français* [small French tuba].[8] The result has been the development of a large body of solo literature for the smaller tubas, but little for the larger ones; this literature, hence, is often very suitable for bass trombone and euphonium.

TERMINOLOGY

The use of the term *tenor trombone*, when referred to in this text, exclusively identifies a slide trombone pitched with a fundamental of B♭' (9') without any valves. When the generic term *trombone* is used, then it is assumed that the discussion is appropriate for both tenor and bass trombones.

The term *bass trombone* refers to a large-bore slide trombone pitched with a fundamental of B♭' (9') with a bore size of 0.547" (usually associated with the orchestral tenor) to 0.562" and a bell diameter from 9" to 10.5". A thumb-operated valve lowers the instrument's fundamental to F' (12'), and a second valve, when present, can further lower the pitch. The second valve is operated either by the thumb or by the middle and fourth fingers of the left hand, and it can be found in dependent (those always requiring the use of the first valve) or independent (when either valve can be used by itself or both valves simultaneously) configurations. Tunings of the second valve are so varied that a thorough discussion here is impracticable since no standardized configuration has yet been developed.[9] This instrument is also referred to as a *tenor-bass trombone.*

In this book, the terms *tuba* and *French tuba* both refer to the *petit tuba français en ut*. It was developed to perform virtually any orchestral tuba part and the older ophecleide parts. Since it is pitched with a fundamental of C Great (one whole tone higher than the modern euphonium), French composers have been afforded the opportunity to write very high passages for tuba without hesitation.[10] This tuba uses three upright valves and three side valves. The first valve lowers the pitch one whole tone; the second, a semitone; the third, a major third;[11] and the fourth, a perfect fourth. The fifth valve, also known as a *transpositeur*, lowers the pitch a semitone, and it is used to simplify difficult passages. The sixth valve lowers the pitch a perfect fifth. This instrument remained popular in French orchestras from 1892 until the mid-1960s, although French conservatories still required students to perform almost exclusively on the small tuba until the early 1980s.[12]

The term *bass saxhorn* refers to the *saxhorn-basse en si♭*. In 1843, Adolphe Sax took out patents on a homogenous family of valved brass instruments of which this is one member. Their bore was narrower than other conical brass instruments, and all models had an upright bell with the leadpipe extending horizontally.[13] The bass saxhorn usually contains three upright valves and one or two side valves; they are tuned in the same manner as the corresponding valves on the French tuba. The bore diameter and taper of modern saxhorns differ from the original, and in many ways they resemble the proportions of the Flügelhorn; this among other reasons has contributed to the hopeless confusion in their true identification. The fundamental of the bass saxhorn is B♭', although some models are built a whole tone higher with a fundamental of C Great.[14]

Because of the similarities in the ranges of the bass trombone, tuba, and bass saxhorn, many composers felt that their compositions could be played equally well on any one of the three instruments.[15] While the French tuba and bass saxhorn can generally accommodate more technical passages with greater facility, compositions that exploit this particular facet can usually be adapted for the bass trombone.

METHOD

The core of this text comes from the combination of our two doctoral dissertations.

Lemke, Jeffrey Jon. "French Tenor Trombone Solo Literature and Pedagogy since 1836." D.M.A. diss., The University of Arizona, 1983.

Thompson, John Mark. "An Annotated Bibliography of French Literature for Bass Trombone, Tuba, and Bass Saxhorn Including Solos and Pedagogical Materials." D.M.A. diss., The University of Iowa, 1991.

The collection of materials for this text has been a continual process since the work on our dissertations. A thorough search of French solo and pedagogical editions for all low brass instruments was undertaken through the use of publishers' catalogs, music periodicals, and literature listings in books concerning the trombone, euphonium, and tuba. Correspondence was also conducted with publishers in an effort to learn of recent publications that might be pertinent to this topic.

After the extensive search to explore this literature was concluded, a comprehensive list of solos and study materials was compiled and alphabetized by composer. The annotated chapters of the essay specify the nature and extent of each composition or publication. Since the development of this music is essentially bipartite (the first contest solo for tenor trombone was written over one hundred years prior to the first for bass trombone, tuba, or bass saxhorn), these instruments will be discussed separately with each group having a chapter for solos and a chapter for pedagogical materials.

A list of publishers' codes and addresses appears in Appendix A; this serves as the source for the abbreviated names of publishers used in the annotations and provides a current list of publishers' addresses as of this writing. An extensive discography appears in Appendix B; this serves as the source for the record codes used in the annotations. A cross-reference list of the solos was created and alphabetized by title; this information is inserted in Appendix C. Composers of specific works can then be identified should only the title be available; this format is helpful in identifying works of a similar genre (sonatines, fantaisies concertantes, etc.). Finally, this appendix also serves as a quick reference to solos with orchestral accompaniment.

The method of annotation for each work employs three sections. Descriptive and dedicatory information that is discussed in the first section is as follows: composer, title, publisher, publishing date, duration, range, degree of difficulty, clefs used, special performance techniques, recordings, and dedication. The second section focuses on specific analytical features of the work: style, meter, tempo indication, number of measures within a section or movement, duration of a section or movement, and total measures. The author's comments are contained in the third section, addressing any facts or observations not previously discussed. These include listings of instrumentations for works originally composed with ensemble accompaniment, when that information is available; it also includes the dates for which a piece was used as a *concours* solo of the Paris Conservatory, when known.

Notes

1. Edward Kleinhammer, *The Art of Trombone Playing* (Evanston, IL: Summy-Birchard Company, 1963).

2. Paul G. Anderson and Larry Bruce Campbell, comps. *Brass Music Guide: Solo and Study Material in Print*, 1985 ed., Music Guide Series, no. 4. (Northfield, IL: The Instrumentalist Company, 1984); Robin Gregory, *The Trombone: The Instrument and Its Music*, (New York: Praeger Publishers, Inc., 1973), 165-299; and Denis Wick, *Trombone Technique*, rev. ed. (London: Oxford University Press, 1980), 115-25.

3. Leon F. Brown, *Handbook of Selected Literature for the Study of Trombone at the University-College Level* (Denton, TX: Leon F. Brown, 1972); and John R. Griffiths, *The Low Brass Guide* (Hackensack, NJ: Jerona Music Corporation, 1980), 63-71.

4. Mary H. Rasmussen, *A Teacher's Guide to the Literature of Brass Instruments* (Durham, NH: Appleyard Publications, 1968), 54-60, 69-71, 100-104.

5. Kleinhammer, 107; and Herbert L. Koerselman, "A Comprehensive Performance Project in Trumpet Literature with an Annotated Bibliography of Brass Study Materials Which Deal with Performance Problems Encountered in Contemporary Music" (D.M.A. diss., The University of Iowa, 1976).

6. Thomas G. Everett, *Annotated Guide to Bass Trombone Literature*, 3d ed. (Nashville: The Brass Press, 1985); Harry J. Arling, *Trombone Chamber Music: An Annotated Bibliography*, 2d ed., Brass Research Series, ed. Stephen L. Glover, no. 8. (Nashville: The Brass Press, 1983); Vern Kagarice, *Annotated Guide to Trombone Solos with Band and Orchestra* (Lebanon, IN: Studio P/R, Inc., 1974); Vern Kagarice, et al, *Solos for the Student Trombonist*, International Trombone Association Series, no. 8. (Nashville: The Brass Press, 1979); and Jeffrey J. Lemke, "French Tenor Trombone Solo Literature and Pedagogy Since 1836" (D.M.A. diss., The University of Arizona, 1983).

7. Constant Pierre, *Le Conservatoire National de Musique et de Déclamation; Documents Historiques et Administratifs Recueillis ou Reconstitues Par Constant Pierre* (Paris: Imprimerie National, 1900), 652.

8. Joseph Vaillant, "The Evolution of the Tuba in France," *T.U.B.A. Journal* 5, no.3 (Spring/Summer 1978): 18; and Fernand Lelong and Robert Coutet, "Le tuba en France," *Brass Bulletin—International Brass Chronicle*, no. 13 (1976): 34-35.

9. The current trend seems to indicate the popularity of a B♭/F/D tuning for dependent systems and B♭/F/G♭/D for independent systems, although there is much variation still found.

10. Clifford Bevan, *The Tuba Family* (London: Faber and Faber, 1978), 154-56.

11. In other countries where similar instruments are found (e.g., Germany, England, and America), the third valve lowers the pitch a *minor* third.

12. Philip Bate, "Saxhorn," in *The New Grove Dictionary of Musical Instruments*, ed. Stanley Sadie (New York: Grove's Dictionaries of Music, 1984); and Melvin Culbertson, interview by author, 11 November 1991, telephone conversation from Iowa City, Iowa to Leognan, France.

13. Bate, "Saxhorn"; and Willi Apel, ed., Harvard Dictionary of Music, 2d ed. (Cambridge, MA: The Belknap Press of Harvard University Press, 1977), s.v. "Brass Instruments."

14. The saxhorn family is a direct predecessor of many modern brass instruments including the alto horn, baritone, and euphonium. The use of saxhorns in France is similar to the use of the latter instruments in other countries in that they are primarily used in military and community bands.

15. Euphoniums also share the same playing range, and their performers should equally benefit from this body of literature. In a telephone interview (11 November 1991) with Melvin Culberston, currently Professor of Tuba at the *CNSM de Lyon*, he stated that euphonium players are now being admitted to the Paris and Lyon Conservatories, and that separate prizes are being awarded for each of the three categories of *Saxhorn/Tenor Tuba* (Euphonium), *Tuba-basse* [F Tuba], and *Tuba-contrebasse* [C' Tuba].

2
System of Annotation

This book presents the published solos and pedagogical materials for all low brass instruments written by French composers or those written by composers of other countries specifically for use as a Contest Solo of the Paris Conservatory or other regional French conservatories, or as pedagogical materials for the same. When this project was begun, there was little information available to the performer or teacher about French music for low brass. Because of a general lack of knowledge about this literature, performers and teachers may have been reluctant to order these materials sight unseen. Cost is also a serious factor in the procurement of these foreign editions, because they are generally much more expensive than American editions. As a result, much of this repertoire may have been excluded from the low brass player's library because of such practical matters.

The discussion of each work is presented in three main sections. The first section contains information of a descriptive and dedicatory nature. The second section contains analytical information; this section will be omitted when discussing pedagogical materials. The third section is used for general comments concerning the particular work. To avoid unnecessary redundancy of category headers, a system was devised to unify the presentation of information pertaining to each work. The following outline provides a detailed description of the discussion points with an explanation of each item covered in the main sections.

DESCRIPTIVE AND DEDICATORY INFORMATION

When certain items discussed below are not addressed by a particular work, their presentation will be omitted from the annotation (e.g., if a work does not utilize a mute, no mention will be made).

1. Composer: Gives the composer's name. The composer's dates will be included in parentheses when known.

2. Title: Gives the complete title of the work with opus number and any subtitles. Translations are given for works with descriptive titles.

3. Editor: Gives the names of others responsible for the editing, arranging, adapting, or otherwise altering the work.

4. Publisher and publishing date: Gives the publisher of the work and the date of publication or copyright. The publishers' codes and addresses appear in Appendix A. In cases when no publication date is found, an indication of "n.d." (for "no date") is given.

5. Total measures: Used to show the total number of measures within the entire work.

6. Duration: Gives the approximate length of time, in minutes and seconds, required to perform the work. Although the works have been timed using indicated metronome markings and observing all repeat signs, timings should be considered approximate. No time has been added for pauses between movements of multi-movement works. When the publisher indicates a duration, it will appear in parenthesis.

7. Range: Gives the following pitch designation currently used in the *The New Harvard Dictionary of Music*, in which middle C is designated c'.[1] This section is only concerned with the lowest and highest pitches in the work and not the tessitura. Notes in parentheses indicate optional low or high notes written by the composer.

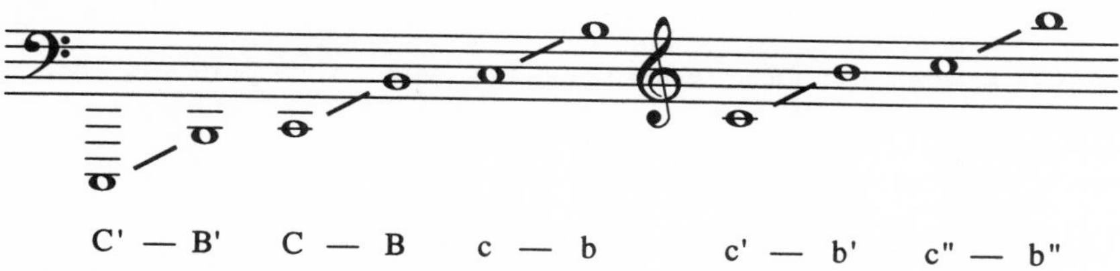

8. Degree of difficulty: This space contains the assigned grade level for the solo part. The grading system used throughout is the European method of assigning difficulty levels. It is as follows:

Easy *(facile)*	Degrees 1-3
Intermediate *(moyen)*	Degrees 4-6
Difficult *(difficile)*	Degrees 7-9

Breakdown by American School Levels

Elementary	Degrees 1-2
Junior High	Degrees 2-3
Senior High	Degrees 3-6
College/Conservatory	Degrees 6-8
Professional/Virtuoso	Degree 9

In recent years, some music in the "Easy" level (Degrees 1-3) has been identified by a different system:

Degree 1	Débutant
Degree 2	Préparatoire
Degree 3	Élémentaire

Each new designation may be further broken into two parts. The pieces that use this system will use a letter and number (if included) to identify its degree of difficulty (e.g., if a piece is graded as "Préparatoire level 2," it will be identified with "P2").

9. Clefs used: Gives a one-letter abbreviation for each clef used.

G — treble (or "G") clef
A — alto clef [rarely used]
T — tenor clef
B — bass clef

While bass saxhorn parts utilize these clefs, they are usually written in a transposed part in B♭ bass clef and sound a major second lower than written.

10. Special performance techniques: Gives a listing of the performance techniques encountered in the piece of a difficult or unusual nature. Included within this section will be indications of a cadenza employed within the solo. Because of a great number of performance techniques associated with modern music, a listing of the techniques found in the works annotated in this document should facilitate the understanding of not only the various terms used but also the performance of these works. They are used by composers to achieve new colors and textures which otherwise would not be possible. An alphabetical listing of the performance techniques of an unusual nature that may be found in the works represented in this study follows.

a. Beam extended from note head (●▬▬▬): Used to show that the pitch indicated by the location of the note head is sustained for the length of the beam. Normally used in proportional notation and timed events.

b. Feathered beaming (♩♩♩♩♩♩♩♩): Used to graphically indicate a gradual change from one rhythmic value to another. Normally used in proportional notation and timed events.

c. Free passages:

(1) A piacere: An indication for the performer to interpret the given passage with his own discretion, with particular regard to tempo and use of rubato.[2]

(2) Cadenza: An "ornamental passage performed by the soloist," usually virtuosic in character.[3]

(3) Quasi cadenza: A passage to be interpreted like a cadenza, but may be in a strict meter and/or with an accompaniment.

(4) Unaccompanied: Any passage not appropriately designated by one of the previous categories but still having no accompaniment. The passage may or may not be in a strict meter.

d. Glissando: Moving from one pitch to another through all the intermediate slide positions without an articulated interruption. The glissando is a simple and effective maneuver on the trombone, provided the pitches involved are within the same partial and slide direction. If not, however, they may be approximated by two or more separate slide movements. While "portamento" is the correct term for this effect, "glissando" is in more common usage.[4]

e. Half valve: An effect produced by engaging one or more valves only half the distance of their full stroke. The resultant sound is an amplified buzzing of the lips, and it can be controlled to produce discreet pitches, if necessary.

f. Meters:

(1) Complex: Any of a number of metric indications in which the main subdivision alternates between two and three within the same measure (e.g., in $\frac{7}{8}$ time, the eighth notes could be grouped as 2+2+3, 2+3+2, or 3+2+2). In general, this technique will not be mentioned unless there is a substantial amount of these meters.

(2) Non-standard meter indication: Any of several ways to indicate a time signature that is a variation of a more common style. The time signature $\frac{4}{4}$ (or C) could be represented by "4," "4♩," by no indication whatsoever, or otherwise.

(3) Proportional notation: Any notation that specifies the time required to perform a line or section of music with respect to the relative durations of the notes. In many cases, all notes exist only as heads with a solid line following it to indicate relative duration. Rests are usually indicated by a blank space.

(4) Timed events: An abbreviated form of proportional notation which defines the duration of a bracketed section of music. The performer must adjust to accommodate all the notes in the bracket within the allotted time, paying respect to the relative durations of the notes.

(5) Unmetered: Any measure that does not contain a discernible time signature, whether actual or implied.

g. Multiphonics (more properly termed "simultaneous chords"): The simultaneous production of two or more tones by playing one pitch and singing another. Two pitches may be heard easily, and often three or four pitches will result from certain intervals correctly tuned to produce the different tones.[5] In this book, all examples require the performer to sing above the played note, although it is possible to sing a note lower than the one being played.

h. Tonguing:

(1) Multiple:

(a) Double: A technique which allows wind instrument performers to play rapid notes with duple divisions (*t-k, t-k...* or other variant).[6]

(b) Triple: A technique which allows wind instrument performers to play rapid notes with triple divisions (*t-t-k, t-t-k... ; t-k-t, t-k-t... ;* or other variant).[7]

(2) Flutter tongue: A rough, growling sound produced by a movement of the tongue, not unlike the rolled "r" in Spanish, as the tone is sustained.[8]

i. Mutes:

(1) Straight: Any of a number of cone-shaped mutes fitting in the bell of the instrument. These usually are made of metal, wood, or cardboard (fiber), and each can produce its own characteristic sound. Metal mutes produce a nasal, penetrating tone; wooden and cardboard mutes produce a more subdued or "dry" sound.

(2) Cup: A mute in the form of a cone that fits in the bell of an instrument that has a cup or bowl attached to the end. The tone is devoid of many of the higher partials, and therefore is quite muffled.

(3) Plunger: A mute that highly resembles the rubber portion of a common toilet plunger. The mute is manipulated by the left hand of the performer over the bell of the instrument to achieve special effects.

j. Ornaments: Because appogiaturas, grace notes, and mordents are used so frequently, each case of their use will not be identified. Other standard ornaments have been omitted because, in this body of literature, they are generally written out in lieu of the use of their corresponding symbol.

(1) Lip trills: Trills played solely with the lip between two closest harmonics in the same slide position.[9]

(2) Trill: "A musical ornament consisting of the rapid alternation of a given note with the diatonic second above it."[10]

k. Tunings:

(1) Approximate pitch (also called "indeterminate pitch"): Pitches that are approximate, or are close to regular pitches and are usually notated with an "x" or similar mark on the staff.[11]

(2) Random pitch selection: Playing pitches at random, either from a set of given pitches or any pitches of the performer's choice.

(3) Quarter tones: "An interval equal to half of a semitone."[12]

11. Recording(s): This space identifies commercial recordings of the work. The numbers correspond to those found in the discography (Appendix B).

12. Instrumentation: This space will identify the instrument(s) for which the piece was originally intended. Instruments will appear in the order presented in the composition. If composed for more than one solo instrument or form of accompaniment, those items will be separated by a slash (/); the solo instrument will be separated from the accompanying instrument(s) by a comma (e.g., a solo written for bass trombone, tuba, or bass saxhorn with the accompaniment being either a piano or an orchestra will appear as "b trbn/tba/b saxhn, pf/orch"). In Chapter 3, "Tenor Trombone: Solos," the instrumentation is assumed as being for trombone and piano unless otherwise indicated.

13. Dedication: This space is for indicating to whom the work was dedicated and/or for whom or what purpose the work was commissioned. The dedications have been included, when present, as a possible means of identifying the general purpose of the solo. They have not been translated.

ANALYTICAL INFORMATION

1. Style: Used to indicate what style(s) are used in a given composition; if there is more than one style in a movement or if the work is one continuous movement, this will describe the various styles therein. This will identify the use of such terms as andante, largo, allegro, etc.

2. Meter: Indicates the meters used within the work, listed from smallest units of measurement to largest (i.e., eighths, quarters, halves, etc.). If there is a cadenza measure, it will be indicated as "cad." Unmetered and proportional sections will be indicated by "n.m." (for "no meter").

3. Tempo indication: Shows the metronome markings of the composer, when noted. The symbol "≈" (meaning "nearly equal to") will be used to show all approximations in tempo given by the composer; these can include markings such as "*env. (environ),*" "±," and "approx." However, if a composer specifies a range of tempos, those limits will be shown.

4. Measures: Used to show the number of measures contained within each section or movement of the work . An (R) indicates that the measures are repeated; with (2R), the measures are repeated twice (i.e., played three times). If, in a work, only some of the measures are repeated, this will be noted in the "General Comments" section indicating the number of repeated measures.

GENERAL COMMENTS

This space is for the author's comments concerning the difficulty of the work and any facets or observations not covered in other discussions. For example, many of the published transcriptions for bass trombone and piano were originally composed with orchestral or band accompaniment. The annotation includes a listing of the instrumentation of the band or orchestra scores in the cases when that information was available. When a dagger (†) precedes a composer's name, it indicates this was one of the Contest Solos of the Paris Conservatory. The dates for which it was used will be indicated within this section.

SAMPLE ENTRY

To illustrate the manner in which solos will be listed, the following example is presented.

Composer (birth and death dates, when known)
Castérède, Jacques (b. 1926)

Title
Fantaisie concertante (contest solo)

Publisher and Publishing Date
Alphonse Leduc, 1960

Duration
7 min. 5 sec. (publisher indicates 7 min. 30 sec.)

Range
B'-a'

Degree of Difficulty
8 (assigned by the publisher)

Clefs Used
bass (omitted if the entire work is in bass clef)

Special Performance Techniques
cadenza, complex meters

Recordings
yes (nos. 18, 56, and 67 in Appendix B)

Instrumentation
bass trombone or tuba or bass saxhorn and piano

This data, combined with the work's analytical information, will appear as follows:

†**Castérède, Jacques** (b. 1926). *Fantaisie concertante.* LED, 1960. 211 meas.; 7'5" (7'30"); B'-a'; 8*; cadenza, complex meters. Recordings: 18, 56, 67. b trbn/tba/b saxhn, pf

"à Paul Bernard, Professeur au Conservatoire National Supérieur de Musique"

Allegro ma non troppo: $\frac{3}{8}, \frac{4}{8}, \frac{5}{8}, \frac{6}{8}, \frac{7}{8}, \frac{2}{4}, \frac{3}{4}, \frac{4}{4}$: ♩ = 104: 57 meas.: 1'50"

Più mosso: $\frac{5}{8}, \frac{8}{8}, \frac{3}{4}$: ♪ = triplet ♪ from previous tempo [♩ = 156]: 69 meas.: 2'15"

Calme e sostenuto: $\frac{6}{8}, \frac{9}{8}, \frac{2}{4}, \frac{3}{4}, \frac{4}{4}, \frac{3}{2}$: ♩. = 66 (♪ constant): 42 meas.: 1'35"

a Tempo I°: $\frac{2}{4}, \frac{4}{4}$: ♩ = 104: 8 meas.: 15"

Più mosso: $\frac{3}{8}, \frac{5}{8}, \frac{6}{8}, \frac{7}{8}, \frac{8}{8}, \frac{9}{8}, \frac{2}{4}, \frac{3}{4}, \frac{4}{4}$: ♩ = 112: 45 meas.: 1'10"

Notes

1. Don Michael Randel, ed., *The New Harvard Dictionary of Music*, rev. ed. of *Harvard Dictionary of Music*, 2d ed., ed. Willi Apel (Cambridge, MA: The Belknap Press of Harvard University Press, 1986), s.v. "Pitch names."
2. Ibid., s.v. "Piacere, a."
3. Ibid., s.v. "Cadenza."
4. Thomas E. Senff, "An Annotated Bibliography of the Unaccompanied Solo Repertoire for Trombone" (D.M.A. diss., University of Illinois (Champaign-Urbana), 1976), 8.
5. Ibid., 9.
6. Randel, s.v. "Tonguing."
7. Ibid.
8. Senff, 8.
9. Ibid., 9.
10. Apel, s.v. "Trill."
11. Senff, 7.
12. Randell, s.v. "Quarter tone."

3

Tenor Trombone: Solos

Amellér, André [Charles Gabriel] (b. 1912). *Belle province: Rivière du loup* [Beautiful Province: Wolf River]. LED, 1973. 2 '; A–c♭"; 3; TB.

"Cordialement à Claude Claquesin"

Marcato assai moderato: 3/4 : ♩ = 84: 46 meas.

——. *Bras d'acier* [Arm of Steel]. EDMT, 1982. A-f; 2.

——. *Kryptos: Étude* [Hidden: Study]. HIN, 1958. 137 meas.; 7'55"; G♭'(A♯'/B♭')–b'(c♯"); 8; TB; mute, unmetered sections. all trbns (t or b)/tba/b saxhn, pf

See entry in Chapter 5.

——. *Ohio.* BILL, 1977. 40 meas.; 1'20"; (B♭')F♯–g'; 2; TB.

Allegro moderato: 3/4 : ♩ = 126: 18 meas.
Andante espressivo: 3/4 : ♩ = 76: 22 meas.

——. *Olivet.* Éditions Philippo, 1977. 2'; F–f'; 2.

"Cordialement à Monsieur Roland Beaulieu"

Andante fieramente: 4/4 : ♩ = 80: 40 meas.

——. *Utah.* BILL, 1977. 40 meas.; 2'; G–f'; 1.

Moderato: 4/4 : ♩ = 92: 20 meas.
Calmo, con espressione: 4/4 : ♩ = 72: 8 meas.
Moderato: 4/4 : ♩ = 92: 12 meas.

Ancelin, Pierre. *La Harangue de Janotus* [Janotus's Speech]. BILL, 1983.

Arrieu, Claude (b. 1903). *Conte d'hiver* [Tale of Winter]. BILL, 1976. 1'; f–c♯"; 6; TB.

Allegretto: 3/4 : ♩ = 104: 32 meas.

†——. *Mouvements.* AM, 1966. 185 meas.; 7'30"; G–c"; 7; TB; quasi cadenza. Recording: 58.

"Gerard Pichaureau"

Andante: 2/4, 3/4, 4/4, 6/4 : ♩ = 56-60: 56 meas.
Allegro: ¢ : 𝅗𝅥 = 80: 32 meas.

Moderato: $\frac{2}{4}$, $\frac{3}{4}$, $\frac{5}{4}$: ♩ = 108: 32 meas.
Allegro: $\frac{2}{4}$, $\frac{3}{4}$, $\frac{4}{4}$: 𝅗𝅥 = 80: 65 meas.

This was the Paris Conservatory contest piece for 1966.

†**Aubain, Jean Marie** (b. 1928). *Aria, scherzo et finale.* LED, 1969. 307 meas.; 7'30"; B♭'–b'; 8*; TB.

"Gerard Pichaureau"

Aria: $\frac{3}{4}$, $\frac{4}{4}$: ♩ = 54: 35 meas.
Scherzo: $\frac{3}{4}$: 𝅗𝅥. = 80: 117 meas.
Finale: $\frac{8}{16}$, $\frac{9}{16}$, $\frac{11}{16}$, etc.: ♪ = 152: 155 meas.

This was the Paris Conservatory contest piece for 1969. The *Aria* is legato throughout, with some difficult intervals and sustained soft playing. It is harmonically, rhythmically and melodically very conservative for its time. The *Scherzo* is technically very difficult, including meter changes and a legato middle section. The *Finale* moves along with many meter changes, but is not as difficult as it may first appear.

Bach, Johann Sebastian (1685-1750). *Suites pour violoncelle seul.* Edited by Raymond Katarzynski. LED, 1977.

See entry in Chapter 4.

——. *Suites de J. S. Bach pour violoncelle seul.* Edited by André Lafosse. LED, 1946.

See entry in Chapter 4.

†**Bachelet, Alfred** (1864-1944). *Morceau de concours* [Contest Piece]. LED; INT, n.d. 163 meas.; 7'30"; G–c"; 6*; TB.

Andante moss: $\frac{4}{4}$: 75 meas.
Maestoso: $\frac{4}{4}$: 32 meas.
Tempo moderato: $\frac{2}{2}$: 56 meas.

This was the Paris Conservatory contest piece for 1901 and again in 1925.

†**Barat, Joseph Edouard** (1882-1963). *Andante et allegro.* LED; Cundy-Bettoney (FISC); INT; Arr. by Loren Marsteller, SOUT, 1964; Arr. by Forrest Buchtel, KJOS, 1967. 169 meas.; 8'; F–b♭'; 7*. Recordings: 16, 28, 30, 41, 43, 46.

"H. Couillaud, Professeur au Conservatoire"

Lent: $\frac{4}{4}$: ♩ = 52: 24 meas.
Tempo I, più vivo: $\frac{4}{4}$: ♩ = 72-76: 34 meas.
Allegro: $\frac{3}{4}$: ♩ = 144-152: 111 meas.

This was the Paris Conservatory contest piece for 1935 and again in 1940, and has since become an established solo in the trombone repertoire. Characterized by elegant harmonic and melodic writing, this piece has two main contrasting sections. The solo opens with a slow, cantabile section that gradually builds and becomes more complex. The calm section again appears to conclude the first part. The second section opens with a fanfare-like theme in total contrast to what has come before. Following this statement, a more lyrical style returns which intensifies and eventually leads back to a final statement of the fanfare-like theme, which concludes the piece.

This frequently performed solo is one of the better examples of nineteenth-century trombone writing in the repertoire. A band transcription of the accompaniment can be obtained from SOUT.

——. *Caprice médiéval.* Arr. by Jean Douay. BILL.

†——. *Pièce en mi bémol.* LED, 1923. 168 meas.; 6'; F–c♭"; 6*; TB. Recording: 7.

Lento: $\frac{3}{4}$: 24 meas.
Andante: $\frac{6}{8}$: 22 meas.
Allegro: $\frac{3}{4}$: 122 meas.

This was the Paris Conservatory contest piece for 1923 and again in 1929. This two-part composition is made up of a lento introduction, an andante section in e♭ minor, and a contrasting allegro in the parallel major. In the slow first section, the melodic and harmonic materials are chromatic and sonorous, with several subtle tempo changes. The second part of the piece shifts to a fast allegro, containing many eighth-note scale patterns. This piece is recommended for the trombonist who is developing a lyric style, as well as technical facility, but who lacks the endurance to perform a long piece. A band transcription of the accompaniment, made by Joe Berryman, can be obtained from the University of Southern Mississippi.

Barraine, Elsa (b. 1910). *Lamento.* GRAS, 1967. 1'30"; G♭'–a♭'; 5; TB.

"Collection 'Villa Medicis' Par Les Premiers Grands Prix de Rome de Musique"

Lent: $\frac{2}{4}$: 37 meas.

——. *Chiens de paille* [Straw Dogs]. JOB, 1966.

See entry in Chapter 5.

†**Baudo, Serge** (b. 1927). *Petite suite* [Little Suite]. SEL, 1953. Recording: 65.

This was the Paris Conservatory contest piece for 1953. It is currently out of print.

Baudrier, Emile. *Relax.* BILL, 1977. 2*.

Beethoven, Ludwig van (1770-1827). *Trio, Op. 20.* Edited by Paul Delisse. Millereau, *ca.* 1882.

†**Berghmans, José**. (b. 1921). *Concertino.* LED, 1954-55. 581 meas.; 13'30"; E–d"; 8*; TB; lip shakes, glissandi, cadenza. t trbn, orch/pf

Aria: $\frac{3}{8}$, $\frac{3}{4}$, $\frac{4}{4}$: ♩ = 60: 41 meas.
Allegro: $\frac{2}{2}$: 𝅗𝅥 = 96: 250 meas.
Vivace: $\frac{3}{8}$, $\frac{2}{4}$, $\frac{3}{4}$: ♩ = 132: 290 meas.

This was the Paris Conservatory contest piece for 1954. This solo is organized in three continuous movements, utilizing driving rhythmic figures and wide melodic leaps. The work begins with a section entitled *Aria,* set in a lyric, chant-like style. This leads to a rhythmically active *Allegro* section which makes use of lip shakes as part of the melodic coloration. The final section, marked *vivace,* is similar in rhythmic style and character to the middle section. Performance of the solo requires excellent range and control. The most difficult part of the solo is its high tessitura. The orchestral accompaniment parts are avallable on rental from LED. The instrumentation of the accompaniment is as follows: 2 fls, 2 obs, 2 cls, 2 bns, 2 hns, 2 trpts, 2 trbns, tba, 3 timp, perc, xylo, pf (obbligato), strgs.

†——. *La femme à barbe* [The Bearded Lady]. LED, 1958. 6'; A–a'; 6*; TB; cadenza. Recording: 60.

Lent: $\frac{3}{4}$, $\frac{4}{4}$
Allegretto: $\frac{5}{8}$, $\frac{2}{4}$, $\frac{3}{4}$, $\frac{4}{4}$
Tempo I: $\frac{4}{4}$

This solo is part of a collection of solos for various wind instruments entitled *Tabteaux forains* [Scenes From a Traveling Circus]. The parts of the complete suite are as follows:

I. Wrestlers (for horn in F)
II. The Tight-Rope Walker (for clarinet in B♭)
III. The Maze (for oboe)
IV. The Bearded Lady (for trombone)
V. The Sultan's Favorites (for flute)
VI. Performing Bears (for bassoon)
VII. The Caterpillar (for trumpet in C or B♭)

The one-movement work begins in a slow chant-like lyrical style. The middle section is in a stately, moderate tempo circus march, featuring a cadenza at its conclusion. This cadenza acts as a connecting link, and brings back the opening chant-like theme. The slow, smooth melody ends the solo quietly. Although quite conventional when compared to most twentieth-century works, it represents a style similar to that of Francis Poulenc. The orchestral accompaniment parts are available on rental from LED. The instrumentation of the accompaniment is as follows: 2 timp, 2 perc, strgs (min. 6-4-3-3-2).

†**Bernaud, Alain** (b. 1932). *Exponentielles.* Société Éditions Musicales Internationales, 1980. 170 meas.; 7'20"; G'–d"; 8; TB; straight and cup mutes, flutter tongue, glissandi.

"Gerard Pichaureau"

Recitativo, Tempo rubato: $\frac{11}{8}$, $\frac{13}{8}$, $\frac{4}{4}$, $\frac{5}{4}$, $\frac{3}{2}$: 𝅗𝅥 = 72: 24 meas.
Lent: $\frac{5}{8}$, $\frac{4}{4}$: ♩ = 66: 58 meas.
Tempo giusto deciso: $\frac{7}{16}$, $\frac{11}{16}$, $\frac{12}{16}$, $\frac{13}{16}$, $\frac{14}{16}$, $\frac{17}{16}$, $\frac{2}{4}$, $\frac{3}{4}$, $\frac{4}{4}$: ♩ =96: 68 meas.
Lent: $\frac{4}{4}$: ♩ = 66: 20 meas.

This was the Paris Conservatory contest piece for 1980. It contains many twentieth-century techniques, but it uses traditional notation.

Berthelot, René (b. 1903). *Le Roi Renaud, varitations* [King Reginald]. LED. 4*.

Bertholon, L. *Variétés*. LED. 6*.

Bessonet, Georges. *Andante dans un style classique*. BILL, 1981. 3.

———. *Comme un air d'opera* [Like an Opera Tune]. BILL, 1981. 3.

———. *Récitatif et petit allegro*. BILL, 1982. 2'30". 3.

†**Bigot, Eugène** (1888-1965). *Impromptu*. LED, 1927. 190 meas.; 4'30"; E–c"; 7-8*; TB. Recordings: 58, 63.

"André LaFosse"

Allegro/Recitative: ¢ : 𝅗𝅥 = 112: 16 meas.
Allegro agitato: ¢ : 𝅗𝅥 = 120: 82 meas.
Andante: $\frac{3}{4}$: ♩ = 66: 22 meas.
Allegro: $\frac{6}{8}$: ♩. = 120: 70 meas.

This was the Paris Conservatory contest piece for 1931, 1943, 1974, and 1982. The first section begins with two short recitativo passages for solo trombone with a homophonic accompaniment, followed by an allegro agitato section. The agitation occurs in the broken chord patterns of the piano, while the trombone plays a smooth, expressive melody made up of whole and half notes. The second section is a through-composed andante, also in a smooth, legato style. The third section consists of an articulated allegro section in $\frac{6}{8}$ meter, which provides the soloist with an area for technical display and a flashy ending. The orchestral accompaniment parts are available on rental from LED. The instrumentation of the accompaniment is as follows: 2 fls, 2 obs, 2 cls, 2 bns, 2 hns, 2 trpts, 2 timp, hp, strgs.

†———. *Variations*. LED, 1949. 239 meas.; 5'30"; F–d♭"; 7*; TB; straight mute, glissandi, trills.

"André LaFosse"

Cantabile: $\frac{4}{4}$: ♩ = 56: 25 meas.
Comodo: $\frac{2}{4}$: ♩ = 92: 41 meas.
Gracioso: $\frac{2}{4}$: ♩ = 80: 44 meas.
Scherzando: $\frac{3}{8}$: ♪ = 184: 52 meas.
Impetuoso: $\frac{6}{8}$, $\frac{2}{4}$: ♩. = 168: 77 meas.

This was the Paris Conservatory contest piece for 1949 and 1981.

†**Bitsch, Marcel** (b. 1921). *Ricercare*. LED, 1970. 220 meas.; 6'30"; E–b♭'; 8-9*; TB.

"Gerard Pichaureau"

Andante maestoso: $\frac{3}{4}$: ♩ = 54: 47 meas.
Allegro: $\frac{2}{4}$: ♩ = 104: 63 meas.
Vivo: $\frac{3}{8}$: ♩. = 112: 40 meas.
Allegro moderato: $\frac{3}{4}$: ♩ = 96: 70 meas.

This was the Paris Conservatory contest piece for 1970.

Bleger, Marcel. *Le rêve de Jeanne d'Arc* [Joan d'Arc's Dream]. René Margueritat, *ca.* 1900.

†**Bleuse, Marc** (b. 1937). *Acclamation concertino.* CHO, 1977. 84 meas.; 7'; A♭'–d♭"; 9; TB; Harmon mute, flutter tongue, glissandi, cadenza.

"Gerard Pichaureau"

Vivo: $\frac{2}{8}$, $\frac{3}{8}$, $\frac{4}{8}$, $\frac{5}{8}$: ♪ = 92: 20 meas.
Moins vite: $\frac{3}{4}$, $\frac{5}{4}$, $\frac{6}{4}$: ♩ = 80: 22 meas.
Tempo Primo: $\frac{2}{8}$, $\frac{3}{8}$, $\frac{4}{8}$, $\frac{5}{8}$: ♪ = 92: 28 meas.
Vivo: $\frac{5}{8}$ + $\frac{4}{8}$: ♪ = 192: 14 meas.

This was the Paris Conservatory contest piece for 1977.

Bon, André. *Canzone.* AM, 1977. Duration varies; G♯'–d♭"; 7; GTB; plunger, glissandi, trills, slide clicks.

This is one of a very few solos written by a French composer for unaccompanied trombone. It features many techniques which place it into an "avant garde" category. The notational system is proportional, although relative note values are used.

†**Bondon, Jacques** (b. 1927). *Chant et danse* [Song and Dance]. ESC, 1974. 115 meas.; 5'30"; E–d♭"; 7; TB; cadenza.

Adagio: $\frac{2}{4}$, $\frac{3}{4}$, $\frac{4}{4}$: ♩ = 58: 25 meas.

Allegro: $\frac{2}{4}$, $\frac{3}{4}$, $\frac{4}{4}$: ♩ = 116-118: 90 meas.

This was the Paris Conservatory contest piece for 1974.

†**Bonneau, Paul** (b. 1918). *Capriccio.* LED, 1946. 224 meas.; 8'; E–d♭"; 9*; TB; straight mute, cadenza, glissandi.

"H. Coulliaud, Professeur au Conservatoire National de Paris"

Modérément animé: $\frac{4}{4}$: ♩ = 126: 57 meas.
Mouvement de Blues: $\frac{3}{4}$, $\frac{4}{4}$: 54 meas.
Animé: $\frac{2}{4}$: ♩ = 132, ♩ = 120: 40 meas.
Légèrement plus vif: $\frac{2}{4}$: ♩ = 126: 28 meas.
Vif: $\frac{2}{4}$: ♩ = 138: cadenza: 11 meas.
Lent: $\frac{4}{4}$: ♩ = 60: 3 meas.
Vif: $\frac{2}{4}$: ♩ = 132-138: 31 meas.

This was the Paris Conservatory contest piece for 1946. It is a work typical of the French Impressionistic style common during the first half of the twentieth-century. This three-part, single-movement piece opens with a detached quick moving section. The middle section, entitled *Blues,* is a smooth slower section, with the soloist playing in a swinging manner, thus interpreting the notation as though it was a jazz tune. The final section returns back to the quick detached style of the beginning. The solo part requires a good command of the low and high register.

——. *Fantaisie concertante* [Concert Fantasy]. LED, 1950. 241 meas.; 5'30", B–c"; 7*; TB; Robinson mute, flutter tongue.

"H. Couillaud, Professeur au Conservatoire National de Paris"

Moderato: $\frac{2}{4}$, $\frac{3}{4}$: 94 meas.
Lento: $\frac{4}{4}$: 22 meas.
Marche: $\frac{2}{4}$, $\frac{3}{4}$: 45 meas.

Moderato: ¢ : 18 meas.
Allegro: 2/4 : 16 meas.
Vivace: 3/4 : 46 meas.

This solo utilizes chromatic materials, both melodically and harmonically, thus suggesting an influence from the Impressionistic era. The principal motive, an interval of a third, appears in the first bar of the solo as part of a fanfare-like introduction. Interspersed within the fast sections of this work are short legato or moderato sections. A Robinson mute is required during the lento section of the solo. This mute is similar in appearance and tone quality to a solo-tone mute. The fast section of the piece returns in a march-like style, utilizing flutter tongue, and this style prevails to the end of the solo. The orchestral accompaniment parts are available on rental from LED. The instrumentation of the accompaniment is as follows: 2 fls, 2, obs, 2 cls, 2 bns, a saxphn, 3 hns, 3 trpts, 3 trbns, tba, 4 timp, perc, cel, glock, vib, hp, strgs.

Bosseur, J. Y. *En quatre actes* [In 4 Acts]. Arr. by Jean Douay. BILL.

Boudry, G. *Je voulais vous dire* [I Want You to Speak]. Arr. Jean Douay. BILL.

Bouny, Jean-Pierre. *Chanson d'autrefois* [Bygone Song]. BILL, 1973. 54 meas.; 3'30"; c–f'; 2; cadenza.

"Prix de Composition de la Confédération Musicale de France"

Andante: 4/4 : ♩ = 60: 20 meas.
Andantino: 4/4 : ♩ = 69: 16 meas.
Andante: 4/4 : ♩ = 60: 18 meas.

†**Boutry, Roger** (b. 1932). *Capriccio*. LED, 1957. 297 meas.; 6'; B♭'–c♯"; 7*; TB; cadenza. Recording: 60.

"André LaFosse, Professeur au Conservatoire National de Musique"

Allegro: 5/8 : ♩. + ♩ = 50: 24 meas.
Andante: 2/4, 3/4, 4/4 : ♩ = 66-69: 37 meas.
Vivace: 2/4 : ♩ = 120-126: 16 meas.
Vivace: 3/8, 2/4, 3/4 : ♩ = 96-104: 114 meas.
Presto: 3/8 : ♩. = 104-108: 68 meas.
A Tempo: 3/8 : ♩. = 120-126: 38 meas.

This was the Paris Conservatory contest piece for 1957. It is very fragmented, both melodically and rhythmically. As might be expected, the player must be skilled in displaying lyrical playing, accuracy of articulation, possess a good range, and understand many varied rhythmic patterns.

——. *Choral varié* [Varied Chorale]. LED, 1956. 4-5*. Recording: 20.

†——. *Concerto*. LED, 1963. 175 meas.; 7'; B♭'–d♭"; 8*; TB.

"Gerard Pichaureau, Professor at the Conservatoire Supérieur de Musique"

Moderato: $\frac{4}{4}$: ♩ = 66: 20 meas.
Allegretto: $\frac{3}{4}$: ♩ = 72: 55 meas.
Adagio: $\frac{4}{4}$, $\frac{5}{4}$, $\frac{7}{4}$: ♩ = 56: 17 meas.
Presto: $\frac{8}{8}$: 𝅝 = 42-48: 83 meas.

The term concerto generally carries the implication of having an orchestral accompaniment. However, this piece was composed for trombone and piano, and no orchestral accompaniment exists.

This was the Paris Conservatory contest piece for 1963.

——. *Fantasia.* BILL, 1985.

——. *Trombonera.* LED, 1956. 6*.

†**Bozza, Eugène** [Joseph] (b. 1905). *Ballade, Op. 62.* LED, 1944. 137 meas.; 9'; F–d♭"; 7*; TB; straight mute, cadenza, glissandi. Recordings: 2, 11, 13, 64, 68, 72.

"H. Couillaud, Professeur au Conservatoire National de Paris"

Andantino ma non troppo: $\frac{3}{4}$, $\frac{4}{4}$: ♩ = 66: 56 meas.
Maestoso: $\frac{4}{4}$: 12 meas.
Dolce: $\frac{4}{4}$: ♩ = 108: 30 meas.
Allegro moderato: $\frac{4}{4}$: ♩ = 96-100: 34 meas.
Largo: $\frac{4}{4}$: 5 meas.

This modern French showpiece has definite Impressionistic connotations through its harmonic and melodic language. The entire work is through-composed, with the melodies being constructed in phrases. The trombone part is soloistic throughout, with much of the accompaniment being homophonic, thus more important as rhythmic ostinato under the solo line than as melodic counterpoint. This work is, at the same time, a serious piece and a parody on several symphonic works. Following three short sections in contrasting styles and characters, a long involved cadenza appears. A long blues section, providing an effective contrast, leads into a typical Bozza-style fast section, featuring repeated rhythmic and pitch patterns. The orchestral accompaniment parts are available on rental from LED. The instrumentation of the accompaniment is as follows: fl, ob, cl, bn, 2 hns, trpt, trbn, timp, perc, hp, strgs.

A band transcription of the accompaniment, made by Dennis Smith, can be obtained from the University of Michigan.

This was the Paris Conservatory contest piece for 1944.

——. *Ciaccona* [Chaconne]. LED, 1967. 6*.

——. *Hommage à Bach.* LED, 1957. 127 meas.; 5'; F–c"; 5*; TB.

"Monsieur Bourez, Professeur au Conservatoire National de Valenciennes"

Maestoso moderato: $\frac{4}{4}$: 8 meas.
Allegro moderato: $\frac{4}{4}$: 28 meas.
Moderato: $\frac{4}{4}$: 19 meas.
Allegro ma non troppo: $\frac{3}{8}$: 72 meas.

The title of this work suggests a tribute to Johann Sebastian Bach, but the music is not in the style of J. S. Bach. "Neo-Baroque" with many melodic motifs similar to some Bach materials. Harmonies are not similar, but phrases, rhythms and texture are. The opening measure is similar to Bach's *Partita No. 3* for solo vlolin *(Preludio).* The work contains three sections; fast, slow, fast with an introduction.

——. *Trois essais.* LED, 1977. 231 meas.; 14'; E–d"; 7-8*; TB; straight mute, flutter, glissandi.

I. Allegro: $\frac{3}{8}$, $\frac{2}{4}$, $\frac{3}{4}$, $\frac{4}{4}$, $\frac{5}{4}$: 126 meas.
II. Calme: $\frac{4}{4}$: 32 meas.
III. Allegro con moto: $\frac{3}{16}$, $\frac{5}{16}$, $\frac{2}{8}$, $\frac{3}{8}$: 73 meas.
(Scherzando)

This piece is for trombone solo accompanied by percussion ensemble. The instruments in the ensemble include:

three chinese blocks
three cow bells
two wood blocks
two suspended cymbals
two bongos
large tam-tam
gong
bass drum with foot pedal
snare drum
triangle
tambourine

Breuil, Helene. *Essai.* BILL, 1978. 1*.

Brouquières, Jean. *Par les chemins* [By the Way]. MAR, 1982. 2'40"; G-d', 2.

——. *Trombonaria.* SAL, 1983. 3.

Brown, Charles (b. 1893). *Méditation.* LED, 1955. 2'45"; c–f♯'; 3*. t trbn, pf/org.

"René Bellet"

Andante: $\frac{2}{4}$: 85 meas.

†**Büsser, Henri** (1872-1973). *Cantabile et scherzando, Op. 51.* LED; BEL. 115 meas.; 4'; E–b'; 7*; TB; trill.

Molto moderato: $\frac{6}{4}$, $\frac{7}{4}$, $\frac{9}{4}$: ♩ = 72: 26 meas.
Allegro: $\frac{3}{4}$, $\frac{4}{4}$: ♩ = 126: 9 meas.
Più allegro: $\frac{3}{4}$: 𝅗𝅥. = 126: 80 meas.

This was the Paris Conservatory contest piece for 1913, 1924, 1936, and 1979. The composition gives the performer the opportunity to demonstrate his ability in musical interpretation, technique, sonority, and intonation. The *Cantabile,* written mostly in $\frac{7}{4}$, is both expressive and sentimental. The *Scherzando,* built around hard-driving rhythms, is an effective contrast to the preceeding movement.

†——. *Étude de concert, Op. 79* [Concert Study]. LED, 1927. 93 meas.; 3'30"; E–c♯"; 8*; TB; cadenza, lip trill.

"H. Couillaud, Professeur au Conservatoire"

Moderato maestoso: $\frac{3}{4}$: ♩ = 80: 46 meas.
Più moderado: $\frac{9}{8}$, $\frac{3}{4}$: ♩ = 72: 26 meas.
Tempo I: $\frac{3}{4}$: ♩ = 80: 21 meas.

This was the Paris Conservatory contest piece for 1927, 1971, and 1978.

†———. *Phoebus variations, Op.* 87. LED, 1965. 74 meas.; 3'50"; E–c"; 7*; TB; cadenza.

"Roger Tudesq"

Moderato maestoso: $\frac{3}{4}$: ♩ = 92: 10 meas.
Plus animé: $\frac{4}{4}$: ♩ = 112: 8 meas.
Moderato marcato: $\frac{3}{4}$: ♩ = 88: 12 meas.
Andante: $\frac{9}{8}$: ♩ = 72: 14 meas.
Poco allegro: $\frac{4}{4}$: ♩ = 120: 17 meas.
Più largo: $\frac{3}{4}$: ♩ = 84: 13 meas.

This was the Paris Conservatory contest piece for 1933.

†———. *Pièce en mi bémol, Op. 33.* Evette et Schaeffer, *ca.* 1907; LED; INT, 1973. 141 meas.; 4'10"; E–c♭"; 6*; TB; trill.

Andante poco adagio: $\frac{3}{4}$: ♩ = 72: 58 meas.
Allegro: $\frac{3}{4}$: ♩ = 144-152: 83 meas.

This was the Paris Conservatory contest piece for 1907 and again in 1920.

Capdeville, Pierre (1906-1969). *Sonate concertante.* LED, 1966. 6*.

Casinière, Yves de la (b. 1887). *Thème varié* [Varied Theme]. LED, 1958. 7*.

Castérède, Jacques (b. 1926). *Sonatine.* LED, 1958. 362 meas.; 13'; E–c"; 7*; TB; cup mute; mordent, trill. Recordings: 5, 11, 33, 45.

I. Allegro vivo: $\frac{3}{4}$, $\frac{5}{4}$, $\frac{2}{2}$: 𝅗𝅥 = 112 : 190 meas.

II. Andante sostenuto: $\frac{4}{8}$, $\frac{6}{8}$: ♪ = 72 : 66 meas.

III. Allegro: $\frac{7}{8}$, $\frac{5}{4}$, $\frac{2}{2}$, $\frac{3}{2}$: ♩ = 92 :206 meas.

This composition is both musically and physically demanding, while at the same time being a very interesting and enjoyable piece to listen to. The work is in three movements, the outer two dealing with shifting meters and requiring excellent tonal security and outstanding lip flexibility. The second movement is one of the most beautiful slow movements in the trombone repertoire. It deals with a high tessitura and concludes with a cup-muted passage. The third movement begins wlth a motive that incorporates a mordent, which can become a problem for some players to execute effectively throughout the movement.

†**Chaynes, Charles** (b. 1925). *Impulsions.* LED, 1971. 7'; B♭'–d♭"; 8*; staright, cup, and harmon mutes, random pitch selection, approximate pitch, flutter tongue, multiphonics. Recording: 33.

Mr. Chaynes comments on *Impulsions*:

> The work falls into four distinct sections: Slow-fast-slow-fast, reminiscent of the *sonata da chiesa*. The slow sections make much use of various effects, such as singing through the instrument, tapping on the bell or mute, and inhaling and exhaling through the instrument. The first fast section (Allegro) makes use of an ostinato pattern of 3 + 2 + 2 + 3 in eighth notes, from which as the section unfolds the music deviates into slightly different variations of the pattern. The climax of the section is a semi-improvisational section made up of two boxes of pitches, the first lasting eight and the second fifteen seconds. The second box also serves as a transition back to the softer and more relaxed atmosphere of the openlng. The return to the final fast section is realized by a steady buildup that seems to achieve a high level of tension rather quickly, but doesn't achieve release until the new tempo is reached, backed again by an ostinato pattern. The contrasts between the two sections of fast and slow is based not only on tempo but also in the use of materials: the slow movements are also most arhythmical, very free, improvisational—the fast very pattern oriented, one could say neo-classical and obstinate.

This was the Paris Conservatory contest piece for 1971.

Chopin, Frédéric (1818-1849). *Nocturne.* Edited by Paul Delisse. Millereau, *ca.* 1886.

Chrétien, Hedwige (1859-1944). *Grand solo.* Millereau, *ca.* 1886.

†**Clergue, Jean** (1896-1966). *Impromptu.* LEM, 1938. 216 meas.; 5'10"; E–c"; 6; TB; straight mute.

"Henri Couillaud, Professeur au Conservatoire National de Paris"

Allegro: $\frac{2}{4}$: ♩ = 120: 66 meas.

Andante: $\frac{4}{4}$: ♩ = 60: 34 meas.

Allegro: $\frac{2}{4}$: ♩ = 120: 74 meas.

Più vivo: $\frac{2}{4}$: ♩ = 138: 42 meas.

This was the Paris Conservatory contest piece for 1938.

Clérisse, Robert (b. 1899). *Idylle.* SOUT, 1973. 86 meas.; 2'45"; G–e♭'; 3.

Moderato: $\frac{3}{4}$: ♩ = 80: 50 meas.

Moderato: $\frac{2}{4}$: ♩ = 80: 36 meas.

———. *Poeme.* BILL.

———. *Prélude et divertissement* [Prelude and Divertimento]. Éditions Musicales Andrieu Frères; RUB, n.d. 154 meas.; 4'30"; G♭–g'; 4.

Andante: $\frac{3}{4}$: 52 meas.

Allegretto (quasi allegro): $\frac{6}{8}$: 102 meas.

——. *Prière* [Prayer]. LED, 1959. 3'30"; d–f♯'; 3*.

"Morceau de Concours des Fédérations, Division Élémentaire"

Andante moderato: 3/4 : 68 meas.

——. *Thème de concours* [Contest Theme]. LED, n.d. 81 meas.; 4'; B♭–f♯'; 5*.

"Morceau de Concours des Fédérations, Division Supérieur"

Large et soutenu: 4/4 : 40 meas.
Allegro: ¢ : 41 meas.

†**Clostre, Andrienne** (b. 1921). *Dialogue II.* CHO, 1979. 90+ meas.; 7'30"; B♭–c"; 9; TB; flutter tongue, cadenza.

Adagio—Declamato: n.m.
Allegro giocoso: 5/8, 2/4, 3/4 : ♩ = 132: 62 meas.
Ritmico: 5/16, 7/16, 2/8, 3/8, 4/8, etc.: ♪ = 152: 28 meas.
Adagio—Declamato: n.m.
Maestoso—Declamato: n.m.

This was the Paris Conservatory contest piece for 1979.

Cohen, Jules (1835-1901). *Andante (Musique du XIXe siècle).* BILL.

Coiteux, F. *Pharaon des mers* [Pharoah of the Seas]. MAR.

Constant, F. *Plaisance* [Pleasure]. BILL, 1978. 7'.

Constant, Marius (b. 1925). *Concerto "Gli elementi."* RICP, 1977.

This piece was especially written as the final test piece for the International Trombone Competition held in Toulon, France from May 22–May 27, 1977. The concerto is in four movements, taking its title *"Gli elementi"* from the four medieval elements—water, air, earth and fire. This piece encompasses every technical and musical demand that could be required of the well-schooled trombonist.

†**Cools, Eugène** (1877-1936). *Allegro de concert, Op. 81* [Concert Allegro]. BILL, n.d. 172 meas.; 4'10"; E–c"; 5; TB. Recording: 28.

"Allard, Professeur au Conservatoire"

Allegro risoluto: ¢ : 𝅗𝅥 = 80: 52 meas.
Allegro: 𝅗𝅥 = 84: 120 meas.
This was the Paris Conservatory contest piece for 1911.

Coriolis, Emmanuel de. *Aria.* LED. 3-4*.

——. *Quartre piècettes* [4 Little Pieces]. BILL, 1973.

——. *Quartre récréations.* BILL, 1976. 119 meas.; 4'; C–f'; 2*.

I.. Moderato: 4/4 : ♩ = 72: 19 meas.
II. Marziale: 2/4 : ♩ = 80: 40 meas.
III. Andantino: 3/4 : ♩ = 84: 36 meas.
IV. Allegro: 4/4 : ♩ = 120: 24 meas.

This solo is in four movements. The rhythmic structure is simple with the work being highly tonal and diatonic. This work is well constructed and would be an excellent introduction for the young trombonist to the "French School" of trombone playing.

†**Croce-Spinelli, B.** (b. 1871). *Solo de concours* [Contest Solo]. Evette et Schaeffer; LED; BEL, *ca.* 1903. 99 meas.; 5'; F–c"; 6*; TB; lip trill. Recording: 39.

Lento: $\frac{4}{4}$: ♩ = 50: 17 meas.
Andante: $\frac{2}{4}$, $\frac{4}{4}$: ♩ = 69: 36 meas.
Allegro moderato: $\frac{4}{4}$: ♩ = 126: 46 meas.

This was the Paris Conservatory contest piece for 1903. The solo demonstrates both legato control and detached technical facility.

Dachez, Christian. *Ébauche* [Rough Draft]. Collection Rougeron. LED, 1985. P1-2*.

———. *Étrange ballad* [Strange Ballad]. Collection Rougeron. LED, 1985. P1-2*.

———. *Mélodica.* Collection Rougeron. LED, 1985. 2'5"; B-c'; D1-2*.

———. *Poursuite* [Pursuit]. Collection Rougeron. LED, 1985. A-a'; E1*.

———. *Résonances.* Collection Rougeron. LED, 1985. F-a'; P1-2*.

———. *Trombonica.* Collection Rougeron. LED, 1985. D1-2*.

†**Dautremer, Marcel** (b. 1906). *Coulissiana.* CHO, 1966. 184 meas.; 7'45"; B♭'–c"; TB; straight and cup mutes, flutter tongue, glissandi, trills.

Lent: $\frac{4}{4}$: ♩ = 54: 36 meas.
Vif: $\frac{2}{4}$, $\frac{4}{4}$: ♩ = 160: 41 meas.
Moderato: $\frac{2}{4}$, $\frac{3}{4}$, $\frac{4}{4}$: ♩ = 88: 38 meas.
Vif: $\frac{3}{4}$, $\frac{4}{4}$: ♩ = 138: 46 meas.
Lent: $\frac{4}{4}$: ♩ = 50: 18 meas.
Vif: $\frac{2}{4}$, $\frac{4}{4}$: ♩ = 160: 5 meas.

This was the Paris Conservatory contest piece for 1967.

Defaye, Jean-Michel (b. 1932). *À la manière de Bach* [In the Manner of Bach]. LED.

———. *Concerto pour trombone et orchestre.* LED. 8*.

———. *Deux danses.* LED, 1954. 120 meas.; 8'; A–f"; 8*; GTB; cup mute, cadenza, glissandi. Recordings: 5, 25, 33, 52, 60, 65.

"Gabriel Masson, Soloist for Orchestra of the Paris Opera"

I. *Danse sacrée* [Sacred Dance], Lent: $\frac{4}{4}$: ♩ = 60: 76 meas.
II. *Danse profane* [Secular Dance], Movement de Samba: $\frac{2}{2}$: 44 meas.

About *Deux danses* Mr. Defaye writes:

> These two dances, dating from 1954, were written especially for Gabriel Masson, then soloist for the Orchestra of the Paris Opera. My main purpose was to demonstrate the great possibilities of the trombone. The first dance, *Danse sacrée*, has a rather classical style and includes many technical difficulties, such as large intervals, long phrases, rapid detached notes, and overall endurance. *Danse profane* is a brilliant piece *par excellence* and was inspired by jazz. Over a samba beat, the trombone soars in the highest tessitura of the instrument. As in the first dance, this movement poses the problems of suppleness and endurance.

There is also an edition for bass trombone by Donald Knaub and published by LED (see entry in Chapter 5).

†———. *Mouvement.* LED, 1972. 198 meas., 6'; E–d"; 8*; TB; straight mute, cadenza, glissandi.

"Gerard Pichaureau"

$\frac{3}{8}$, $\frac{2}{4}$, $\frac{3}{4}$: ♩ = 132: 164 meas.
Moderato: $\frac{4}{4}$: ♩ = 92: 34 meas.

This was the Paris Conservatory contest piece for 1972.

Defossez, René (b. 1905). *Concerto.* MET, 1951. 354 meas.; 11'30"; G–c"(d"); 6; TB.

I. Scherzando: Allegro: $\frac{4}{4}$: ♩ = 96-104: 99 meas.
II. "Elegie": Adagio: $\frac{3}{4}$, $\frac{4}{4}$: ♩ = 60: 54 meas.
III. Rondo: $\frac{3}{8}$: ♪ = 200: 201 meas.

This solo is in three movements, combining a romantic expressiveness with modern harmonies and dissonances. The first movement is an ABA form, starting with a scherzando-like introduction, followed by a slower section consisting of block chords over a free legato line, and concludes with a return of the opening. The second movement resembles the middle section of the first movement in terms of legato style, harmonic texture, and general expressiveness. The final movement resembles the first movement, consisting of melodic materials based on fast scale passages with added chromatic alteration. The orchestral accompaniment parts are available on rental from ELKH.

Delbecq, Laurent (b. 1905). *Trombonite.* MAR. 1*.

"Série Très Facile Pour Débutants"

Délcroix, Léon (1880-1938). *Légende, Op. 64.* Evette et Schaeffer; LED, 1921. 6*; TB.

"Morceau de Concours du Conservatoire de Liege (1921)"

Delerue, Georges (b. 1925). *Concerto.* BILL, 1980. 356 meas.; 16'; E–d"; 6*; TB; cup mute, flutter tongue, glissandi, cadenza.

"Michel Becquet"

I. Allegro moderato: $\frac{3}{4}$, ¢, $\frac{3}{2}$: 𝅗𝅥 = 84: 152 meas.
II. Poco lento: $\frac{4}{4}$, $\frac{3}{2}$: ♩ = 50: 60 meas.
III. Alelgro vivace: $\frac{2}{4}$, $\frac{3}{4}$, $\frac{4}{4}$, $\frac{5}{4}$, $\frac{3}{2}$: ♩ = 120: 144 meas.

This solo is in three movements, containing many features not typical of many of the other compositions in the "French School" of trombone literature. There are virtually no tempo changes, little use of changing meter, and a lower tessitura than usual. However, it does contain its share of running sixteenth notes that make great technical demands, and also contains awkward leaps in either direction. This solo seems most appropriate for the student who has above average technique and moderate endurance, but who doesn't possess a solid high register. The orchestral accompaniment parts are available on rental from BILL.

Delgiudice, Michel (b. 1924). *Sérénité* [Serenity]. MAR, n.d. 3*.
"Morceaux de Forces Diverses"

Delisse, Paul (1817-1888), ed. *12 transcriptions pour trombone et piano.* Auguste O'Kelley, *ca.* 1878.

1. Sonate en si bemol de Mozart
2. Andante et menuet de Haydn
3. Theme varié de Beethoven
4. Theme varié en ré mineur de Mozart
5. Adagio de Mozart
6. Sonate en fa de Mozart
7. Theme varié en sol
8. Sonate en fa de Beethoven
9. Theme varié sur Judas Macchabee
10. Ariette de Mozart
11. Theme varié en la
12. Theme varié en fa

——, ed. *Tyrolean Air.* Recordings: 54, 55.

Demersseman, Jules (1833-1866). *Cavatine, Op. 47.* BILL, n.d. Recording: 62.

——. *Introduction et polonaise, Op. 30.* BILL; BEL, n.d.

Denisov, Edison. *Choral varié.* LED, 1979. 8*.

Depelsenaire, Jean-Marie (b. 1914). *Ce que chantait l'æde.* CHO.

——. *Impromptu.* SCHF.

——. *Jeux chromatiques* [Chromatic Games]. BILL, 1960; COM.
See entry in Chapter 5.

——. *Légende nervienne.* Éditions Philippo; COM.

——. *Le vieux berger raconte* [The Old Shepherd Recounts]. Éditions Philippo; COM.

——. *Prélude et danse.* LED. 4*.

†**Désenclos, Alfred** (b. 1912). *Plain-chant et allegretto.* LED, 1965. 162 meas.; 8'; B♭'–b'; 8*; TB; quasi-cadenza.

"Gerard Pichaureau, Professeur au Conservatoire de Paris"

Andante molto moderato: 3/4, 4/4 : ♩ = 66: 57 meas.
Allegretto non troppo vivo: 4/8, 5/8, 6/8, 2/4, 3/4 : ♪ = 144: 105 meas.

This was the Paris Conservatory contest piece for 1965.

Desportes, Yvonne (b. 1907). *Des chansons dans la coulisse* [Songs Within the Slide]. BILL, 1981. 5'; G–a'; 5; TB.

Moderato: 3/4 : ♩ = 72
Meno: 3/4
Allegro moderato: 2/4 : ♩ = 92
Tempo primo: 3/4 : ♩ = 72

This solo is one movement and constructed in binary form. The melodic material is modally based, primarily mixolydian and aeolian. The challenges for the trombonist exist in clearly defining the articulation patterns, and alternating between staccato and legato passages .

——. *L'exploit de la coulisse* [The Feat of the Slide]. BILL, 1981. t trbn, orch (pf red)

†——. *Fantaisie in B♭.* FISC. 104 meas.; 4'30"; B♭'–c♭"; 6*; cadenza.

Andante: 4/4 : ♩ = 58: 14 meas.
Allegro scherzando: 6/8, 12/8, 3/4, 4/4 : ♩ = 112: 52 meas.
Più lento: 4/4 : ♩ = 63: 18 meas.
Allegro scherzando: 12/8 : ♩ = 112: 20 meas.

This was the Paris Conservatory contest piece for 1932.

——. *Un petit air dans le vent* [A Little Tune in the Wind]. BILL, 1981. 2'; A-e'; 3.

Destanque, Guy. *Romance en ré mineur.* LED. 1-2*.

Destanque, Guy, and **Larguèze, Jacques**. *Ballade.* Edited by Philippe Rougeron. LED, 1985. P1-2*.

Devogel, J. *Volupté* [Sensual Pleasure]. MAR.

Dewanger, Anton. *Humoresque, Op. 89.* LED, 1954. 4-5*.

Dhaene. *Andante.* LED.

Domrœse, Wilhelm. *Les ours, suite métamorphique* [The Bears]. LED, 1985. 3-4*.

Dondeyne, Désiré (b. 1921). *Cantabile et caprice.* LED, 1958. 7*.

Dorsselaer, Willy van. *À Longchamp, Op. 117*. BILL, 1972. 2'30"; d–d'; 1*.

"Louis Potters, ex. trombone-solo au Stadttheater de Colmar/Prix de Composition de la Confédération Musicale de France, 1972"

Maestoso: $\frac{2}{4}$: 75 meas.

——. *Le grand duc* [Eagle Owl]. BILL, 1971. 42 meas.; 2'10"; c–d'; 2.

"Albert Ehrmann/Prix de Composition de la Confédération Musicale"

Maestoso: $\frac{4}{4}$: 30 meas.
Allegro décido (Grandeur): $\frac{4}{4}$: ♩ = 92: 12 meas.

——. *Introduction et allegro martial*. BILL, 1964. 75 meas.; 2'30"; F–f'; 3.

"Henry Dessauvage, Professeur a L'École National de Musique de Mulhouse/Prix de Composition 1964 de la Confédération Musicale de France"

Moderato: $\frac{4}{4}$: 24 meas.
Allegro Martial: $\frac{4}{4}$: ♩ = 112-126: 44 meas.
Grandioso: $\frac{4}{4}$: 7 meas.

——. *Jericho*. MOLE.

——. *Pour la promotion*. BILL, 1971. 2'; d–d'; 2.

"Prix de Composition de la Confédération Musicale de France, 1971"

Maestoso: $\frac{2}{4}$: 78 meas.

Douay, Jean. *Pièces classiques*. 5 vols. Edited by P. Sciortino. BILL.

Douay, Jean, and **Christian Gouinguene**. *Divertissement*. BILL, 1976. B♭–g♭'; 4; TB.

This solo is a short composition that is tonal in style. Its rhythmic structure is very simple and relies on sequential repetition to develop its material. The composition is without tempo markings or style indications.

——. *Thème et variations*. BILL, 1976. 3'; F–f'.

This piece consists of the statement of the theme, followed by three variations, and a restatement of the opening theme. The first variation uses canonic imitation, while the second variation uses the trombone as an extension of the ideas presented in the piano. In the third variation the trombone arpeggiates the theme in quarter notes, while the piano plays a running eighth note figure.

Dubois, Pierre Max (b. 1930). *Concerto dit "l'Irrespecteux"* [called "The Disrespectful"]. LED, 1970. 489 meas.; 16'; G'–d"; 7*; TB; lip trills, lip smears, flutter tongue.

"Pierre Ambach, Professeur au Conservatoire de Bescancon"

I. Allegro: 4/4 : ♩ = 104: 51 meas.
Modéré: 3/4, 4/4, 5/4 : ♩ = 86: 70 meas.
II. Vivo: 3/8, 2/4 : ♩ = 88: 160 meas.
III. Andante: 3/8, 3/4, 4/4, 5/4 : ♪ = 76: 45 meas.
IV. Allegretto tranquillo: 3/8, 2/4, 3/4, 4/4 : ♩ = 88: 163 meas.

This solo is in four movements and lacks the usual impressionistic tendencies found in many of the other solos of the "French School." The first movement, *Allegro*, has two principal themes, each being repeated, to form an ABBA pattern. The accompaniment to this movement is comprised only of percussion instruments. The second movement requires excellent tonguing facility, with meter changes moving frequently between 2/4 and 3/8. The third movement, *Andante*, has a slow harmonic pattern in addition to the legato approach of the trombone part. The final movement is similar to the second movement, featuring short phrases as well as a delicate style. The performer needs excellent technique, range, and flexibility to perform this virtuoso work. The orchestral accompaniment parts are available on rental from LED. The instrumentation of the accompaniment includes: timp, perc, strgs.

——. *Cortège*. LED, 1959. 4'15"; A♭–g'; 6*; TB.

Maestoso: 4/4 (3/8, 5/8, 2/4, 3/2): ♩ = 92

This one movement solo provides the young trombonist with an introduction to music with variable time signatures. The melodic content of the solo is very simple, being based generally in diatonic lines.

——. *Deux marches*. LED, 1960. 113 meas.; 6'; F–c"; 6-7*; TB.

I. Lento: 4/4 : 50 meas.
II. Allegro moderato: 4/4 : 63 meas.

——. *La danse du Herisson*. BILL.

——. *En coulisse* [On Slide]. Rid, 1969. 2'30"; G–g'; 3.

Maestoso: 4/4 : 45 meas.

This solo begins with a march-like theme, based in C Major. This is contrasted by a short, soft, legato section which then returns to the opening theme.

——. *Histoire de trombone*. BILL, 1978. F–b♭'; 5*; TB; straight mute.

I. *Rumba*. Andante
II. *Parade*. Allegro Moderato: 3/8, 2/4

The *Rumba* consists of a stepwise lyrical theme in the trombone with the piano playing a chordal syncopation underneath. The middle section has the trombone and piano exchanging rhythmic patterns, with a return of the original theme. The *Parade* is march-like in character, featuring trombone fanfares. Shifting 2/4 and 3/8 meters shape much of this movement, adding a lopsided feeling to its march-like form.

——. *Menuet d'automne* [Autumn Minuet]. BILL. 2*.

——. *Pour le trombone élémentaire* [elementary], *9 pièces en un recueil.* LED, 1967. 12'40"; 2-3*.

1. Polka
2. Romance
3. Intermezzo
4. Berceuse
5. Air ecissais
6. En fanfare
7. Passepied
8. Petite valse
9. Sicilienne

——. *Pour le trombone moyen* [intermediate], *8 pièces en forme d'études en un recueil.* LED, 1967. 10'45"; 5*.

1. Humoresque
2. Ritournelle
3. Fanfare
4. Vocalise
5. Burlesque
6. Tango
7. Slow
8. Tambourin

——. *Pour le trombone préparatoire* [preparatory], *dix pièces progressives avec accompagnement de piano.* LED, 1967. 405 meas.; 20' (2'/piece); B♭–f'; 1*.

"Pierre Ambach, Professeur au Conservatoire de Besancon"

1. Entrée. Maestoso: $\frac{4}{4}$: ♩ = 100: 32 meas.
2. Lai. Lent: $\frac{4}{4}$: ♩ = 76: 28 meas.
3. Virelai. Moderato: $\frac{4}{4}$: ♩ = 80: 32 meas.
4. Suite à l'ancienne. Allegro: $\frac{3}{4}$: ♩ = 120: 57 meas.
5. Cortège. Tranquille: $\frac{2}{4}$: ♩ = 72: 48 meas.
6. Canon. Alla breve: ¢ : 𝅗𝅥 = 69: 34 meas.
7. Intermède. Allegro: $\frac{3}{4}$: ♩ = 104: 45 meas.
8. Passepied. Allegretto: $\frac{2}{4}$: ♩ = 72: 41 meas.
9. Berceuse. Lento: ¢ : ♩ = 80: 40 meas.
10. Marche. Allegretto: $\frac{2}{4}$: ♩ = 63: 48 meas.

——. *Sonatine impromptu.* LED, 1985.

——. *Suite.* LED, 1965. 9'; E–c"; 6-7*; TB.

I. Humoresque. Allegretto.
II. Galop—Fantaisie. Presto.
III. Pastourelle. Andante.
IV. Complainte. Molto lento.
V. Rondeau. Allegro moderato.

†**Dubois, Théodore** (1837-1924). *Solo de concert (Concertpiece).* Evette et Schaeffer, 1907; LED; INT, 1965. 162 meas.; 5'50"; A♭–c"; 6*; TB.

"L. Allard, Professeur au Conservatoire"

Andante: $\frac{4}{4}$: ♩ = 72: 72 meas.
Allegro Vivo: $\frac{4}{4}$: ♩ = 152: 90 meas.

This was the Paris Conservatory contest piece for 1909.

†**Duclos, René** (1899-1964). *Doubles sur un choral* [Variations on a Chorale]. LED, 1939. 100 meas.; 4'45"; E–b'; 7*; TB.

"H. Couillaud, Professeur au Conservatoire"

Allegro moderato: $\frac{4}{4}$: 29 meas.
Allegro scherzando: $\frac{4}{4}$: 16 meas.
Andante cantabile: $\frac{4}{4}$: 29 meas.
Allegro moderato: $\frac{12}{8}$, $\frac{4}{4}$: 26 meas.

This was the Paris Conservatory contest piece for 1939, 1945, and again in 1973.

†———. *Sa majesté le trombone* [His Majesty the Trombone]. LED, 1948. 114 meas.; 5'10"; E–d♭"; 7*; TB.

"Henri Couillaud"

Molto lento ed sostenuto: $\frac{3}{4}$: ♩ = 40: 37 meas.
Allegretto: $\frac{6}{8}$: ♪ = 104: 20 meas.
Moderato: $\frac{3}{4}$: 8 meas.
Allegro: ¢ : 𝅗𝅥 = 100: 49 meas.

This was the Paris Conservatory contest piece for 1948 and again in 1977.

†**Durand, Pierre**. *Parcours*. RID, 1975. 81 meas.; 5'; B♭'–c♯"; 8; GTB; cadenza.

"Gerard Pichaureau"

Andante: $\frac{4}{2}$, $\frac{5}{2}$, $\frac{6}{2}$, $\frac{4}{1}$: 𝅗𝅥 = 48: 26 meas.
Allegro: $\frac{4}{4}$: ♩ = 112: 50 meas.
Andante: $\frac{4}{2}$: 𝅗𝅥 = 48: 5 meas.

This was the Paris Conservatory contest piece for 1975.

†**Dutilleux, Henri** (b. 1916). *Choral, cadence et fugato* [Chorale, Cadenza, and Fugato]. LED, 1950. 132 meas.; 5'; B♭'–c"; 8*; TB; cadenza. Recordings: 5, 44, 58, 59, 67, 68.

"Andre LaFosse"

Chorale: $\frac{3}{2}$, $\frac{4}{2}$: 𝅗𝅥 = 52: 42 meas.
Fugato: $\frac{2}{4}$: ♩ = 84-88: 90 meas.

This was the Paris Conservatory contest piece for 1950. The *Choral* opens with a soft, legato statement of the melody. In the *Cadence* section of the solo, the accompaniment sets up some of the subject ideas which will be developed in the *Fugato*. The subject of the *Fugato* utilizes a series of intervals widening from a minor second to a minor ninth. The end of the *Fugato* builds to an exciting conclusion by the use of rapid triplets and repeated pitches in duple groupings.

Fiche, Michel (b. 1939). *Ballet pour un kangourou* [Ballet for a Kangaroo]. BILL, 1977. 2*.

Fiche, Michel, and **Claude Pichaureau**. *En vacances* [On Vacation]. BILL. 1*.

"Collection de la Fédération Nationale Des Unions de Conservatoires Municipaux de Musique"

Fievet, Paul (b. 1892). *Légende celtique* [Celtic Legend]. BILL.

†**Franck, Maurice** (b. 1892). *Fanfare, andante et allegro.* SAL, 1958. 247 meas.; 8'50"; B♭'–d"; 7; TB.

Allegro moderato: $\frac{2}{4}$, $\frac{4}{4}$: ♩ = 88: 11 meas.
Large: $\frac{4}{4}$, $\frac{3}{2}$: ♩ = 60: 13 meas.
Lent: $\frac{2}{4}$: ♩ = 50: 75 meas.
Allegro non troppo: $\frac{6}{8}$: ♩ = 100: 148 meas.

This was the Paris Conservatory contest piece for 1958.

Gabaye, Pierre (b. 1930). *Complainte* [Lament]. LED, 1957. 1'30"; d–e♭'; 2*.

Moderato: $\frac{2}{4}$: ♩ = 80: 60 meas.

———. *Spécial.* LED, 1969. 190 meas.; 6'15"; E–d"; 8*; TB; cadenza.

Très vif: $\frac{4}{4}$: ♩ = 152: 94 meas.
$\frac{4}{4}$: ♩ = 66: 25 meas.
Tempo primo: $\frac{4}{4}$: ♩ = 152: 52 meas.
Coda: $\frac{4}{4}$: ♩ = 152: 19 meas.

This solo is a one movement work, structured in an ABA-Coda form. The A sections feature fast tempos, with melodic materials requiring double-tonguing as well as good slide technique. The B section features a beautiful cantabile melody, including a totally improvised cadenza. This cadenza, appearing near the end of the cantabile section, must be considered a unique point in the trombone solo literature. The accompaniment, scored for chamber orchestra, is available on rental from LED. The instrumentation of the accompaniment is as follows: 2 hns, 3 trpts, 3 trbns, timp, cel (or pf), hp, guitar (ad lib), strgs, jazz set (cymbals, bass drum, snare drum, and triangle).

Gabitchvadzé. *Deux pièces.* LED. 5-6*.

I. Motif lyrique.
II. Scherzo—Toccata.

Gagnebin, Henri (1886-1977). *Sarabande.* LED, 1953. 1-2*.

Gallet, Jean. *Légende.* BILL, 1973. 64 meas.; 1'30"; c–d'.

"Prix de Composition de la Confédération Musicale de France 1973"

Moderato: $\frac{2}{4}$: 36 meas.
Poco più lento: $\frac{2}{4}$: 11 meas.
Tempo I: $\frac{2}{4}$: 17 meas.

Galliègue, Marcel. *Essai I.* LED, 1976. 1'45"; A–d'; 2*.

This solo is basically a two-part song form, the first being in d minor and the second in D Major. The waltz-like melody is lyrical and slow.

———. *Essai II.* LED, 1976. 2'30"; G♯–g'; 3*; cadenza.

$\frac{12}{8}$: ♩. = 60
$\frac{4}{4}$: ♩ = 66-72

This solo appears to be in a type of three-part form, an A section of a sweeping melodic nature, a B section in a more toccata-like structure, then a cadenza, followed by a return to A, but this time in a maestoso style. The cadenza is noteworthy because of its avoidance of rhythmic notation and meter. This utillzes a type of symbolic notation where note lengths and speed are graphically indicated by placement and by relative length lines following the longer tones. However, style and dynamics are conventionally shown.

———. *Essai III.* LED, 1976. 2'30"; E–b♭'; 4*; TB; cadenza.

$\frac{2}{4}$: ♩ = 72
$\frac{7}{8}$: ♪ = ♪
$\frac{2}{4}$: ♩ = 72

This solo appears to be in a type of three-part form, opening with an A section of sustained legato, followed by the B in a light staccato style, then a cadenza utilizing A motifs with a closing section also utilizing A material. The cadenza uses conventional rhythmic notation in contrast to that of *Essai II.*

———. *Essai IV.* LED, 1976. 3'; 5-6*; TB.

Galliègue, Marcel, and **Dupin**. *Quelques chants, huit pièces en quatre cahiers* [Some Little Tunes, 8 Pieces in 4 Notebooks]. LED, 1974. 1-2*.

Cahier I.
1. Fleur de choral.
2. Trialogue.

Cahier II.
3. Canzone.
4. Manège.

Cahier III.
5. Petit choral.
6. En syncope.

Cahier IV.
7. Romance.
8. Deux sur trois.

Galliègue, Marcel, and **Jérôme Naulais**. *Deux ans déjà trombone* [Two Years Before Trombone]. Collection Crescendo. LED.

———. *Très sympa trombone* [Very Likable Trom-bone]. Collection Crescendo. LED.

Gallois-Montbrun, Raymond (b. 1918). *Aria.* LED, 1952. 5*.

Gartenlaub, Odette (b. 1922). *Improvisation pour Trombone.* Recording: 58.

———. *Rite.* BILL, 1977. 2*.

Gaubert, Philippe (1879-1941). *Cantabile et scherzetto.* FISC, 1939. 203 meas.; 5'30"; A♭–g'; triple tonguing.

Lento: $\frac{6}{8}$, $\frac{9}{8}$: 18 meas.
Un peu plus vite: $\frac{6}{8}$, $\frac{12}{8}$, $\frac{2}{4}$: 81 meas.

Un peu moins vite: 3/4 : 33 meas.
Tempo I vif: 2/4 : 57 meas.
Moins vite: 12/8 : 14 meas.

†——. *Morceau symphonique* [Symphonic Piece (*lit.* "Morsel")]. LED; SOUT; INT, 1912. 119 meas.; 5'; A♭–b♭'; 7*; TB. Recording: 50.

Lento: 3/2 : 𝅗𝅥 = 72: 25 meas.
Allegro moderato: 2/4, 4/4 : 22 meas.
Assez lent: 9/8 : 20 meas.
Allegro moderato: 4/4 : 28 meas.
Lento: 3/2 : 𝅗𝅥 = 72: 24 meas.

It is set in the traditional slow-fast concept of the French Contest solos. The opening section is in a slow legato style. The faster section, allegro moderato, needs caution in spacing the notes. This thematic material develops toward the concluding slow legato opening theme.

This was the Paris Conservatory contest piece for 1912, 1921, 1937, and 1972.

Gédalge, André (1856-1926). *Contest Piece.* INT; edited by Christopher Jones, SAL, 1972. 118 meas.; 5'30"; B♭–c"; 6; T.

Maestoso: 4/4 : 11 meas.
Andante: 4/4 : 33 meas.
Allegro maestoso: 3/4 : 84 meas.

†**Gotkovsky, Ida** (b. 1933). *Concerto.* BILL, 1978. 243 meas.; 14'30"; E–d♭"; 8; TB; cup mute, cadenza.

I. Lyrique.
Allegro agitato tumultuoso: 4/4 : ♩ = 96: 42 meas.
Più vivo: 3/8, 2/4, 3/4, 4/4 : ♩ = 120-126: 62 meas.
Calm dolce: 4/4 : ♩ = 69: 15 meas.
II. Dolcissimo.
Dolcissimo con anima: 5/8, 7/8, 3/4, 4/4 : ♩ = 58: 45 meas.
III. Final.
Ostinato: 4/4 : ♩ = 100: 44 meas.
Poco meno: 4/4 : ♩ = 92: 11 meas.
Ostinato: 4/4 : ♩ = 100: 24 meas.

This was the Paris Conservatory contest piece for 1978 (1st mvt. only).

——. *Romance.* MAR, 1983. 50".

Gouinguene, Christian. *Air du saqueboutier* [The Sackbut Player's Tune]. BILL, 1981.

——. *Concerto.* BILL, 1975. 246 meas.; 8'; B–d'; 6*; TB. Recordings: 9, 24.

I. Allegro: 2/4 : 114 meas.
II. Sicilienne: 6/8 : 48 meas.

III. Allegro vivo: $\frac{3}{8}$: 84 meas.

This piece is in three movements and is based upon themes by Johann David Heinichen (1683-1729). The work is Baroque-like in style with sequences, strong fifth relationships, and running sixteenths used throughout. Unfortunately there are no articulation markings contained within this piece.

——. *Ostinato.* BILL.

——. *Trombone circus.* BILL.

Guide, Richard de (1909-1962). *Suite: "Les caractères du trombone," Op. 32, No. 3.* LED, 1958. 146 meas.; 8'; B♭'–b'; 6*; TB; straight mute, glissandi. Recording: 6.

"Jules de Haes, Trombone Solo de L'Orchestra National de Belgique, Professeur de Trombone au Conservatoire Royal d'Anvers"

I. Solennel [Solemn].
Intrada dans le style ancien: $\frac{12}{8}$: ♩. = 66: 23 meas.
II. Funèbre [Funereal, Gloomy].
Largo: $\frac{4}{4}$: ♩ = 50: 24 meas.
III. Burlesque [Comical].
Andantino: $\frac{2}{4}$: ♩ = 76: 20 meas.
Meno mosso: $\frac{6}{8}$: ♩. = 56: 16 meas.
Tempo I: $\frac{2}{4}$: ♩ = 76: 16 meas.
IV. Sentimental [Sentimental].
Largo: $\frac{9}{8}$, $\frac{12}{8}$: ♩. = 46: 22 meas.
V. Triomphant [Triumphant].
Deciso: $\frac{4}{4}$: ♩ = 69: 25 meas.

†**Guilmant, Alexandre** (1837-1911). *Morceau symphonique, Op. 88* (also *Concert Piece, Op. 88*) [Symphonic Piece (*lit.* "Morsel")]. BEL, 1937; Big Hill Music Press; INT; edited by Eugene Watts, LEO; PROA; SCHG, 1963; SCHL; edited by E. Falaguerra, WAR. 158 meas.; 6'; B♭'–c♯"; 5; TB for INT, B for all others; cadenza. Recordings: 2, 17, 21, 27, 30, 32, 36, 38, 46, 51, 57, 58, 60, 62.

Andante sostenuto: $\frac{4}{4}$: ♩ = 63: 38 meas.
Allegro moderato: $\frac{3}{4}$: ♩ = 104: 120 meas.

This solo represents one of the most frequently performed compositions in the trombonist's repertoire. The single-movement work, in two principal parts, restates each theme in a condensed version at the end. The opening section establishes a lyrical, cantabile character in e♭ minor. Following a short cadenza, the allegro section drastically changes the style to a more disjunct feeling. This is an excellent vork for the development of endurance, style, articulation, and rhythmic stability. A band transcription of the accompaniment by W. Sheppard can be obtained from FISC. A performance/accompaniment cassette (Eugene Watts, soloist) comes with the LEO edition. A version for trombone and organ has been prepared by Klemens Schnorr and published by Reift. An orchestral version of the accompaniment is available from Interlochen Press.

This was the Paris Conservatory contest piece for 1902, 1928, and again in 1975.

†**Handel, George Frideric** (1685-1759). *Concerto en fa mineur.* Edited by André Lafosse, LED; SOUT, 1948. 188 meas.; 9'30"; F–b♭'; 7*; TB.

I. Grave: $\frac{4}{4}$: ♪ = 72: 28 meas.
II. Allegro: $\frac{4}{4}$: ♩ = 104: 48 meas.
III. Largo: $\frac{3}{4}$: ♩ = 52: 42 meas.
IV. Allegro: $\frac{3}{4}$: ♩ = 100: 70 meas.

Composed in 1703 by George Frideric Handel, this concerto was originally for oboe and chamber orchestra and played in g minor. This transcription is presented in f minor as a more practical key for the trombone. This concerto is a comparatively early work, composed when Handel was playing the violin in the Hamburg Opera House and beginning to think of composing Italian-style operas, such as were popular in Hamburg. Handel throughout his career would be little interested in the three-movement concerto form, as taken up by Albinoni, Vivaldi and Bach. This work is in the more conservative four-movement form, as developed by Corelli, but at the same time it has a typically Handelian solidity, inspiration and melodic strength. The opening "Grave," in typical dotted rhythm, leads into an "Allegro" which is imitative in form and not strictly fugal. A "Sarabande" of symmetrical phrase lengths is followed by a final "Allegro," the opening theme of which is basically the same as that of the *Organ Concerto, Op. 4, No. 3,* second movement. It is a combination of fugal and concerto grosso principals structurally.

This was the Paris Conservatory contest piece for 1970 and again in 1976.

Haydn, [Franz] **Joseph** (1732-1809). *Trio extrait du deuxieme quatuor, Op. 64.* Edited by Paul Delisse. Millereau, *ca.* 1881.

Holstein, J. P. *Pour rire et pleurer* [For to Laugh and to Weep]. BILL.

†**Houdy, Pierick** (b. 1929). *Largo et toccata.* LED, 1968. 108 meas.; 4'10"; E–c♯"; 7-8*; TB.

$\frac{2}{2}$: 𝅗𝅥 = 40: 25 meas.
$\frac{2}{2}$: 𝅗𝅥 = 56-60: 40 meas.
$\frac{2}{2}$: 𝅗𝅥 = 40: 6 meas.
$\frac{2}{2}$: 𝅗𝅥 = 64-76: 37 meas.

This was the Paris Conservatory contest piece for 1968.

Hugon, Georges (b. 1904). *Élégie.* EDMT, 1976.

†———. *Introduction et allegro.* EDMT, 1961. 180 meas.; 13'; A♭'–d"; 8; TB; straight mute, flutter tongue, glissandi, cadenza.

Lent: $\frac{2}{4}$, $\frac{3}{4}$, $\frac{4}{4}$, $\frac{5}{4}$, $\frac{6}{4}$: ♩ = 52: 25 meas.
Allegro: $\frac{2}{4}$, $\frac{3}{4}$, $\frac{4}{4}$: ♩ = 144: 44 meas.
$\frac{2}{4}$, $\frac{3}{4}$, $\frac{4}{4}$: ♩ = 126: 25 meas.
$\frac{2}{4}$, $\frac{3}{4}$, $\frac{4}{4}$: ♩ = 104: 52 meas.
Allegro: $\frac{2}{4}$, $\frac{3}{4}$: ♩ = 144: 34 meas.

This was the Paris Conservatory contest piece for 1961.

Joubert, Claude-Henry. *Chanson de Blondel.* COM.

——. *Dialogue du captian et du coucou.* MAR, 1985. 3'; G-e'; 2.

Lafosse, André, ed. (b. 1890). *Trois pièces de style.* LED, 1956. 115 meas.; 5'30"; B♭–c"; 7*; TB; mordents.

I. Giuseppe Tartini—*Andante cantabile.* $\frac{4}{4}$: 19 meas.
II. Franz Schubert—*Adagio.* $\frac{6}{8}$: 36 meas.
III. Antonio Vivaldi—*Sonate (fragments).*
Largo: $\frac{3}{4}$: ♩ = 56: 35 meas.
Allegro: $\frac{2}{4}$: ♩ = 100: 25 meas.

Lamy, Fernand (1881-1966). *Choral varié.* LED, 1949. 3*; TB.

Lancen, Serge (b. 1922). *Menuet pour un ours* [Minuet for a Bear]. BILL, 1965. 96 meas.; 3'45"; G–g'; 4; glissandi.

"Prix de Composition de la Confédération Musicale de France (1965)"

Andante: $\frac{2}{4}$: ♩ = 42: 18 meas.
Menuet—Allegretto: $\frac{3}{4}$: ♩ = 86: 78 meas.

Landowski, Marcel. *Improvisation.* SAL, 1983.

Leclercq, Edgard. *Concertino.* LED. 7*; TB.

"Morceau de Concours du Conservatoire d'Anvers"

Legron, Léon. *Grave et cantilène.* BILL, 1977. 76 meas.; 3'30"; B♭–e'; 2.

"À Michel Fiche"

Grave: $\frac{3}{4}$: ♩ = 52: 32 meas.
Cantilene: $\frac{3}{4}$: ♩ = 96: 32 meas.
Grave: $\frac{3}{4}$: ♩ = 52: 12 meas.

This short work is in the common one movement style of slow-fast-slow. The major emphasis of the piece concerns itself with controlled legato playing. The key of B♭ major predominates with a short piano interlude in D♭ major.

†**Lejet, Edith** (b. 1941). *Musique.* EDFR, 1974. 4'30"; A♭'–indefinite; 9; plunger, quarter tones, flutter tongue, glissandi, large vibrato, approximate rhythms.

"Gerard Pichaureau"

$\frac{4}{4}$, $\frac{5}{4}$: 80 meas.

This was the Paris Conservatory contest piece for 1973. It is a difficult piece requiring many changes of mood and the ability to project them through the instrument. It is also made more difficult due to the extreme range, frequent large intervallic skips, and changes from traditional notation to proportional notation.

Lemaire, Jean (1854-1928). *Récit pour un débutant* [Solo for a Beginner]. BILL. 1*.

"Collection de la Fédération Nationale des Unions de Conservatoires Municipaux de Musique"

†**Lepetit, Pierre** (b. 1893). *Pièce de concert* [Concert Piece]. LED, 1955. 172 meas.; 6'; E–d"; 7*; TB.

"André LaFosse"

Moderato: $\frac{4}{4}$: ♩ = 76: 14 meas.
Très lent: $\frac{6}{4}$: ♩ = 80: 39 meas.
Allegro très modéré: $\frac{2}{4}$: ♩ = 96: 64 meas.
Un peu plus vitae: $\frac{2}{4}$: ♩ = 112: 20 meas.
Plus vite: $\frac{2}{4}$: ♩ = 116: 35 meas.

This was the Paris Conservatory contest piece for 1955.

Lesaffre, Charles. *En glissant...* [On Sliding...]. BILL, 1984.

See entry in Chapter 5.

Liagre, Dartagnan. *Souvenir de Calais*. BILL.

Loucheur, Raymond (b. 1899). *Hialmar*. DUR, 1947. 75 meas.; 6'; A-d"; 7*; TB; straight mute.

"Henri Couillaud"

Lento: $\frac{2}{4}$, $\frac{4}{4}$: ♩ = 46: 31 meas.
Animando: $\frac{3}{4}$: ♩ = 72: 6 meas.
Lento: $\frac{4}{4}$: ♩ = 46: 15 meas.
Sostenuto: $\frac{2}{4}$, $\frac{4}{4}$: ♩ = 60: 23 meas.

Louvier, Alain (b. 1945). *Hydre à cinq têtes* [Hydra with Five Heads]. LED. 3*.

Lucie, Robert. *Élégie I*. BILL, 1985.

Lys, Marc. *Cocktail*. MAR, 1984.

Maillard, A. *Ballade*. BILL.

———. *Fantaisie*. BILL.

Margoni, Alain (b. 1934). *Fête à l'abbaye de Thélème* [Saint's Day at the Thélème Abby]. BILL, 1982. G-f"; 4; TB.

———. *Gargantua apprend la sacqueboute* [Gargantua Learns the Sackbut]. BILL, 1982. G-g♭'; 4; TB.

———. *La guerre picrocholine*. BILL, 1982. 5; GT; flutter tongue.

Marie, Jean-Marie (b. 1917). *Labyrinthes (avant garde)*. AM, 1975.

†**Martin, Frank** (b. 1890). *Ballade*. UE, 1940. 347 meas.; 7'30"; B♭'–d"; 7; TB. Recordings: 8, 11, 12, 22, 61, 71.

"Concours National Suisse D'Execution Musicale Geneve 1940"

Largamente, Andante: $\frac{2}{4}$, $\frac{3}{4}$: ♩ = 72: 17 meas.
Tranquillo: $\frac{2}{4}$, $\frac{3}{4}$: ♩ = 54: 39 meas.
Allegro giusto: ¢ : 𝅗𝅥 = 116: 142 meas.
Vivace assai: $\frac{6}{8}$: ♩ = 184: 72 meas.
Grandioso: $\frac{3}{4}$: ♩ = 160: 24 meas.
Più mosso: $\frac{3}{4}$: 𝅗𝅥. = 66: 42 meas.
Molto largamente: $\frac{2}{4}$: ♪ = 76: 11 meas.

This was the Paris Conservatory contest piece for 1959, written for trombone and piano in 1940 and transcribed for orchestra in 1941. The work opens with an accompanied passage for trombone in a fanfare-like style. Although the solo features ballad qualities, it also provides some technical sections. The melodic construction is often motivic, but phrases can be found in passages of the slower tempi. The accompanying textures are contrapuntal, but much of the accompaniment is more important as rhythmic foundations for the solo line than as linear counterpoint. The orchestral accompaniment parts are available on rental from PR. The instrumentation of the accompaniment is as follows: 2 fls, 2 obs, 2 cls, 2 bns, 2 hns, 2 trpts, 2 trbns, timp, pf, strgs.

Massis, Amable (b. 1893). *Impromptu* (Version A: Facile, Version B: Moyenne Force, Version C: Difficile). LED, 1949. 3'50"; B–a♭', F–a', E–b♮'; 3,5,7; TB; cadenza.

Allegro moderato: $\frac{2}{4}$, $\frac{4}{4}$: ♩ = 88: 78 meas.

This solo is very unique due to its three versions for use by the trombonist. The first version is labeled "easy," the second "moderate," and the third "difficult."

Each version becomes progressively more difficult through the use of rhythmic, melodic and range complexities. The piano accompaniment remains the same for each trombone version of the solo.

Maurat, Edmond (b. 1881). *Petites inventions* [Little Inventions], *Op. 21, No. 3.* Esc, 1966.

†**Mazellier, Jules** (1879-1959). *Solo de concours en b mineur.* LED; INT, 1960. 146 meas.; 6'50"; F♯–b'; 7*; TB; straight mute.

"Henri Couillaud, Professeur au Conservatoire National de Musique de Paris"

Andante espressivo: $\frac{3}{4}$: ♩ = 54: 62 meas.
Allegro risoluto: $\frac{4}{4}$: ♩ = 100: 84 meas.

This was the Paris Conservatory contest piece for 1934.

Mendelssohn, Felix (1809-1847). *Capriccioso brilliant, Op. 22.* Edited by Paul Delisse. Millereau, *ca.* 1886.

Meyer, Jean-Michel (b. 1910). *Cordelineété.* Lem.

Mignion, René. *Andante et allegro.* BILL, 1972. 80 meas.; 3'; c–g'; 2.

"Prix de Composition de la Confédération Musicale de France 1972"

Andante: $\frac{4}{4}$: ♩ = 63: 30 meas.
Allegro: $\frac{2}{4}$: ♩ = 100: 50 meas.

——. *Cantabile et minuetto.* BILL, 1978. 95 meas.; 4'; A–f'; 3*.

"Dupart, Professeur au Conservatoire de Bordeaux"

I. Cantabile—Andante: $\frac{4}{4}$: ♩ = 60: 30 meas.
II. Menuetto: $\frac{3}{4}$: ♩ = 96-100: 65 meas.

While this is not a major work for trombone, it has many pedagogical values. The rather narrow range and rhythmic simplicity make this selection accessible to the young trombonist.

——. *Rêverie et ballade.* BILL, 1966. 94 meas.; 3'50"; c♯–f♯'; 3.

"Prix de Composition de la Confédération Musicale de France 1966"

Andantino: $\frac{4}{4}$: ♩ = 65: 44 meas.
Moderato: $\frac{2}{4}$: ♩ = 85: 50 meas.

——. *Sérénade et ballade mosellanes.* BILL, 1978. 68 meas.; 3'15"; B♭–f'; 2*.

"Gilles Senon, Professeur au Conservatoire de Metz"

Andante: $\frac{4}{4}$: ♩ = 60: 24 meas.
Moderato: $\frac{6}{8}$: ♩ = 80-84: 44 meas.

Milhaud, Darius (1892-1974). *Concertino d'hiver* [Winter Concertino]. AS, 1955. 292 meas.; 11'30"; E–c"; 7; TB; straight mute, flutter, glissandi. Recordings: 29, 34, 42, 69, 73.

"Davis Shuman and Hunterdon County Art Center"

Animé: $\frac{2}{2}$: 𝅗𝅥 = 86: 104 meas.
Trés modéré: $\frac{3}{4}$: ♪ = 86: 84 meas.
Animé: $\frac{2}{2}$: 𝅗𝅥 = 86: 104 meas.

Although performed as a continuous one-movement piece, its three large sections function as three separate movements. The movements are entitled, *Animé, Très modéré,* and *Animé,* in ternary form. The first and third movements use the same melodic material and are in a highly disjunct, non-diatonic intervallic style. The melodic construction is phrase oriented, but the phrases are not always clearly defined because of the disjunct nature of the intervallic style. The middle section is quite slow and long because of the slow rhythmic motion. The two strong features of this work are its audience appeal and the technical challenge it presents to the trombonist. This piece was written with string accompaniment; the parts are available from KING. The specific instrumentation of the accompanying string orchestra is as follows: vns I and II, va, vc, db.

†**Missa, Edmond Jean Louis** (1861-1910). *Morceau de concours* [Contest Piece]. Evette et Schaeffer, 1904; LED, 1959. 85 meas.; 3'30"; B♭–c"; 7*; TB.
"Louis Allard"

Moderato ben marcato: $\frac{4}{4}$: 13 meas.
Plus lent et expressif: $\frac{3}{4}$: 22 meas.

Allegretto: $\frac{2}{4}$: 30 meas.
Plus lent et expressif: $\frac{4}{4}$: 20 meas.

This was the Paris Conservatory contest piece for 1904.

Morel, Florentin (b. 1926). *Pièce en fa mineur.* BILL, 1933. 140 meas.; 5'; G♭–c"; 5; TB, lip trills. Recordings: 30, 43.

"Morceau Impose au Grand Concours International de Solistes de Lille (1933)"

Allegro deciso: $\frac{9}{8}$: 25 meas.
Allegro moderato: $\frac{9}{8}$: 45 meas.
Andante: $\frac{3}{4}$: 37 meas.
Allegro deciso: $\frac{9}{8}$: 33 meas.

Muller, J. P. *Concertino, Op. 6.* MAU, 1957. 88 meas.; 2'30"; E♯(D)–d♭"; 7; GB.

Giocoso: $\frac{4}{4}$: ♩ = 120: 36 meas.
Sostenuto: $\frac{4}{4}$: ♩ = 𝅗𝅥: 20 meas.
Tempo I: $\frac{4}{4}$: ♩ = 120: 32 meas.

———. *Concerto minute, Op. 4.* MAU, 1960.

Nicolas, M. *Primo concertino.* BILL.

———. *Rhizome.* BILL.

Niverd, Lucien (1879-1967). *Six petites pièces de style.* BILL.

1. Hymne.
2. Romance sentimentale. 1'45"; G–c'; 3.
   Moderato: $\frac{4}{4}$: ♩ = 76: 36 meas.
3. Complainte [Lament]. 1'10"; E–b; 3.
   Andantino: $\frac{3}{4}$: ♩ = 80: 33 meas.
4. Historiette dramatique. 1'10"; F–d'; 3.
   Modéré, mélancolique: $\frac{4}{4}$: ♩ = 76: 24 meas.
5. Chant mélancolique.
6. Scherzetto.
   Vif et léger: $\frac{3}{4}$: ♩ = 200: 48 meas.

———. *Légende.* BILL. 20 meas.; 1'10"; E–g♭'; 3.

Assez lent: $\frac{4}{4}$: ♩ = 46: 12 meas.
Largement: $\frac{4}{4}$: 8 meas.

Niverd, Raymond (b. 1922). *Maestoso et scherzando.* DEL, 1969. 180 meas.; 5'; E–d♭"(e"); 8; TB.

"Maffei, Professeur au Conservatoire de Troyes"

I. Maestoso: $\frac{2}{2}$: 73 meas.
II. Scherzendo: $\frac{3}{4}$: 52 meas.
Plus lent: $\frac{3}{4}$: 35 meas.
Tempo I°: $\frac{3}{4}$: 20 meas.

†**Nux, Paul V. de la** (1853-1928). *Solo de concours* [Contest Piece]. Evette et Schaeffer; LED; SOUT, 1903, 1961. 111 meas.; 5'; G–b♭'; 6*; cadenza, lip trills. Recordings: 16, 28, 40, 53.

Andante: $\frac{4}{4}$: 51 meas.
Allegro: $\frac{6}{4}$: ♩. = 60: 16 meas.
$\frac{4}{4}$: ♩ = 72: 44 meas.

This was the Paris Conservatory contest piece for 1900 and again in 1919. This solo contains the typical slow legato section followed by a fast articulated portion. A band accompaniment is available from FISC.

Pares, Gabriel (1860-1934). *Crépuscule* [Twilight]. BILL; BEL. 2'15"; c♭–g♭'; 4.

Moderato: $\frac{9}{8}$: 68 meas.

Pascal, Claude (b. 1921). *Improvisation en forme de canon.* DUR, 1959.

†——. *Pastorale héroïque.* DUR, 1952. 5'; B♭'–c♯"; 5; TB; cadenza.

"Andre LaFosse, Professeur au Conservaeoire National de Musique"

Allant: $\frac{2}{4}$: ♩ = 126: 312 meas.

This was the Paris Conservatory contest piece for 1952.

——. *Sonate.* DUR, 1958. 6'30"; F'–b'; TB.

Perrin, Jean (b. 1920). *Introduction et allegro.* BILL.

†**Pfeiffer, Georges-Jean** (1835-1908). *Solo de trombone.* LED; SOUT, 1941. 168 meas.; 7'; F–c"; 6*; TB; trills, cadenza.

"U.S.A. School Music Competition-Festivals"

Adagio: $\frac{4}{4}$: 66 meas.
Allegro eroico: $\frac{3}{4}$: 102 meas.

This was the Paris Conservatory contest piece for 1899 and again in 1906. The work, in two large parts, begins with a series of adagio sections, incorporating recitative-like cadenzas at the beginning and end of the first part. The fast section begins with an articulated technical passage, followed by a short expressive phrase. Following a cadenza, a final statement of the fast theme and a short coda complete the piece. A band transcription of the piano accompaniment, made by Lee Hope, is available from the music department at the University of Notre Dame.

Pichaureau, Claude. *Marine.* RID, 1969. 8'; B♭'–c♯"; 7; TB; plunger, harmon, and velvet mutes, quarter tones, trills, glissandi, proportional notation.

This solo is accompanied by violin and piano. The work is sectional, harmonically tertian oriented, with chromaticism and an abundance of thirteenth chords. The texture is contrapuntal with frequent meter changes being employed throughout.

——. *Cinc concerti "minute."* CHO.

Poot, Marcel (b. 1901). *Étude de concert* [Concert Study]. LED, 1958. 160 meas.; 3'30"; F–g; 6*; TB.

Andante: $\frac{2}{4}$, $\frac{3}{4}$, $\frac{4}{4}$: ♩ = 72: 17 meas.
Allegro deciso: $\frac{2}{2}$, $\frac{3}{2}$: 𝅗𝅥 = 126: 116 meas.
Andante: $\frac{4}{4}$: ♩ = 72: 9 meas.
Allegro: $\frac{2}{2}$, $\frac{3}{2}$: 𝅗𝅥 = 126: 18 meas.

——. *Impromptu.* ANDE; ESC, 1933. 4' G–b'; 6; TB. Recording: 68.

Porret, Julien (b. 1896). *Concertino No. 7.* BILL, 1950; MAR. 86 meas.; 5'30"; B♭–f♯'; 3.

"René Dhaene, Professeur au Conservatoire de Lille"

Andantino sans lenteur: $\frac{4}{4}$: 41 meas.
Dolce e poco più lento: $\frac{4}{4}$: 45 meas.

——. *Concertino No. 8.* MAR.

——. *Concertino No. 10.* BILL, 1950. 108 meas.; 5'30"; A–a'; 4.

"Louis Delforge, Professeur au Conservatoire de Tours"

Moderato e energicamente: $\frac{4}{4}$: 32 meas.
Andantino semplice: $\frac{9}{8}$, $\frac{4}{4}$: 76 meas.

——. *Concertino No. 23.* BILL; MAR.

——. *Concertino No. 24.* BILL; MAR.

——. *Six esquisses* [Six Sketches]. BARO, 1935. 231 meas.; 10'40"; E–a♯'; 7; TB. Recording: 38 (Nos. I and II only).

"Baron, Musique de Chambre No. 3"

I. Andantino: $\frac{6}{8}$: ♩. = 60: 42 meas.
II. Andantino, dolce: $\frac{3}{4}$: ♩ = 60: 52 meas.
III. Andantino, dolce e con espressione: $\frac{9}{8}$: ♩. = 63: 26 meas.
IV. Moderato: $\frac{4}{4}$: ♩ = 88: 42 meas.
V. Andantino: $\frac{4}{4}$: ♩ = 60: 33 meas.
VI. Moderato: $\frac{2}{4}$, $\frac{4}{4}$: ♩ = 96: 36 meas.

——. *Solo de concours No. 15.* MOLE, 1963. 2'50"; c–e'; 2.

"Pierre Ambach, Soliste au Theatre et Professeur au Conservatoire National de Musique de Besancon"

Moderato: $\frac{4}{4}$: 65 meas.

——. *Solo de concours No. 16.* MOLE, 1964. 167 meas.; 5'45"; F–g'; 3.

Allegro moderato: $\frac{3}{4}$: ♩ = 120: 70 meas.
Allegro moderato: $\frac{4}{4}$: ♩ = 76: 13 meas.
Andantino: $\frac{4}{4}$: ♩ = 72: 36 meas.
Andantino: $\frac{3}{4}$: ♩ = 120: 43 meas.

———. *Solo de concours No. 29.* MOLE, 1964. 5'; c–g'; 3.

"Pierre Goigou, Professeur au Conservatoire de Musique de Rennes"

Andantino semplice: $\frac{4}{4}$: 100 meas.

———. *Solo de concours No. 30.* MOLE, 1964. 195 meas.; 6'45"; B♭'–d'; 4; cadenza.

"Henri Dupart, Professeur au Conservatoire, Soliste au Grand Theatre de Bordeaux"

Allegretto: $\frac{4}{4}$: ♩ = 88: 18 meas.
Lento: $\frac{9}{8}$: ♩. = 50: 57 meas.
Allegretto: $\frac{6}{8}$: ♩. = 96: 120 meas.

———. *Solo de concours No. 31.* MOLE, 1966. 97 meas.; 4'45"; c–f'; 3.

"Robert Bouffier, Professeur au Conservatoire de Musique de Toulon"

Moderato: $\frac{4}{4}$: 52 meas.
Poco più lento: $\frac{4}{4}$: 20 meas.
Moderato: $\frac{4}{4}$: 25 meas.

———. *Solo de concours No. 32.* MOLE, 1966. 122 meas., 5'45"; A–a♭'; 4.

"Henri Borel, Professeur au Conservatoire National de Musique d'Arras"

Allegretto: $\frac{4}{4}$: ♩ = 88: 60 meas.
Andantino: $\frac{4}{4}$: ♩ = 80: 40 meas.
Allegretto: $\frac{4}{4}$: ♩ = 88: 22 meas.

Pucci, Alain. *Pièce en fa majeur dans le style de W. A. Mozart.* BILL, 1988.

———. *Pièce en ré mineur dans le style de Haendel.* BILL, 1985. 2'10"; F-f'; 4.

———. *Pièce en si bémol majeur dans le style de Brahms.* BILL, 1985. 3'; G-e'; 4.

Rasse, François (1873-1955). *Concertino.* Evette et Schaeffer; LED, 1921. 8'; A♭'–b♭'; 5.

"Morceau de Concours du Conservatoire de Bruxelles"

Moderato: $\frac{4}{4}$
Andantino: $\frac{3}{4}$
Cantabile: $\frac{2}{4}$
Allegro deciso: $\frac{2}{4}$

This work consists of four connected sections, all of which are through-composed. The intervallic style used throughout is non-diatonic, often outlining chords, while the melodies are constructed in phrases which are not disjunct. The orchestral accompaniment parts are available from the Fleisher Collection, Catalog #748m. The instrumentation of the accompaniment is as follows: 2 fls, 2 obs, 2 cls, 2 bns, 2 hns, 2 trpts, timp, strgs.

Reichel, Bernard (b. 1901). *Choral, canon I et II.* BILL, 1973. 3.

Reutter, Hermann (b. 1900). *Étude polyphonique.* LED. 4*.

——. *Ostinato.* LED, 1957. 3'; F–d♭'; 3*.

Poco grave: $\frac{3}{4}$: ♩ = 60: 60 meas.

†**Rieunier, Jean-Paul** (b. 1933). *Silences.* LED, 1976. 8'; A♭'–f"; 8*; GB; plunger mute, multiphonics, quarter tones, glissandi.

"Gerard Pichaureau"

(Circa): $\frac{4}{4}$: ♩ = 60

This was the Paris Conservatory contest piece for 1976. It is an expressive piece requiring a sensitive performance to bring out the contrast of material. This piece utilizes many of the new music devices for trombone in a most cohesive way with the materials flowing together smoothly. It wlll require an experienced player who has had some experience with this idiom, multiphonics in particular. This is the first contest piece to employ the technique of multiphonics. It is notably late when comparing it to the compositions of Berio, Alsina, and Globokar, which used the technique in the mid-1960's.

Rivière, Jean-Pierre (b. 1929). *Burlesque.* LED, 1958. 7*.

——. *Rhapsodie.* BILL, 1984. 67 meas.; 10'; E-d"; 8; TB; straight mute, cadenza, trills, glissandi.

"Gilles Millière"

Maestoso: $\frac{12}{8}$: 15 meas.
Poco più mosso: $\frac{3}{4}$, $\frac{4}{4}$: 26 meas.
Più mosso: $\frac{3}{4}$: 18 meas.
Allegro ritmico: $\frac{3}{4}$, $\frac{4}{4}$: 18 meas.
Poco meno: $\frac{3}{4}$, $\frac{4}{4}$: 120 meas.

This was the Paris Conservatory contest piece for 1984.

Robert, Jacques. *Air noble.* BILL, 1970. 78 meas.; 2'; B♭–f'; 2*.

"Prix de Composition de la Confédération Musicale de France 1970"

Allegretto: $\frac{4}{4}$: ♩ = 104-108: 20 meas.
Un poco più mosso: $\frac{2}{4}$: ♩ = 116: 47 meas.
Allegretto: $\frac{4}{4}$: ♩ = 104-108: 11 meas.

Robert, L. *Élégie I.* BILL.

——. *Élégie II.* BILL.

Roche, G. *L'Olympienne.* René Margueritat, *ca.* 1886.

Roizenblatt, A. *Comme un souvenir* [Like a Souvenir]. BILL.

Ropartz, J. Guy (1864-1955). *Andante et allegro.* FISC. 5'; A♭–a'. Recording: 16.

†——. *Pièce en mi bémol mineur.* LED; BEL, 1908; INT, 1953. 166 meas.; 8'; F–c"(e♭"); 6*; T; lip trill. Recordings: 50, 60.

Lento: $\frac{4}{4}$: ♩ = 56: 48 meas.
Allegro: $\frac{4}{4}$: ♩ = 132: 118 meas.

This was the Paris Conservatory contest piece for 1908. The work contains two connected sections, marked *Lento* and *Allegro*. The intervallic style of the composition is non-diatonic and the melodies are constructed in phrases. There is little contrapuntal writing with the accompaniment generally involving ostinato rhythmic patterns. Only the orchestral score is available from the Fleischer Collection, Catalog #747m. The instrumentation of the accompaniment is as follows: 2 fls, 2 obs, 2 cls, 2 bns, 4 hns, 2 trpts, timp, strgs.

Rossini, Gioacchino (1792-1868). *Air de pharaon dans "Moïse"* [Pharoah's Aria in "Moses"]. Edited by Pierre Signard (1829-1901). Millereau, *ca.* 1885.

This work is edited for use by the valve trombone.

Rougeron, Philippe. *Pièce en fa.* BILL, 1978. 3'; F–f'; 3.

†**Rousseau, Samuel-Alexandre** (1853-1904). *Pièce concertante.* HEU, *ca.* 1898; FISC, 1938; LED. 180 meas.; 5'30"; F♯–c"; 6; cadenza. Recordings: 30, 40, 58.

Allegro moderato: $\frac{3}{4}$: 86 meas.
Larghetto: $\frac{3}{4}$: 42 meas.
Allegro moderato: $\frac{3}{4}$: 52 meas.

This was the Paris Conservatory contest piece for the years 1898, 1918, 1926, and 1980.

†**Rueff, Jeanine** (b. 1922). *Rhapsodie.* LED, 1962. 284 meas.; 7'10"; B♭–d♭"; 8*; TB; cadenza.

Quasi recitativo: $\frac{3}{4}$: 23 meas.
Lento expressivo: $\frac{4}{4}$, $\frac{2}{2}$, $\frac{4}{2}$: ♩ = 92: 31 meas.
Allegretto scherzando: $\frac{3}{8}$: ♩. = 66: 110 meas.
Allegro energico: $\frac{3}{4}$, $\frac{2}{2}$: 𝅗𝅥 = 104: 76 meas.
Presto: $\frac{3}{8}$: 44 meas.

This was the Paris Conservatory contest piece for 1962.

†**Saint-Saëns, Camille** (1835-1921). *Cavatine, Op. 144.* DUR, 1915. 220 meas.; 5'; A♭'–d♭"; 6; TB. Recording: 1, 37, 50, 60, 70.

Allegro: $\frac{3}{4}$: 70 meas.
Andantino: $\frac{3}{4}$: 52 meas.
Allegro: $\frac{3}{4}$: 98 meas.

This was the Paris Conservatory contest piece for 1922.

†**Salzédo, Carlos** (1885-1961). *Pièce concertante, Op.* 27. LED, 1958; INT, n.d. 215 meas.; 6'10"; c–c"; 7*; T; straight mute. Recordings: 33, 60, 64.

Largo: $\frac{6}{4}$: ♩ = 96: 34 meas.
Più vivo: $\frac{6}{4}$: ♩ = 168: 40 meas.
Molto più lento: $\frac{6}{4}$: ♩ = 168: 28 meas.
Più vivo: $\frac{3}{4}$: ♩. = 72: 72 meas.
$\frac{6}{4}$: ♩. = 138: 41 meas.

This was the Paris Conservatory contest piece for 1910. This is one of the few compositions of Salzédo that does not include a harp. The main theme, *Largo* is stated by the trombone.after a short piano introduction. Upon its immediate return, the second measure of the theme undergoes a rhythmic variation which later becomes the principal motive of the following *Più vivo* section. The *Più vivo* ends abruptly and the opening section returns *Molto più lento,* the trombone now muted. The second *Più vivo* leads to a true virtuosic ending.

Sciortino, Patrice (b. 1922). *Ergies (à Paraitre).* BILL. 5*.

——, ed. *Pièces classiques.* 4 vols. BILL.
Vol. 1. Very easy.
Vol. 2. Moderately easy.
Vol. 3. Medium.
Vol. 4 Moderately difficult.

Lively, varied series which presents arrangements from master works by master composers, including Bach, Chopin, Beethoven, Schumann, and others. For studios, conservatories. (quoted from PR catalog)

Séguin, Pierre. *Chanson d'août* [Song of August]. Collection Rougeron. LED. P1-2*.

——. *Confidence.* Collection Rougeron. LED, 1984. 1'20"; P1-2*.

——. *Étreinte.* Collection Rougeron. LED, 1984. 1'20"; D1-2*.

——. *Marine.* Collection Rougeron. LED, 1983. 1'20"; D1-2*.

——. *Rupture.* Collection Rougeron. LED, 1987. P2-E*.
See entry in Chapter 5.

——. *Tubavardage.* Collection Rougeron. LED, 1987. D1-2*.
See entry in Chapter 5.

†**Semler-Collery, Jules** (b. 1902). *Fantaisie lyrique.* ESC, 1960. 117 meas.; 7'; B♭'–c♯"; 6; TB; Robinson mute, cadenza. Recording: 1. "Andre LaFosse"

Tempo guisto: $\frac{3}{4}$: ♩ = 104: 39 meas.
Tempo più lento: $\frac{3}{4}$: ♩ = 80: 38 meas.
Tempo guisto: $\frac{3}{4}$: ♩ = 104: 31 meas.
Vivo—Coda: $\frac{3}{4}$: 9 meas.

This was the Paris Conservatory contest piece for 1960. The one-movement solo begins with a long unaccompanied cadenza in a free, improvisatory style. The composer has created themes that sound rhythmically free and improvisatory by mixing duple and triple rhythmic figures together, and incorporating them with a smooth melodic style.

Sendrez, M. *Capricorne.* BILL.

——. *Prélude.* BILL.

Senon, Gilles (b. 1932). *Ambiances.* BILL. 6*.

——. *Blues, reflets et cabriolets.* MAR, 1984.

——. *Cantilène et baladine.* MAR, 1984.

——. *Chevauchée* [Cavalcade] BILL, 1977. 2'15"; E–g'; 3*.

Allegretto: $\frac{6}{8}$, $\frac{9}{8}$, $\frac{2}{4}$: ♩ = 104: 73 meas.

This short piece utilizes a mixture of quartal and triadic harmonies. There are numerous passages of a fanfare-like nature with a moderate amount of chromaticism and disjunct intervals.

——. *Mélodie.* BILL, 1977. 2'20"; G–a♭'; 3*.

Andante: $\frac{2}{4}$, $\frac{4}{4}$: ♩ = 66: 39 meas.

——. *Océane et parodie.* MAR, 1984.

——. *Prière* [Prayer]. BILL. 6*. Recording: 24.

This work is unusual in that the accompaniment is written for the organ, as opposed to the traditional piano accompaniment.

Sichler, J. *Avenue Washington.* Collection Rougeron. LED. P1-2*.

——. *Trombone blues.* Collection Rougeron. LED. D1*.

†**Spisak, Michel** (1914-1965). *Concertino.* LED, 1951. 282 meas.; 10'; B♭'–d"; 5*; TB; straight mute, cadenza.

Allegro moderato: $\frac{2}{4}$: ♩ = 96-100: 147 meas.
Andante tranquillo: $\frac{3}{4}$: ♩ = 72: 64 meas.
Allegro moderato: $\frac{2}{4}$: ♩ = 96-100: 71 meas.

This was the Paris Conservatory contest piece for 1951. It is a one movement work structured into an ABA formal pattern. The work begins with a fast section which exploits the performer's technical facility. The B section utilizes materials from the beginning, but with a much slower smoother style. The fast A section returns, and following a short coda, the solo ends. The soloist can ease some of the difficulty of this solo by using a trombone with an F attachment. The orchestral accompaniment parts are available on rental from LED. The instrumentation of the accompaniment is as follows: fl, ob, cl, bn, hn, trpt, tba, 2 timp, strgs.

†**Stojowski, Sigismond** (1869-1946). *Fantaisie.* Evette et Schaeffer, 1905; edited by Keith Brown, INT, 1972; LED, 1953. 126 meas.; 6'; B♭'–b♭'; 7*; TB. Recordings: 50, 70.

Allegro risoluto poco maestoso: $\frac{4}{4}$: 25 meas.
Lento: $\frac{4}{4}$: 39 meas.
Tempo I: $\frac{4}{4}$: 62 meas.

This was the Paris Conservatory contest piece in 1905 and again in 1914.

Tamba, Akira. *Fantaisie.* LED, 1965. 4*.

Tillet, Louis. *Hypnose.* BILL, 1986. unacc t trbn.

——. *Ignéscence.* BILL, 1986.

Tisné, Antoine (b. 1932). *Élégie et burlesque, Op. 32, No. 1.* LED, 1965. 3*.

†**Tomasi, Henri** (1901-1971). *Concerto.* LED, 1956. 468 meas.; 14'; F–d"; 8*; TB; straight and cup mutes, cadenza. Recording: 8.

I. Antante et Scherzo—Valse
Lento assai rubato: $\frac{6}{8}$, $\frac{9}{8}$, $\frac{12}{8}$: ♩. = 54: 66 meas.
Allegro: ¢ : 𝅗𝅥 = 80: 4 meas.
Tempo di valse: $\frac{3}{4}$: 𝅗𝅥. = 60: 158 meas.
Tempo I : $\frac{6}{8}$, $\frac{9}{8}$, $\frac{12}{8}$, $\frac{3}{4}$: ♩. = 54: 5 meas.
Subtotal: 233 meas.

II. Nocturne
Andante: $\frac{2}{4}$, $\frac{3}{4}$, $\frac{4}{4}$, $\frac{5}{4}$: ♩ = 60: 36 meas.
Tempo di Blues: $\frac{2}{4}$, $\frac{3}{4}$, $\frac{4}{4}$: 28 meas.
Lent: $\frac{4}{4}$: ♩ = 52: 10 meas.
Subtotal: 74 meas.

III. Tambourin
Allegro giocoso: $\frac{2}{4}$, $\frac{3}{4}$, $\frac{4}{4}$: ♩ = 144: 161 meas.

This was the Paris Conservatory contest piece in 1956. The work is in three movements, and reflects a strong impressionistic influence through its melodic and harmonic organization. The first movement is composed in two connected sections and is through-composed, except for a five measure restatement of the opening theme at the end. The second movement, with a slow tempo involving several short sections, is in ternary form. A *Tempo di Blues* section, similar to some of Gershwin's writing, appears near the end of this movement. The third movement, in a quasi-rondo form, consists of a fast movement in an articulated style. The orchestral accompaniment parts are available on rental from LED. The instrumentation of the accompaniment is as follows: 2 fls, 2 obs, 2 cls, 2 bns, 2 hns, 2 trpts, 2 timp, perc, cel, vib, xylo, hp, strgs.

——. *Danse sacrée.* LED, 1960. 42 meas.; 3' (11'30" total); G–a♭'; 5*; GB. Recording: 56.
"À Mr. Baptiste Mari, amicalement"

Lent: $\frac{3}{4}$, $\frac{4}{4}$, $\frac{5}{4}$: ♩ = 52: 17 meas.
Con moto: $\frac{3}{8}$, $\frac{2}{4}$, $\frac{3}{4}$, $\frac{4}{4}$: ♩ = 60: 16 meas.
Tempo I (Lent): $\frac{2}{4}$, $\frac{3}{4}$, $\frac{4}{4}$, $\frac{5}{4}$: ♩ = 52: 9 meas.

This work represents one part of a collection of pieces entitled *Cinq dances profanes et sacrées* [Five Secular and Ritual Dances]. The five pieces for examination and performance represent five levels of difficulty that correspond to the five years of study, according to the programs of the Paris Conservatory and High Schools of Music in France. The solo for the trombone represents the third level:

I. *Danse agreste* [Rustic Dance]—oboe
II. *Danse profane* [Secular Dance]—horn in F
III. *Danse sacrée* [Sacred Dance]—trombone
IV. *Danse nuptiale* [Bridal Dance]—clarinet
V. *Danse guerrière* [War Dance]—bassoon

Although the solo requires only a limited amount of technical facility and range, a mature and sensitive musician is needed for an effective performance of this piece. The orchestral accompaninent parts are available on rental from LED. The instrumentation of the accompaniment is as follows: pf, 3 timp, perc, strgs (min. 6-5-4-3-3).

Toulon, Jacques. *Collection enfants—Décidé* [Decided]. Piano accompaniment by L. Mallie. MAR, 1978.

——. *Collection enfants—Enfant de chœur* [Naïve Person]. Piano accompaniment by L. Mallie. MAR, 1978.

——. *Collection enfants—Gai* [Merry]. Piano accompaniment by L. Mallie. MAR, 1978.

——. *Collection enfants—Rêveur* [Pensive, Dreamy]. Piano accompaniment by L. Mallie. MAR, 1978.

——. *Collection enfants—Triste* [Sorrowful, Mournful]. Piano accompaniment by L. Mallie. MAR, 1978.

——. *Pièce No. 1.* Piano accompaniment by Jacqueline Vernier. LED, 1982. 3'20"; A-g♭'; 4*.

Toulon, Jacques, and **Jean Brouquières**. *En allant.* MAR, 1984.

——. *Marche et danse.* MAR, 1984. 2'; G♯–f'; 4.

——. *Récitative.* MAR, 1984. 2'; A-f'; 4.

——. *Romance.* MAR, 1984. 2'; d-f'; 4.

†**Tournemire, Charles** (1870-1939). *Légende.* LED, 1920. 70 meas.; 2'; B♭'–c"; 7*; TB; straight mute; lip trills.

"Henri Couillaud"

Assez largement: $\frac{4}{4}$: ♩ = 54: 12 meas.
Retenez: $\frac{4}{4}$: ♪ = 88: 4 meas.

Allegro moderato: $\frac{4}{4}$: ♩ = 108: 12 meas.
Meno: $\frac{4}{4}$: ♩ = 96: 16 meas.
Assez largement: $\frac{2}{4}$, $\frac{4}{4}$: ♩ = 54: 14 meas.
Plus vif: $\frac{4}{4}$: ♩ = 80: 12 meas.

This was the Paris Conservatory contest piece for 1930.

Tournier, Franz (b. 1923). *Aerème.* RID, 1968. 183 meas.; 5'15"; A'–c"; TB; cadenza.

"Solo de Concours"

Con espressione: $\frac{6}{8}$: ♪ = 126: 47 meas.
Giocoso: ¢ : 𝅗𝅥 = 100: 136 meas.

Tremblot de la Croix, Francine. *Le Tombeau de Goya, sur des thèmes de T. Aubin* [Goya's Tomb]. LED, 1982. 99 meas.; 5'30"; E-d"; 3*; TB; flutter tongue, glissandi, cadenza.

"Gérard Pichaureau"

Adagietto: $\frac{2}{4}$, $\frac{4}{4}$: ♩ = 100: 21 meas.
Allegro: $\frac{2}{4}$, $\frac{3}{4}$, $\frac{4}{4}$: ♩ = 126: 32 meas.
Molto più lento: $\frac{2}{4}$, $\frac{3}{4}$, $\frac{4}{4}$: ♩ = 76: 14 meas.
Maestoso: $\frac{3}{4}$, $\frac{4}{4}$: ♩ = 88: 32 meas.

This was the Paris Conservatory contest piece for 1982.

Uga, Piérre. *Promenade.* BILL, 1978.

See entry in Chapter 5.

Vachey, Henri. *Deux interludes.* LED, 1966. 4*.

Vallier, Jacques (b. 1922). *Aria.* RID, 1969. 71 meas.; 2'; F–g'; 4.

"Gerard Pichaureau"

Andantino: $\frac{3}{8}$: ♪ = 72-76: 30 meas.
Allegretto: $\frac{2}{4}$: ♩ = 96-100: 41 meas.

——. *Fantaisie.* CHO.

†**Vidal, Paul** (1863-1931). *Solo de concert No. 2.* Girod, *ca.* 1897; LED, 1921. 5'30"; G–c"; 7*; TB.

Allegro: $\frac{4}{4}$: ♩ = 126
Andante: $\frac{9}{8}$: ♩. = 56
Allegro moderato: $\frac{4}{4}$: ♩ = 126

This was the Paris Conservatory contest piece for 1897. This is a one movement work which contains three connected sections, forming an ABA pattern. Although the tempo indications change at the section points, a cantabile style remains constant through the entire solo. There are no unusual rhythmic complexities, and the indicated tempi create no unusual technical difficulties. The orchestral accompaniment parts are available on rental from LED. The instrumentation of the accompaniment is as follows: 2 fls, 2 obs, 2 cls, 2 bns, 2 hns, 2 trpts, 2 timp, strgs.

†**Villette, Pierre**. *Fantaisie concertante*. LED, 1962.
See entry in Chapter 5.

Vivaldi, Antonio (1678-1741). *Concerto in si-bémol*. Edited by Jean Thilde. BILL, 1979. 6'30".

†**Weber, Alain** (b. 1930). *Allegro, 1er mouvement du Concerto*. LED. 8*.

†——. *Concerto*. LED, 1964, 1968. 17'; B♭'–d"; 8*; TB; straight mute, flutter tongue, glissandi, lip trills.

I. Allegro
II. Lento
III. Allegro

The first movement of this work, entitled *Allegro*, was the Paris Conservatory contest piece for 1964. This work contains three movements, and shows characteristics which are different from most twentieth-century solos of the "French School." An atonal harmonic organization and a melodic organization based on a major seventh and a tritone are some of the characteristics. The orchestral accompaniment parts are available on rental from LED. The instrumentation of the accompaniment is as follows: 2 fls (2d doubles pic), 2 obs, 2 cls, 2 bns, cbn, 2 hns, 2 trpts, 2 trbns, tba, perc, strgs.

Weiner, Stanley (b. 1925). *Phantasy, Op. 42*. BILL, 1973. 7.

Wurmser, Lucien (1877-1967). *Solo de concours* [Contest Solo]. Éditions Andrieu, 1955. 85 meas.; 3'30"; G–f'; 4.

"Fernand Anne, President Fon Stes Mles le Normandie"

Largement: $\frac{4}{4}$: 16 meas.
Allegro: $\frac{4}{4}$: 7 meas.
Andantino: $\frac{4}{4}$: 23 meas.
Allegro: $\frac{2}{4}$: 39 meas.

——. *Tendres mélodies*. Éditions Andrieu, 1956. 40 meas.; 2'; F–f'; 3.

"Andrien Maltete, President de la Fédération des Societies Musicales du Sud-Ouest"

A—Lent: $\frac{3}{4}$: 24 meas.
B—Andante: $\frac{4}{4}$: 16 meas.

Zbar, Michel. *Contacts*. HEU, 1973. Varies; B♭'–f'; plunger mute, glissandi, flutter tongue, indefinite pitch.

"Commissioned by the National School of Music in Boulogne"

This work exists on a single enlarged page, 48" long and 38" wide. The general compositional style is in the new music idiom. Its appearance is much like a road map in that frames, containing musical passages, are reached by following various paths. At the top and bottom of the score are staves which contain music with which the piece may begin and end, with the boxes being situated between the two.

4

Tenor Trombone: Pedagogical Materials

Because of the nature of this section, durations of exercises will not be included, and any special techniques discussed or used will be detailed in the "General Comments" portion of each annotation. For studies only, an overall range and degree of difficulty will be indicated. The total number of pages will be reflected at the end of the "Descriptive Information."

Bach, Johann Sebastian (1685-1750). *Suites pour violoncelle seul.* Edited by Raymond Katarzynski. LED, 1977. F-c", 5-6, 27 pp.

This edition of the Bach *Suites for Violoncello Alone* is written in the bass clef and has been transposed to higher keys than the original suites. Suite I has been transposed up a fourth from G to C Major. Suite II is transposed up a third from the original. Suite III is transposed up a fourth from C to F Major and Suite IV is transposed up a fourth from E♭ to A♭ Major. Suite IV does not include the original Bourree II. Instead, Katarzynski adds the "Sarabande" and the "Gigue" of Suite V set up a fourth from E♭ to A♭ Major and the "Courante" of Suite VI set up one-half step. Suites V and VI are not included in their entirety.

The phrase markings of these suites are editorial and do not follow the original manuscript of Bach. The Katarzynski edition follows the LaFosse edition in dynamics, phrasing, and metronome markings.

———. *Suites de J. S. Bach Pour Violoncelle Seul.* Edited by André LaFosse. LED, 1946. E-c", 5-6, 24 pp.

The set of Bach cello suites is transposed a major fourth higher than the original notation. LaFosse has edited the suites in terms of articulation markings, dynamic markings, and alternate positions. The tessitura lies generally in the middle and middle upper register and therefore it is appropriate for the trombonist without an F attachment. The placement of the musical material in the middle and upper registers allows the tenor trombonist greater technical and musical possibilities than would be available in the original keys.

Bitsch, Marcel. *Quinze études de rhythme.* Edited by Gabriel Masson. LED, 1952. E-d", 6, TB, 16 pp.

The fifteen etudes in this volume are primarily concerned with the metric difficulties encountered in contemporary writing. This excellent book of studies may well be used as a source book of complex and difficult rhythms for trombone. Many of the rhythms included in this book will be found in the contemporary solo and orchestral literature for trombone.

Included in these studies are many unusual meters, mixed meters, and superimposed, irregular rhythms. The etudes, written with key signatures, vary from tonal to quasi-tonal. Although several etudes start and end on the same tonal center, tonal hierarchies within the etudes are frequently disregarded. The melodic writing is generally angular and includes disjunct melodic lines with numerous accidentals to contribute to the difficulty. Also common are passages with erratic uses of rests and ties and passages with sudden changes in the rhythmic divisions of the beat.

The etudes in this volume, written in tenor and bass clef, should be reserved for the advanced student.

Blecer [Bléger], Marcel. *Ten Caprices for Trombone.* INT, n.d. F-b♭, 4, 8 pp.

Similar to the *Thirty-One Studies* of the same composer but more dramatic in style with emphasis on accented and staccato technique. These harmonically conservative etudes are suitable for developing accuracy in tonguing, a fast slide technique, variations in articulations, centering of detached notes, and overall technique at faster tempos. The etudes are generally very idiomatic for the trombone.

———. *Thirty-One Studies for Trombone.* INT, n.d. F-b♭, 4, 19 pp.

This Blecer (Bléger) etude book consists of traditional and predictable technical etudes which mix staccato with legato techniques. The etudes progress frequently in sixteenth-note scale-like patterns with occasional passages which include wide skips and arpeggiated writing. The studies are a good source for the development of clean articulation and slide technique. The rhythms often include dotted patterns in a variety of traditional meters. These etudes may also be found in the complete Cornette *Method.*

———. *Trente et une études.* LED, 1946. E-b♭, 4, 19 pp.

This set of Bléger etudes is slightly more difficult than the *Thirty-One Studies* and *Ten Caprices* of the same composer; however, the three books are very similar in style and difficulty. Excellent for the development of detached tonguing technique, slide technique, velocity, and general technique, this set of etudes would be useful for the student needing technical drill.

Bléger, Marcel, and **Henri Couillaud**. *10 caprices.* LED, n.d. F-b♭, 4, 8 pp.

The same studies as those published by INT under the name "Blecer." Alternate positions are edited into this edition.

Bléger, Michel, and **M. Job**. *Méthode de trombone à coulisse.* LED, 1946. E-b♭, 4, 99 pp.

This method begins with middle range notes and moves fairly quickly to scale and etude material arranged in progressive order. Following several pages of revolving scale exercises and lip slurs are "30 Classical Airs," selected by M. Job. These song studies, taken from melodies of master composers from the 1600-1900s, are followed by 31 etudes of Bléger. The etudes are excellent technical studies, dealing with work in a detached tonguing style. Following the 31 etudes are 12 concert duets ideally suited for teaching tonguing and technique. The duets are followed by ten increasingly more difficult technical etudes.

Bleicher, Jacques. *Le tromboniste commencant.* COM, 1980. E-a, 1-2, 49 pp.

Le tromboniste commencant is a good, basic French method book. It is comprised of 100 progressively more difficult studies.

In part one, Bleicher introduces studies in the seven positions of the trombone starting with first position and progressing to seventh position. There are three pages of etude material for each position. Part One concludes with easy studies in tone production, studies to develop legato tonguing, lip slurs, studies in alternate positions, and chord studies.

Part Two includes etude material in varying keys (1-3 flats and 1-3 sharps), rhythms, and articulations. The book concludes with easy duos in the style of Glück, Handel, and Mozart.

From the very first pages, it is evident that proper use of the breath is very important to Bleicher. He uses dynamics, long tones, and glissandi in the opening pages of the book. Bleicher also introduces an excellent variety of articulations and rhythms arranged in a logical and carefully planned progression.

Although the music is generally easy and confined to the middle register, the progression to more difficult keys, rhythms, and accidentals is much faster in comparison with other beginning American method books.

An excellent book for the older beginner or for the player with a basic background in music theory. Well-planned, high quality musical materials.

Bordères, Yves. *Special syncopes: cinquante études progressifs.* BILL, 1988.

——. *Trente petites études techniques.* BILL, 1985. 1-3.

——. *Trente-cinq petites études techniques.* BILL, 1986.

——. *Vingt pièces mélodiques.* BILL, 1992. 6-8.

Advanced melodic etudes. For colleges and conservatories. Difficult. (quoted from PR catalog)

——. *Vingt-cinq petites pièces mélodiques.* BILL, 1986.

Boutry, Roger. *Douze études de haut perfectionnement pour trombone.* LED, 1958. E-e♭, 6, TB, 19 pp.

This etude book consists of complicated, taxing studies which could serve as preparatory studies for contemporary orchestral trombone passages. Each study is constructed with one specific technique to be developed, such as a difficult interval, the high register, quick arpeggiated playing, a difficult key, an unusual rhythmic figure, or a combination of these techniques. The studies frequently involve mixed meters, unusual meters, or meter changes. The melodic writing is often disjunct in nature and frequently involves the intervals of a major 7th, 9th, or 11th. Tempo and style changes occur frequently in these etudes.

Extremely difficult etudes that are recommended only to the highly advanced player. Particularly well suited to the study of advanced rhythmic techniques.

Bozza, Eugéne. *Graphismes.* LED, 1975. B♭ (opt.), 6, GTB, 4 pp.

The subtitle indicates this material is "preparation for the reading of different contemporary musical graphic notations." Many types of new notation are used in the four studies in this volume. The performer must choose at times whether to play notes within brackets, or in other circumstances, must decide the order of several pitches. There are many notes of long duration, where the length is notated in seconds. In other etudes the performer must choose the order of several predetermined pitches. Also included in the context of this study are passages of glissandi, quarter-tones, rhythmic accelerandos, and passages which must be played as fast as possible.

An excellent set of etudes for the trombonist who wishes to develop skills in reading new symbols employed in the contemporary music. The coverage of techniques is selective, although many of the important twentieth-century techniques are represented.

———. *Onze études sur des modes karnatiques.* LED, 1972. B♭-d", 6, GTB (only 3 meas. of G), 12 pp.

The preface includes twenty-four modes taken from the Carnatic or southern area of India together with suggestions for practicing the modes. The composer suggests that the student learn the modes before practicing the subsequent etudes.

The eleven etudes in the volume are very difficult. Many are written without meter signatures or bar lines. Others utilize rapid and complex meter shifts. The rhythmic complexities within sections or beats is often very involved. The lower portion of the meter signature is written with a note instead of a number to indicate the value of the beat. Due to poor engraving, the shifting-meter etudes are sometimes difficult to read.

These contemporary etudes will be technically and musically challenging for the advanced player. Although they have the same name as the etudes for trumpet, they are different etudes but similar in style.

———. *Treize études caprices.* LED, 1958. E-e", 6, TB, 15 pp.

The thirteen etudes in this volume require extensive technical skill for proper performance. While only one involves the use of frequent meter changes, many of the etudes have rhythmic complexities within the measure. One of the etudes, written without meter signature, is marked "recitativo."

The melodic line is often disjunct, employing large leaps and broken chords. The range is often quite high but the low range will not require a trombone equipped with an F-attachment. Most of the etudes are tonal, with chromaticism being used extensively. The melodic writing includes many imitative clusters, with a tendency toward chromatic passage work. There is some use of glissandi.

Requires a secure technique at all tempos and a secure upper register. Excellent studies for the skilled player.

Clodomir, P. *Études et exercises.* MOLE, n.d. A-a', 3-4, 52 pp.

These exercises include a considerable amount of useful technical material and numerous appealing duets. The etudes are of varying lengths, several being short and tuneful, while others are long and more technical. Most of the etudes and the more technical exercises are marked to be played staccato, although a few etudes and exercises are marked to be played with varied articulations.

The duets range from short half-page study duets to two-page concert duets. About half of the book is comprised of duet material; the other half includes traditional, tonal etudes and exercises in the easier flat or sharp keys.

Keys, rhythms, range, and scale-like patterns are especially idiomatic for trombone and ideally suited for the intermediate-advanced player.

———. *Méthode complète pour trombone à coulisse, Vol. I.* LED, n.d. E-a', 2-4, 56 pp.

The beginning pages of this method book are comprised of explanatory material (in French only) relating to the elements of music, clefs, names of notes, rhythmic values, time signatures, keys, dynamics, scale construction, the conductor's main beat patterns, and several other topics. Also included is a chart showing the overtone series in each of the seven positions of the trombone, and a page on the fundamentals of trombone playing.

The method begins with exercises in each of the seven positions, starting with first position and proceeding very rapidly through the positions. The scale exercises in the first three lessons take the trombonist to an a' above the staff, clearly too high for a beginning player. The remainder of the book covers syncopation in eighth-notes and quarter-notes, articulation, several types of embellishments, minor scales, quarter-note triplets, sixteenth-notes, and legato tonguing.

There is no song material in this volume, but it includes a variety of traditional etude materials and duets. The concluding etudes will be difficult for any player. The wealth of technical material is well suited to the preparation of traditional French trombone solo material.

——. *Méthode complète pour trombone à coulisse, Vol. II.* LED, 1949. F-b', 4-5, 56 pp.

Book II begins with a review of scales and arpeggios in all major and minor keys. The remainder of the book consists of etudes and duets, most of which are in a traditional, tonal idiom. Etudes are typically marked "Theme with Variations," "Polka," "Tempo di Bolero." Much of the material is comprised of scale-like patterns or tonal arpeggio passages. Three extended concert duets are also included.

This method lacks the variety of etude material needed for a well-rounded trombonist, but offers a considerable amount of technical material suitable for building technique.

Couillaud, Henri. *Études de style d'après Bordogni, Vols. I, II, et III.* LED, 1927. E-c"; 4-5; TB; Vol. I, 18 pp.; Vol. II, 18 pp.; Vol. III, 25 pp.

Most of these etudes are duplicated in the Bordogni-Rochut *Melodious Etudes, Vol. II*, with several studies not found in any other popular edition. The Couillaud edition of the Bordogni etudes offers a more expansive variety of articulation possibilities than the same etudes transcribed by Rochut, the latter being edited primarily for use as legato studies.

There are twelve etudes in each book, arranged in progressive order from the moderately-difficult to difficult level. These are primarily expressive studies suitable for the development of tongued and legato phrasing, breath control, tone quality, and style. Piano accompaniments to these studies are available from the RICI.

——. *Exercises progressifs.* LED, 1937. E-b♭', 3-4, TB, 19 pp.

A short book of studies that is divided into three parts. Part I includes a one-page theoretical discussion in French, relating to the make-up of major and minor scales, together with one-octave scales and scale variation patterns which incorporate both legato and detached tonguing styles. The scale patterns are composed primarily in eighth- and sixteenth-note rhythmic patterns.

The keys covered in Part I range from 1-5 flats and 1-5 sharps. Part II includes a variety of moderate to moderately-difficult studies, including etudes comprised mainly of scale-like patterns in major and minor keys (four flats-four sharps) presented in eighth- and sixteenth-notes, dotted-quarter- and dotted-eight-note figures. There are several exercises designed to improve articulation and attacks. Part III is comprised of vocalises that are moderate in difficulty, tonal in style, and similar to the easier vocalises included in the Bordogni-Rochut or Fink collections of legato studies.

This material could be used by many high school students who are familiar with tenor clef or college players. It has scales, scale exercises, and etudes in both detached and legato tonguing styles. *Exercises progressifs* is generally at the level of the Bordogni-Rochut *Melodious Etudes, Vol. I.*

———. *Méthode.* LED, 1946. E-c", 1-5, TB, 92 pp.

Emphasis of this French method book is on the rudiments of trombone playing. The method begins at the beginning level, but progresses very quickly through scales, scale studies, exercises in legato and staccato tonguing, lip slurs, ornaments, and etude material culminating in material that is quite advanced. The intermediate to advanced etudes and duets are in a variety of tonal styles and were extracted from the vocalises of Bordogni, Kruetzer, and others. All of the editorial text is in French. Several excellent duets are included.

This is a questionable beginning method book for the trombone student due to its rate of progression through the material. It contains good etude material in both legato and detached tonguing styles and might best be used as etude material for high school or college level students.

———. *Pièces mélodiques, Vols. I, II, et III.* LED, 1946. E-b♭', 4-5, TB, 15 pp./vol.

This three-volume set of trombone studies includes original pieces for trombone and, vocalises by Dukas, Gaubert, Lefebre, Paray, Buesser, and other French composers who were contemporaries of Couillard. The melodies are typically in a French Impressionistic style and include short rapid legato flourishes, legato chromatic passages, turns and mordents, rubato phrases, and modal writing characteristic of French vocal lines.

These are not overly difficult etudes, and are typical of a great deal of the French writing in the solo de concours style for brass instruments. Piano accompaniments to these etudes are available from the publisher. Interestingly, Volume II is slightly easier than Volumes I and III.

———. *Trente études modernes.* LED, 1946. E-d", 4-5, TB, 51 pp.

The thirty etudes can be easily divided into two parts. The first includes progressively more difficult scales and arpeggio patterns with little rhythmic variety or interest. The format of these scales (written on successive tones of the scale) is similar to those used by LaFosse in his *Vade Mecum*.

The second part of the book includes a variety of technical studies ranging from lyric phrasing studies of moderate difficulty to music of a more majestic nature similar in style to a great deal of the standard orchestral literature for trombone. The etudes in the beginning of the second part begin rather predictably in traditional tonal scale-like patterns, but become increasingly more contemporary in style and proceed to etudes involving meter change and more unusual meters within a traditional tonal context. The melodic content of the etudes becomes more angular during the course of the book and includes intervals that are often difficult to hear and play. Sudden dynamic changes occur more frequently as the etudes progress. The concluding etudes are also rhythmically difficult.

An extensive book of etudes offering a good variety of moderate to moderately-difficult material for the advancing college student, they are written in tenor and bass clefs with only a small amount of alto clef.

Recommended as preparatory study material for the standard orchestral literature for trombone.

——. *Vingt études de perfectionnement.* LED, 1929. E-c", 4-5, TB, 23 pp.

Similar in style to the etudes of Tyrell, these exercises are taken from the cello etudes of Dotzauer, Duport, and Lee. Each study focuses on one technique to be mastered, such as a continuous, smooth legato style in eighth-notes, continuous arpeggios in triplet-figures, strong, accented articulation at a slow tempo, rapid and detached tonguing in sixteenth-note figures.

This basic book of traditional tonal studies will be suitable technical studies for the improvement of articulation, slide-tongue coordination, and overall technique.

Couillaud, Henri, and **L. Allard**. *Vingt-six études techniques d'après Bordogni.* LED, 1927. E-b♭', 4-5, T, 28 pp.

Includes a good variety of tonal etudes in both detached tonguing and legato tonguing style. Preceding the main section of the book are several studies for trombone involving long tones, slow legato playing, and detached tonguing patterns in thirds and fourths, and other exercises in scale-like patterns which would prove valuable for the development of a smooth legato style and slide-tongue coordination. Many of the exercises are similar, but not identical, to the Clarke *Technical Studies*. The studies may be played in different tempos and in different ranges and are, therefore, suitable for the intermediate through advanced levels.

Following the section of study material are several etudes in a lyric and detached tonguing style. These tonal, melodic studies, written in the style of Bordogni, are not overly difficult, and will be playable by many high school students who read tenor clef. An excellent book of varied etudes and exercises.

Dhellemmes, Raymond. *Vingt-cinq études de perfectionnement.* LEM, 1961. E-c", 4-5, TB, 28 pp.

This book includes etudes which emphasize traditionally difficult rhythmic patterns, studies with rhythmic changes from three to four pulse beat patterns, exercises in wide intervals (octaves, tenths, and twelfths), exercises in alternate positions, exercises comprised of fast chromatic passages, flexibility studies (lip slurs), legato scale patterns, exercises designed to compare notes in regular and alternate positions, exercises designed to compare intervals with the legato tongued and natural slide slurs, studies in chromatic scale patterns, major scale patterns, and minor scale patterns with numerous rhythmic variations. Editorial comment is in French only.

Included is a wide variety of basic rhythmic studies, scale patterns, lip slurs, and other routines which could be useful to the trombonist in improving overall technique.

——. *Vingt-cinq études méthodiques.* LEM, 1960. E-c", 1-5, TB, 38 pp.

This book begins with very easy study material and progresses rapidly to the moderately difficult level. It contains well-designed studies for clean attacks, scale studies, long tone exercises, and legato studies. *Vingt-cinq études méthodiques* also includes short-scale studies and exercises that advance very rapidly into the high register. Editorial comment is in French only.

Dieppo, A. G. *Nine Progressive Studies.* FISC, n.d. F-d", 4, GB (only 12 meas. in G), 7 pp.

This book consists of short, tonal pieces similar to short operatic arias. They are written in a variety of tempi, but are typically marked "Andante Affetuoso," "Cavatina," or "Moderato." The etudes are suitable for the development of song style and phrasing techniques in both detached and legato tonguing styles. Even though these studies are clearly those of an older publication, they should be enjoyable material for the trombonist who desires to play etudes in a highly expressive, late nineteenth century operatic style.

Douay, Jean. *L'ABC de jeune tromboniste, Vol. I.* BILL, 1975. E-g', 1-2, 37 pp.

This French trombone method book includes a well-planned balance of study and etude material which progresses at an average rate. The preface is in French and has no further editorial comment accompanying the study material.

The materials presented in the book should cover approximately two years of trombone study. Unlike many other French method books, this book is concerned with the musical, as well as the technical progress of the student.

It includes short pieces titled simply "Solo," with dynamic markings and phrase indications. New rhythmic concepts, legato, as well as staccato technique, are introduced gradually, and there is ample opportunity for review of new concepts through the exercise, etude, and "solo" material.

The material is organized by keys so that after every four or five lines the player is introduced to a new key. By the conclusion of the book, the player has covered from the key of C to four flats in both major and minor keys, legato style, staccato articulations, and various kinds of accented articulations. Solo, duet, and etude material was written by Jean Douay.

——. *L'ABC du jeune tromboniste, Vol. II.* BILL, 1977. E-g', 2-3, TB, 51 pp.

Volume two is a complete and thorough intermediate book which progresses less rapidly than most French method books. There are numerous progressive etudes and "solos" designed for the development of musicality at the intermediate level. These short solos are well designed and typically include dynamic markings, variations in articulations, and logical tempo changes.

The book includes an excellent balance of material designed to improve tone quality (exercises in longer note values), as well as lip slurs, interval studies, arpeggio studies, rhythm studies, and articulation studies. Several exercises are contemporary in style, including exercises which incorporate sudden dynamic changes, ternary and binary rhythms, and misplaced accents. These techniques are incorporated into material that is at the intermediate level. Tenor clef is introduced with this volume.

Duets cover one and two pages, and are well designed in several diverse styles. The $\frac{5}{8}$ meter is introduced, and there are many good exercises in dotted note values in $\frac{12}{8}$ meter and $\frac{4}{4}$ meter. Chromatic patterns and sixteenth-note scale patterns are included near the end of the method.

———. *12 études de grande technique.* BILL, 1977. E-d", 5-6, T, 18 pp.

Many of these technical etudes are sequential, with each sequence modulating to a new key center. The etudes are organized with a short lyrical introduction followed by a technical middle section and concluding with another lyrical section.

The book covers a variety of technical areas such as alternating thirds, chromatic scales, slurs, tonguing, high tessitura, technical formulas taken through several keys and rapid, scale-like passages.

This work requires an advanced player with excellent technique who is looking for a challenge. It is excellent for the development of fluency, rapid legato, and general technique.

———. *à propos du...trombone: Pédagogie fondamentale sur l'enseignement du trombone* [On the Subject of the...Trombone: Fundamental Pedagogy on Teaching Trombone]. BILL, n.d. 135 pp.

Although entirely in French, this text provides useful information pertinent to the school of thought at French conservatories in the 1980s. Similar to Lafosse's *Traité*, this book includes articles that are required for a person to become a good teacher. Chapters include: (1) brief history and general characteristics of the instrument, (2) pedagogical summary (basics of trombone playing), (3) the trombone family, (4) the different schools (including foreign, French, and Paris Conservatory), and (5) the mastery of one's profession. The discussions of the bass and contrabass trombones are more detailed than in Lafosse, and the discussion of the Paris Conservatory gives keen insight on the way the French prepare for a career in music. A chronological listing of the tenor trombone contest solos from 1842-1982 is interesting.

Dubois, Pierre Max. *Quatorze études de moyenne difficulte pour trombone.* LED, 1964. E-d", 5, TB, 11 pp.

This book contains an excellent set of intermediate to advanced etudes in a variety of traditional and contemporary idioms. About half of the etudes are tonal, with the other half being freely atonal. The melodic lines typically involve disjunct intervals, with passages comprised of augmented and diminished intervals. Rhythms range from conservative to contemporary, with the more difficult ones including concealment of stress beats and repeated syncopation.

Although there are a few passages which extend to c" and d", the tessitura is generally much lower. Each study is written in a distinctly new style and technique such as multiple tonguing, syncopation, or disjunct melodic lines.

This is a useful book of short varied etudes especially recommended for the development of rhythm and articulation at the advanced-intermediate level player.

Flandrin, Gaston. *Method for Trombone, Vols. I and II.* SAL, 1923. F'-d", 2-6, ATB, 163 pp.

This method begins with the first notes in the middle register, but progresses very quickly through interval and scale studies to notes in the very high and very low registers.

This book is typical of other method books in its inclusion of scales, arpeggios, interval studies, lip slurs, etc. Of special interest to the trombone student are several lyric pieces of extended length transcribed from the works of Beethoven, Mendelssohn, and other masters. It also contains vocalises of Bordogni, etudes in a variety of traditional styles, and selected orchestral excerpts. The introductory pages include a position chart, explanation of music terms, and general information about the trombone, all in French.

Volume II is noteworthy for its inclusion of lyric etude material and several duet and trio transcriptions of the works of J. S. Bach.

Galiégue, Marcel, and **Jérôme Naulais**. *Quarante petites études.* LED, 1987. A-f'; 4-5.

Gallay, J. F. *12 études pour trombone ou tuba.* Edited by Estavan Dax. GERV, n.d. E-b♭', 4-5, 15 pp.

These tonal etudes are written in an early nineteenth century harmonic vocabulary. They are not particularly idiomatic for trombone as they include wide skips and quick arpeggiated figures characteristic of the writing used for bassoon. Also typical are many very fast tongued scale-like passages in both slurred and tongued articulations. The writing is generally in the middle and upper-middle trombone register with optional notes given for the pedal and trigger registers. The editor has suggested alternate positions for several of the passages.

Most of the studies are at the intermediate level and are not overly difficult to perform.

Job, M. *Trente airs classiques.* LED, 1949. E-b♭', 2-4, 11 pp.

This collection of pieces is suitable for nearly all levels of ability from junior high school through college level. All of the selections are very short (about thirty-two measures each). The pieces are taken from the song and operatic literature of J. S. Bach, Beethoven, Glück, Mozart, Haydn, Peri, Lully, Monteverdi, Schubert, and other masters. Job has prefaced the edition with several suggestions (in French) to the trombonist for playing these pieces in the proper song style. The airs lie generally in the middle and upper-middle registers with only occasional skips to b♭'.

This is an excellent book for the development of phrasing, interpretation, style, and general musicianship.

Katarzynski, Raymond. *Étude complète des gammes, Book I.* LED, 1975. E-e♭', 5, TB, 18 pp.

This book is comprised of a complete set of major and harmonic minor scales written in two octaves to be played in a detached tonguing style.

Pages 1-7 include all scales in whole-notes. Pages 8-12 include all scales written in eighth-notes, together with several suggested variations in articulation. Pages 13-18 include scale patterns at the interval of a third, a fourth, and a fifth.

Occasional editorial comment can be found written in French, German, and English.

This is an excellent source of scale studies for the trombone player.

———. *Étude complète des gammes, Book II.* LED, 1975. E-f", 5, TB, 18 pp.

Book II is a continuation of Book I consisting entirely of interval studies (fifths-ninths) and concluding with two pages of chromatic scales.

All of the studies contained within this volume are written in eight-note or quarter-note values in detached tonguing style. All major and minor scales are covered during the course of work.

These scale studies and interval patterns will serve to improve technique, attacks, tone placement, tonguing, and evenness of tone quality.

LaFosse, André. *Méthode complète de trombone, Vols. I et II.* LED, 1921. F'-d", 2-6, ATB, 280 pp.

One of the most complete and thorough method books in print from the French, it covers a wide variety of styles, incorporates interesting musical material, and includes helpful editorial suggestions in French, German, and English. The method progresses very rapidly (similar to the progression of the Arban method), and includes scales, arpeggios, intervals, slurs, legato studies, multiple tonguing, etude material, and duets. All styles of trombone playing are covered in a thorough manner.

Volume II covers multiple tonguing, pedal tones, use of the F-attachment, and uses of the bass trombone. Of special interest are several difficult etudes in style. These etudes, in the tenor clef, are diverse in style and techniques and cover a wide variety of musical idioms. The etudes are taken from the vocalises of Bordogni and the French solo literature for trombone. Also included are several pages designed as preparatory studies to the standard orchestral repertoire for the trombone. These preparatory studies are followed by several pages of orchestral excerpts from the standard repertoire and the French orchestral repertoire.

Excellent editorial commentary throughout the book relates to many facets of trombone playing including multiple tonguing, the F-attachment, legato style, glissandi, ornaments, and other topics. The duets are especially noteworthy. Several duets are transcriptions from the works of Bach, Mozart, and other masters.

The LaFosse method would be best used by highly motivated junior high school beginners or as a source book for etude material at the college level.

——. *Méthode complète de trombone, Vol. III.* LED, 1946. F'-c", 5-6, TB, 53 pp.

Written in four languages: French, English, German, and Spanish and recently revised by LaFosse, Volume III covers material on double and triple tonguing , pedal tones, glissandi, and use of various types of mutes (all with appropriate orchestral examples). In addition there are twelve studies involving the complete technical requirements of the instrument, transcriptions of two sonatas by Handel, transcriptions of six vocal studies of Bordogni, and five pages of music and explanatory material relating to the bass trombone.

The twelve technical studies (pp. 162-176) are similar in style to the twelve *Characteristic Studies* of Arban, but slightly easier. The LaFosse studies would serve nicely as preparatory pieces to the more difficult Arban studies. The etudes cover a variety of rhythms, articulations, and keys..

LaFosse has preceded each new chapter with short introductory comments. Book III was the last book to be added to the original LaFosse method which initially consisted of only two parts.

——. *School of Sight Reading and Style, Vols. I-V.* BARO, 1948. E-c", 2-6, ATB, 18-20 pp./vol.

The five volumes of books in this series are intended to increase facility in sight reading. Each volume contains thirty half-page studies ranging from relatively easy-to-play etudes in the first volume to very difficult in the last. The etudes are written in manuscript which is sometimes difficult to decipher. The etudes are comprised of a great variety of musical and technical styles.

While only bass clef is used in the first book, both bass and tenor clefs appear in the other books. The last volume also includes alto clef. The clef changes occur with greater frequency than would be found in most writing. In addition, the clef changes do not coincide with changes of range as one might expect.

Although key signatures are utilized in all of the etudes, the melodies often move far from the original tonic before returning. Many accidentals appear in the etudes, often with much frequency. Due to the unusual problems of reading in these etudes, one who could play these well would be much better prepared to cope with such aspects of contemporary music.

The book labeled as “easy” is not easy, and would be challenging for most high school players. The etudes become longer and more technically difficult. Book V is very difficult in terms of technique, rhythm, and endurance.

Varied in style and technique, the style of the pieces ranges from romantic and impressionistic to more contemporary etudes in a popular idiom. These five books include a wealth of useful sight reading material.

——. *Vade Mecum du Tromboniste.* LED, 1956. E-d♭", 4-5, TB, 55 pp.

This etude was written and designed to assist in preparing advanced students for the final examinations at the Paris Conservatory. It is divided into three sections. Part One is comprised of technical etudes in major and minor scales, diminished sevenths, chromatic scales, and scale patterns in thirds. Both the very high and very low registers of the tenor trombone are utilized.

In Part Two the author presents a scale of one octave in sixteenth-notes. Each degree of the scale is then the starting point for a further, sequential scale. Each scale is then followed by its chords: major, minor, diminished and augmented. The seventh degrees and the octave are dealt with in ascending and descending order in triplet figures.

Part Three consists of 26 moderately-difficult studies covering the main technical areas of trombone playing. This section includes staccato exercises, legato studies, studies in varied articulations, arpeggio studies, interval studies, etc. All of the studies are in a traditional, tonal style. The concluding studies include several etudes comprised of transcriptions of pieces in varied styles by Schubert, Bach, Vivaldi, and Tartini.

Manna, G. *Douze études.* BILL, n.d. F-b', 5, 12 pp.

These twelve etudes are written in an eighteenth-century classic style of Haydn and Mozart. Although the etudes are one page in length each, they are not taxing due to their use of the middle register. The etudes are characterized by predictable melodies in a very conservative harmonic and rhythmic framework, similar to the etudes of Vobaron and Bleger. These studies are suitable for the development of articulation and general technique.

Masson, Gabriel. *Douze études variées.* LED, n.d. E-d', 5, TB, 15 pp.

The twelve studies which comprise this etude edition are based on difficult technical passages extracted from the trombone and cello literature of a variety of composers. Included within the work are arpeggio studies that are intended to be played in several different articulations, octave studies, studies in rubato, studies in more challenging keys (b minor and g♯ minor, for example), interval and chord studies (which are similar to the first movement of the Bach *Suites for Cello, No. 1),* capriccio studies which involve rapid scale and arpeggio figures (again similar to movements of the Bach *Suites for Cello, No. 1),* studies involving contrasts between legato and detached tonguing styles, studies in light, fast staccato styles, and studies in extended legato playing (primarily in sixteenth-note scale patterns).

Millière, Gilles. *Exercises sur deux octaves.* LED, 1988.

Parès, G. *Méthode de trombone à coulisse.* LEM, 1914. E-a', 2-4, 45 pp.

This is basically a progressive method using the famous Parès's scale book as its basis. The instructional material is written entirely in French beginning with a long descriptive section covering clefs, rhythmic values, conducting patterns, intervals, key signatures, the modes, and other general musical or trombone information. The book is organized into three parts of material, progressing very quickly in its approach to introducing fundamental techniques. It is an older style method book consisting primarily of technical and drill style material.

——. *Scale Studies.* Edited by Whistler. RUB, 1963. E-b♭', 3-4, 48 pp.

This book is a series of studies representing various scale patterns and articulations organized around one key. The scale patterns are mainly detached with some mixture of slurred and detached patterns. (Patterns are very similar to those found in the scale section of the Arban method.) The book also consists of lip slurs, long tone studies, a set of chromatic scales, and three etudes of moderate difficulty written in a harmonically conservative style. These traditional scale studies are well suited to the intermediate or advanced-intermediate trombone student.

Pichaureau, Gérard. *Préambule.* LED, 1971. E-g', 2-3, 36 pp.

The material contained in this volume progresses fairly quickly and concludes with rather some rather difficult advanced-intermediate exercises. *Préambule* also includes traditional lip slurs, scale patterns, and a variety of etudes. The final study is comprised of relatively difficult intermediate passages requiring good flexibility and control. Changing meters are introduced toward the end of the book.

The first half of the book is comprised of intermediate technical studies, the second half of etudes in detached and legato tonguing styles at the advanced-intermediate level. Also included are etudes in march styles, etudes in song-like styles, and a daily routine and warm-up studies. This book is most likely too difficult to use as a book for the beginning trombonist.

——. *30 récréations en forme d'études.* LED, 1960. E-a'(b♭'), 3-4, TB, 19 pp.

This work consists of thirty short etudes written in every major and minor key. The melodic writing is not mainly contemporary but does include unexpected melodic leaps approaching atonality. The melodic progressions frequently outline the major 6th, major 7th, major 9th, and major 11th chords, giving a "popular" quality to these advanced-intermediate studies. Phrases are rarely organized into neat four-bar groups; this results in melodies whih are rarely balanced or shaped regularly. Rhythmic patterns are sometimes freely organized as in chant or rhapsodic writing but do not contain complex rhythmic structures.

Several etudes rely on a more traditional stylistic approach similar to the easier Blazhevich *Clef Studies.* It also includes several legato studies which are traditional in their basic structure, but which include occasional leaps and unexpected melodic contours.

These well-designed etudes provide material for the development of traditional musical styles and serve as an introduction to contemporary solo and orchestral literature.

———. *Trente études dans tous les tons.* LED, 1963. E-f", 6, TB, 29 pp.

These etudes explore a wide variety of difficult techniques including rapid legato passages, multiple tonguing, passages in the very high and very low trombone registers, difficult or unusual embellishments, wide skips, rapid chromatic passages, unusual meters, and changing meters. Each exercise is composed in a different tonality. The studies contained within this book are clearly intended as extremely difficult virtuoso studies.

———. *Vingt études.* LED, 1963. E-d", 6, TB, 20 pp.

It is suggested that the twenty etudes of this volume be used following completion of the *Vignt-et-une études* by the same author. These exercises progress in difficulty from moderately-difficult to very-difficult.

There are several etudes in this collection which rely on the less common meter signatures such of $\frac{3}{1}$, $\frac{3}{16}$ and $\frac{2}{16}$. They provide excellent practice material in realizing rhythms of highly varied notational values. The works within the collection use a contemporary melodic style within their structure.

The contemporary melodic style is centered around the use of angular lines, large leaps, and the disjunct appearance of the melodic line. Key signatures are utilized in all of the etudes. These contemporary etudes should prove challenging and interesting to the moderately-advanced student.

———. *Vingt études pour trombone.* LED, 1962. E-d", 6, TB, 20 pp.

These etudes are designed to stretch the technical limits of the advanced trombonist's ability. They are taxing, difficult studies which emphasize many different trombone techniques. Although these are primarily tonal, traditional studies, designed for general technique, there are several studies which involve contemporary techniques, such as $\frac{5}{8}$ and $\frac{5}{4}$ meter, some use of complex rhythms, and melodic writing involving disjunct melodic passages and wide intervals.

Vingt études is intended to follow the *Vingt-et-une études* by the same composer.

———. *Vignt-et-une études de technique general.* LED, 1960. E-d", 5, TB, 21 pp.

The twenty-one etudes in this volume are designed for work in general technique. They progress in difficulty from moderate to moderately-difficult with the studies being notated in both the tenor and bass clefs. The three studies written in odd meter are in either $\frac{5}{8}$ or $\frac{5}{4}$. Rhythms become more complex as one progresses through the book.

There are instances of varying divisions of the beat and uneven note groupings, but these are not extensive.

The etudes all appear with key signatures although there is considerable use of chromaticism in the melodic compositional style. The melodic lines exhibit contemporary style in their disjunct construction and large leaps. These mostly traditional etudes would be useful for the student who has had little exposure to contemporary etude material.

———. *Vingt-quatre études pour trombone tenor* (Special Legato Studies). LED, 1978. E-c#", 4-5, TB, 22 pp.

This book consists of unique slur and legato studies not arranged progressively. Each etude centers around one legato problem and thus may be used in any order. These exercises are designed for the player who already possesses a good foundation in legato playing.

The beginning pages consist of slur exercises in arpeggiated form based on the primary triads of all the major and minor scales. The studies are followed by several etudes in a variety of intervals, keys, clefs, meters, and rhythms designed to keep the player "in shape" with challenging material for the embouchure, slide, and legato tongue. Also included are etudes involving unexpected wide intervals, major and minor ninth and eleventh chords, rapidly changing clef signs, and frequent use of accidentals. The musical style of the etudes might best be described as late impressionistic.

This is an excellent book of etudes and exercises ideally suited to the challenge of matching natural slurs with legato slurs.

Porret, Julien. *Vingt-quatre déchiffrages manuscrits.* Le Chant du Monde, 1946; republished by BILL, 1960. F-a', 5, TB, 14 pp.

This book of etudes, written in manuscript, is characterized harmonically by loosely related tonal centers or extended passages of atonality. Rhythmically, the etudes involve extended syncopation in compound bars, and constantly changing divisions of the beat. Meters used include $\frac{4}{1}$, $\frac{21}{8}$ and $\frac{15}{8}$. Although the material is intended for sight reading, it is difficult and would serve more appropriately as practice material in working with the contemporary techniques of the trombone. These etudes are similar in many ways to the Dufresne sight reading material, but never become as difficult as the Dufresne book. The manuscript is very similar to that found in the LaFosse sight reading books.

Rieunier, Françoise. *Vingt-deux déchiffrages rythmiques instrumentaux pour tous les instruments* [22 Rhythmic Instrumental Sight-reading Exercises for All Instruments]. LED, 1972. 7-9, 15 pp.

A book of difficult contemporary studies, including new notational symbols and difficult rhythmic patterns. The preface includes a glossary of notation signs and terms used in the main body of the book. With no clef sign given, the player may use any clef he chooses. Since these studies are written without clef signs, they are playable by all instruments. The range remains generally within the staff. The studies are also written so that tempos and articulations may be altered to suit the performer.

The etudes within this work are characterized by a variety of contemporary metric and rhythmic writing. Nine of the studies have no meter signs, four out of the nine employ non-traditional notation, and one etude is written without the use of bar lines. Changing meter is characteristic throughout these etudes, with unusual meters designated in a number of different ways, including $\frac{31}{16}$, $\frac{11}{32}$, and $\frac{33+22}{32}$.

This is an excellent book of contemporary studies designed for the very advanced player.

Senon, Gilles. *Le déchiffrage méthodique et progressif pour le trombone, Vol. I (A), Vol. II (B), Vol. III (C).* BILL, 1981. A: F-f', 2-3; B: F-f', 3-4, TB; C: F-g#', 4-5, ATB; D: ???

Le déchiffrage méthodique et progressif is conceived in four books: Cahier A. *Preparatoire. Élémentaire 1;* Cahier B. *Élémentaire 2;* Cahier C. *Moyen;* Cahier D. *Supérieur.* The books are similar in concept and format to the older and more widely used manuscript sight-reading books of LaFosse *(School of Sight Reading and Style)* and Porret *(24 Dechiffrages manuscrits).* Unlike the LaFosse and Porret books, the Senon books offer but one style of manuscript throughout all the volumes.

The present collection starts at an easier level than either LaFosse or Porret books. The Senon preparatory book is not, however, a beginning book and assumes that the student has had about one year of previous study on the trombone. The *Preparatoire* book is written in bass clef only; the range is conservative and the manuscript is not difficult to read. The writing is mainly tonal although Senon employs some chromatic writing, together with sudden dynamic changes and other expressive musical markings. Because the book progresses quickly from short, simple studies to more difficult ones, the book will be challenging for most junior high school and many high school players.

Élémentaire 2, or Book B, becomes progressively more difficult. The etudes remain short and include more unusual meters ($\frac{5}{8}$ and $\frac{7}{8}$), shifts in meter, a more interesting variety of styles, articulations, and keys, together with sudden dynamic changes, crescendos and diminuendos, and a wide variety of accents or stress markings. The notes in the second book are smaller and placed more closely together giving the lines a crowded appearance and making the reading more difficult. The second book uses primarily the bass clef but includes some writing in tenor clef.

At the beginning of *Moyen* (Book C) Senon has included an excellent table which isolates the rhythmic problems to be encountered in each of the 49 etudes. A student might play the rhythms on any pitch, clap the rhythms, or use the table as a study guide before playing each etude.

The etudes in the *Moyen* and *Supérieur* (Book D) become progressively more difficult in terms of technique, rhythm, range, and clef changes (bass, tenor, and alto). A student who is able to play these etudes will be prepared to play a great deal of contemporary solo, band, and orchestral literature.

——. *25 études rhythmo-techniques.* BILL, 1979. E-c#", 5, TB, 27 pp.

This book contains a collection of one-page rhythmic studies employing contemporary techniques. Melodically the lines are based largely on fourths and fifths, as well as thirds and seconds. Rhythmically the studies are difficult but not as difficult as one might expect at first appearance. The sudden dynamic changes in quick tempos and frequent meter changes add to the difficulty of many of the etudes.

Each of the etudes has an interesting title such as "Music Hall," "Barcarolle," or "Arithmétique," which describe the character of the pieces. These are high quality, fascinating etudes many of which could be programmed.

——. *24 études divertissantes.* BILL, 1978. F-f', 3-4, 12 pp.

This work contains melodious, dramatic pieces which constantly change mood within each etude. Each line is typically marked with a shift in articulation, a dynamic change, and a new tempo marking. The phrases are melodic and often irregular in structure, where one etude may involve long wandering melodies, another may center on the marked, majestic intervals of the fourth, fifth, or seventh.

Although contemporary techniques are involved (easy meter changes such as $\frac{3}{4}$ to $\frac{2}{4}$, or $\frac{3}{1}$ to $\frac{2}{1}$, and some disjunct melodic writing), these etudes are in the easy-moderate to moderate level and are not technically demanding in general. Several of the etudes may even be performed by talented junior high school trombonists.

Although the composer's intent appears to be that of great variety, his over-maniuplation of expression marks results in a kind of predictable monotony. There is, however, a great deal the young player may learn about phrasing, legato technique and musical style from these etudes.

——. *Vingt-quatre petites études mélodiques.* BILL, 1976. A-a', 4, 24 pp.

Diverse in style, interesting musically, and ideally suited for the development of musical concepts free of technical demands, each etude in this collection involves frequent dynamic changes, numerous articulation variations, rubato, accent markings, and dramatic changes in phrasing and in mood.

Although the etudes are generally romantic in idiom, several of them include contemporary techniques such as modulations, syncopation, a variety of tied note values, and disjunct melodic writing.

Perhaps one of the more musically stimulating Senon books, each piece could serve as miniature, unaccompanied solo. The pieces are not overly difficult and the range is consistently conservative. The pieces are also edited with the appropriate alternate positions for ease of performance.

———. *23 esquisses.* BILL, 1977. G-g', 4, 14 pp.

The *23 esquisses* of Senon are stylish, short, melodic pieces comprised of chordal or sequential patterns. For example, a two-measure legato melody will typically be repeated up a half-step, then up another half-step, etc. Many of the etudes are built around natural lip slurs with the use of the slide added to fill in certain chords. One or two notes of a sequential pattern are often changed so that the patterns do not become predictable.

These etudes encompass the keys of one to three flats and one to three sharps. Senon has composed these pieces primarily for conception of tone and practice in breathing technique. This book is perhaps comparable in difficulty to the first book of etudes in the Bordogni-Rochut series, although the Senon exercises are generally shorter.

Some of these Senon pieces appear to be designed as training or technical exercises, while others in the series appear to be more melodious in the manner of an unaccompanied solo.

The pieces are excellent for ear training, intonation, tone and breath control, relaxation, and a fluid legato style.

Thévet, Lucien. *Soixante-cinq études-déchiffrages pour trombone.* LED, 1981. E-d", 4-5, TB, 30 pp.

Thévet indicates in the introduction that these sight-reading studies have been written for students at the moderate to advanced grade levels. Thévet provides suggestions on how best to use the material to improve sight-reading skills. The etudes are intentionally short since Thévet feels that exercises which are too long are unnecessarily tiring and make it impossible for the student to cover the complete range of daily technical work.

Soixante-cinq études begins at the intermediate level and progresses rather quickly to the advanced level. The book is technically and rhythmically more difficult than the Senon sight-reading books but the music is easier to read since it isn't written in manuscript.

The advanced player will be challenged by the variety of rhythms, changing meters, and, toward the end of the book, by intervals which are difficult to hear and play. There is also an abundance of rapid, florid legato passages for the advanced trombonist to work on.

Toulon, Jacques. *10 études d'après le prélude de la Ire suite pour violoncelle seul de J. S. Bach.* LED, 1976. E-c", 4-5, TB, 11 pp.

This work will serve to introduce the player to many of the techniques found in the Bach *Suites for Violoncello Alone, No. 1.* Using similar scale and arpeggio patterns as those found in the "Prelude" movement of the Bach *Suites for Violoncello Alone, No. 1,* Toulon introduces patterns which begin at the intermediate level and proceed to a more advanced level. Typically, the arpeggio formulas move in patterns from the very low to very high register, or move up and down the scale in rhythmic patterns which Bach employed in the "Prelude" movements of his *Suites for Violoncello Alone, No. 1.* Both consist largely of continuing sixteenth-note scale and arpeggio figures.

This book accomplishes what it sets out to do by preparing the student for the technical difficulties found in the "Prelude" of *Suites for Violoncello Alone, No. 1,* as transcribed by LaFosse and Katarzynski.

——. *J'apprends le trombone.* MAR, 1978. E-d", 1-4, TB, 98 pp.

An excellent but expensive method book, it has a simple yet progressive approach which moves more slowly than most older French methods. It includes a short history of the trombone and provides excellent photographs on the correct way to hold the trombone.

Included within the method is an excellent variety of etudes, study, and song material, some of the easier orchestral excerpts, scales and arpeggios in all keys, and duets, trios, and quartets from the sixteenth to nineteenth century masters. In addition, there are many practical exercises to develop facility in the performance of embellishments.

The book, divided into three main parts and twenty-eight shorter lessons, approaches a different facet of trombone playing in each new lesson. Part One includes a wide variety of expression markings, attacks, legato tonguing, and extensions in range. Part Three includes more difficult etudes, scale studies, and arpeggios.

This is an excellent French method for younger players, and the range is conservative. The variety of high-quality materials is unusual for a beginning method book, and the print is especially clean and clear.

Vobaron, Edmond "Felix." *Four Lessons and Seventeen Studies, Op. 1.* FISC, n.d. F-b♭', 2-4, 19 pp.

This book begins with half-page, easy exercises in quarter and half-notes. The exercises are written primarily in detached, scale-like, and arpeggio patterns and are very conservative tonally. Although these studies are not difficult, the etudes ascend rapidly into the high register with the succeeding lessons becoming increasingly more difficult.

The lessons and studies are both similar in style, with the lessons being slightly more difficult and longer than the studies. The pieces contained within this book are slightly easier than a similar book of traditional, tonal studies by the same composer, entitled *Thirty-four Etudes for Trombone.*

——. *Méthode de trombone.* BILL, n.d. E-b♭', 1-3, 71 pp.

Vobaron, the first professor of trombone at the Paris Conservatory of Music, has left us several study and duet books which have been important in the training of trombone players for over a hundred years. His *Méthode de trombone* is a small "march-size" book and which begins with five pages of explanatory material. These pages relate to the embouchure, the seven positions, breathing, the ranges of alto, tenor, and bass trombone, and a six-measure trio for the alto, tenor, and bass trombone.

The method book proper commences with the study of the basic notes in each position and progresses to exercises using first position, first and second positions, first, second, and third positions, etc., until all seven positions have been covered in one exercise. The exercises are then organized by keys progressing from one flat to seven flats, the key of C, the relative minor flat keys, and finally proceeding to exercises in one sharp to seven sharps in both major and minor keys. Within the study of keys there is some variety of rhythms, meters, tonguing styles, and slurs.

———. *Quarante études pour trombone, 1e suite.* BILL, n.d. F-c", 4, 20 pp.

This is a collection of studies in the middle register with a supplementary bass trombone accompaniment part. Rhythmic melodies typify most of the etudes, with the harmonies being traditional and predictable. A few studies explore varied articulations and several make some demands on the player in terms of speed and technique.

Most of the etudes are in the easier flat keys and are very idiomatic for trombone.

———. *Quarante études pour trombone, 2e suite.* BILL, n.d. F-a', 4, 20 pp.

This work is a collection of traditional technique studies primarily concerned with the detached tonguing style. The book includes a supplemental bass trombone accompaniment part. Book II is not markedly more difficult than Book I, but Book II includes faster tempos such as "Vivace" and "Agitato Vivace" and an etude in four sharps in $\frac{5}{4}$ time.

These etudes are tonal and melodic studies that should be enjoyable to play. These pieces are excellent for the development of clean articulation, general technique, and a fluid tonal quality.

———. *32 Celebrated Melodies.* FISC, 1960. F-b♭', 4-5, 34 pp.

This book contains traditional, tonal etudes that are suitable for developing rhythmic accuracy, articulation, and endurance. In a style similar to the studies of Kopprasch and Tyrell, these etudes are not overly difficult but will be challenging due to their extended length.

These studies generally deal with scale and arpeggio-like patterns being melodically akin to melodies found in the early twentieth century trombone band parts.

———. *34 études mélodiques.* BILL, n.d. E-b♭', 4, 41 pp.

Similar to the Bleger *Ten Artistic Recreations* and the Tyrell *Forty Progressive Studies,* these etudes are traditional staccato pieces suitable for the development of articulations, slide technique, and general technique involving detached tonguing. Characteristically, the etudes move in scale-like progressions, with shifts from major to minor modes, recurring diminished chords, and frequent predictable interval skips. Aside from a certain historic interest, these are not particularly noteworthy technical studies.

5

Bass Trombone, Tuba, and Bass Saxhorn: Solos

Albinoni, Tommaso (1671-1750). *Sonate en fa majeur.* Adapted by André Goudenhooft. BILL, 1981. 146 meas. (R); 10'40" (11'); C-d'; 8; trills, written-out ornaments. b trbn, pf

I. Adagio: C : ♩ = 48-52: 21 meas.: 1'40"
II. Moderato: C : ♩ = 80: 34 meas. (R): 3'25"
III. Adagio: C : ♪ = 60: 16 meas.: 2'10"
IV. Allegro vivace: $\frac{3}{4}$: ♩ = 132: 75 meas. (R): 3'25"

This edition was prepared by André Goudenhooft, currently bass trombonist with *l'Orchestre National de France.* This adaptation is an extension of Mr. Goudenhooft's use of earlier works in order to develop musical feeling as well as technique.

——. *Sonate en ré majeur.* Adapted by André Goudenhooft. BILL, 1981. 157 meas. (R); 11' (11'); A'-e'; 8; trills. b trbn, pf

I. Grave: C : ♪ = 66-72: 21 meas.: 2'25"
II. Allegro moderato: C : ♩ = 76: 35 meas. (R): 3'40"
III. Adagio: $\frac{3}{4}$: ♪ = 80: 25 meas.: 1'55"
IV. Allegretto: $\frac{2}{4}$: ♩ = 100-104: 76 meas. (R): 3'

This edition was prepared by André Goudenhooft, currently bass trombonist with *l'Orchestre National de France.* This adaptation is an extension of Mr. Goudenhooft's use of earlier works in order to develop musical feeling as well as technique.

Amellér, André [Charles Gabriel] (b. 1912). *Bassutecy.* Collection Rougeron. LED, 1984. 1'40" (1'30"); B♭-f'; P2-E1*. tba/b saxhn, pf

Moderato: $\frac{3}{4}$: ♩ = 76: 31 meas.

Although the range may seem high, the expressive qualities of this solo could be used to benefit young bass trombonists. The mental preparation for rhythmic precision must be high, while at the same time allowing the musical aspects to predominate. The tessitura is at the top of the bass clef staff, and there are few rests; endurance should not be a major problem, though, because of its relatively short length.

——. *Batifol.* Com. 3*.

——. *Belle province: Hauterive* [Beautiful Province: High Bank]. LED, 1973. 2'35" (2'30"); E♭-e♭'; 2-3. tba/b trbn/saxhn (B♭ treb clef)/ b saxhn (B♭ and E♭ b clef), pf

"Cordialement à Jean Arnoult"

Andante expressivo: $\frac{3}{4}$: ♩ = 60-66: 54 meas.

Written in a lyrical style, this piece employs a mood which remains constant throughout. A simple melody is repeated twice with a small developmental interlude in between. There are only a few eighth-note patterns, and the range can be easily handled by most young players. The editing is good, and the many dynamic changes and slurs are helpful for developing expressive playing.

†——. *Irish-Cante* [Irish Song]. LED, 1977. 114 meas.; 4'20" (≈ 5'15"); E♭'-g'; 7*. tba/b saxhn/b trbn, pf

"Cordialement à Paul Bernard, Professeur au Conservatoire National Supérieur de Musique"

Assai vivo agitato: $\frac{3}{4}$: ♩ ≈ 120: 12 meas.: 20"
Tranquillo: $\frac{3}{4}$: ♩ ≈ 86: 4 meas.: 10"
A Tempo Primo: $\frac{3}{4}$: ♩ ≈ 120: 7 meas.: 10"
Tranquillo: $\frac{3}{4}$: ♩ ≈ 86: 6 meas.: 15"
A Tempo Primo: $\frac{3}{4}$: ♩ ≈ 120: 10 meas.: 15"
Molto lento: $\frac{4}{4}$: ♩ = 54: 11 meas.: 50"
Moderato: $\frac{6}{8}$: ♩. ≈ 84: 17 meas.: 25"
Lento: $\frac{6}{8}$: ♩. = 54: 4 meas.: 10"
Simplice: $\frac{6}{4}$: ♩ ≈ 92: 14 meas.: 55"
A Tempo moderato: $\frac{6}{8}$: ♩. = 84: 20 meas.: 30"
Lento: $\frac{6}{8}$: ♩. = 54: 9 meas.: 20"

As the number of "sections" may indicate, there is a great deal of tempo fluctuation. The large number of ritards can easily account for the large discrepancy in the duration estimate. This work truly demands a sensitive player to effectively interpret all musical indications. There is a mistake in solo part: add *"a Tempo moderato"* 7 meas. before rehearsal number "6."

†——. *Kryptos: Étude* [Hidden: Study]. HIN, 1958. 137 meas.; 7'55"; G♭'(A♯'/B♭')-b'(c♯"); 8; TB; mute, unmetered sections. all trbns (t or b)/tba/b saxhn, pf

"en Hommage à:

Paul Bernard, professeur au Conservatoire National Supérieur de Musique de Paris

René Poinsard, professeur au Conservatoire National de Musique Dijon

Maurice Smith, Trombone Professor at the Royal College of Music, London"

Largamente: n.m.: 20"
Largo: $\frac{3}{4}$: ♪ = 63: 19 meas.: 1'50"
Scherzando: $\frac{2}{4}$: ♩ = 104: 60 meas.: 1'10"
Lento espressivo: $\frac{6}{8}$: ♪ = 92: 24 meas.: 1'35"

Come prima: 3/4, 4/4, 5/4 : ♪ = 63: 9 meas.: 1'
Lento: 3/4, 4/4, n.m.: 20 meas.: 1'30"
Come prima: 3/4, 4/4, n.m.: 5 meas.: 30"

This is the only contest piece in this collection that was not originally published in France. The form of the work is ABCA'A", preceded by a Prologue that later returns as an Epilogue. The A theme is based on material in the Prologue. The A' returns a major third lower than the original statement, and it ends with a retrograde of the A theme. The A" is loosely based on the second half of the original A theme. Though there is no cadenza, there is plenty of room for expression and interpretation within the metrical framework. In general, endurance is not a problem because there are sufficient rests; the "Lento espressivo" is the only exception, because the tessitura is rather high.

†———. *Logos* [Speech]. LED, 1982. 190 meas.; 5'20" (≈ 7'); E'-(f')a♭'; 7*; cadenza, double and triple tonguing. tba (C or F)/b saxhn, pf

Allegro vivace: 4/4, 6/4, cad.: ♩ = 112: 20 meas.: 1'30"
Vivace: 6/8, 3/4 : ♩. = 104: 67 meas.: 1'15"
Molto lento: 6/8, 9/8 : ♩. = 50: 20 meas.: 1'5"
Vivace: 3/8 : ♩. = 84: 42 meas.: 30"
a Tempo: 6/8 : ♩. = 104: 30 meas.: 35"
a Tempo Vivace: 4/4 : ♩ = 112: 11 meas.: 25"

This piece begins with an opening one-measure "Largamente" in the piano that contains the motive upon which the rest of the piece is based. A brief "Espressivo lento" in the piano part serves as a bridge between the cadenza and the first "Vivace." The opening "Largamente" returns as an epilogue, this time in the solo part. The work is in arch form (ABCBA), and the principal tonalities stay close to D Major, although there are many brief excursions as one would expect in a French piece. The cadenza contains several slurs of about three octaves, one being three octaves plus a minor third. There are a few small discrepancies between the solo and piano parts. Though the A sections are technically oriented, this work is entirely feasible for performance on bass trombone.

†———. *Thème et variations*. AM, 1975. 213 meas.; 9'25"; F'-b♭'; 8; TB; cadenza. b saxhn/tba/b trbn, pf

"À Monsieur Paul Bernard, Professeur au Conservatoire National Supérieur"

Thème: Allegro con spirito: 4/4 : ♩ = 120: 19 meas.: 40"
Var. 1: Lo Stesso Tempo: 2/4, 4/4 : 10 meas.: 20"
Var. 2: Lo Stesso Tempo: 4/4 : 18 meas.: 35"
Var. 3: Allegretto: 6/8 : ♩. = 108: 39 meas.: 45"
Var. 4: Lento, cantabile: 2/4, 3/4, 4/4 : ♩ = 40: 13 meas.: 1'
Var. 5: Con Spirito: 2/4, 3/4, 4/4 : ♩ = 120: 25 meas.: 45"
Var. 6: Grave: 6/8 : ♪ = 120: 40 meas.: 2'
Var. 7: Quasi Allegro: 4/4, 5/4 : ♩ = 108: 12 meas.: 30"

Var. 8: Allegro maestoso, con brio: 4/4 : ♩ = 72: 6 meas.: 20"
Var. 9: Allegro moderato, giocoso: 2/8, 2/4, 3/4, 4/4, cad.: ♩ = 96: 31 meas.: 2'30"

This is one of only a few pieces from the repertoire of this genre. The quality of writing is high, and much facility and musicality is required to perform the work effectively. The layout is generally very good; there are only a few problems with vertical spacing. The piano cues are exceptional.

This was the Paris Conservatory contest piece for 1975.

——. *Tuba-abut.* ESC, 1975. 5'30".

†——. *Tuba-concert, Op. 69.* ESC, 1952. 154 meas.; 6'55"; D♯'/E♭'-(b')c"; 8; GB. tba/b saxhn, pf

"Amicalement à Paul Bernard, Professeur au Conservatoire National de Musique de Paris"

Agitato: 4/4, 5/4 : ♩ = 104-108: 32 meas.: 1'15"
Meno mosso: 4/4 : ♩ = 76-80: 11 meas.: 35"
Tempo I°: 4/4, 5/4 : ♩ = 104-108: 11 meas.: 25"
Tempo meno mosso: 4/4 : ♩ = 76-80: 6 meas.: 20"
Scherzando: 3/4 : ♩ = 120-126: 43 meas.: 1'5"
Tempo meno mosso: 4/4 : ♩ = 76-80: 6 meas.: 20"
Lento espressivo: 4/4, 5/4, 6/4 : 27 meas.: 2'
Largo: 3/4, 4/4 : ♩ = 66-70: 9 meas.: 30"
Più mosso: ¢, 3/4 : 5 meas.: 10"
Largo: 4/4 : ♩ = 66-70: 4 meas.: 15"

This is a concerto in one continuous movement, and the frequent style changes can become distracting. The work is unified through variation of a theme first heard completely at the first "Meno mosso." Although the range demands are obvious, there are few technical problems that prohibit the performance of this piece on bass trombone. There is a mistake in the tuba part in the measure before "16"—the first note after the treble clef change should be a concert d♭' (vice b♭").

This was the Paris Conservatory contest piece for 1952.

Bach, Johann Sebastian (1685-1750). *Sicilienne d'après la 1re Sonate en Sol mineur (BWV 1,001) pour Violin seul* [Sicilienne after the 1st Sonata in g minor for Violin Solo]. Edited by Philippe Rougeron. LED, 1983. 3'30" (3'30"); F-(e♭')f'; E2*.

Lent: 12/8 : ♪ = 69: 20 meas.

This piece is included because of its potential benefit in developing expressive playing. Although the LED catalog lists this piece under the "Tuba, Trombone basse, Saxhorn basse" section, the range of this piece allows for its performance on a tenor trombone. The performer of this piece would be well advised to consult an *Urtext* edition of the violin solo to discern which material is the most important.

Barat, Joseph Edouard (1882-1963). *Introduction et danse*. LED, n.d.; *Introduction and Dance*. Edited by Glenn Smith, SOUT, 1973. 84 meas.; 4'10"; C(E)-g'; 2* (LED) [5]; cadenza. Recordings: 3, 16, 49. b saxhn, pf (LED); bar, pf (SOUT)

Introduction: Lento: C, cad.: ♩ = 60: 31 meas.: 2'05"
Danse: Allegro: C : ♩ = 116-120: 23 meas.: 50"
Meno mosso: ♩ = 92: 18 meas.: 50"
Tempo primo (Danse): 12 meas.: 25"

Perhaps the main reason Glenn Smith created this edition is that the Leduc version is only in B♭ bass clef. The difficulty level has been raised in consideration of the bass trombonist. While many technical passages would be relatively easy for the French tuba or bass saxhorn, these passages would demand considerable slide technique for the bass trombone. The optional passage makes this work equally playable on a tenor trombone.

———. *Introduction et sérénade*. LED, 1957 (reprinted, 1963). 107 meas.; 3'30"; F'(F)-f'; 6*; cadenza. tba/b saxhn/bar saxhn, pf

Introduction: Lent: $\frac{3}{4}$, cad.: ♩ = 66: 33 meas.: 1'30"
Sérénade: $\frac{2}{4}$: ♩ = 72-76: 74 meas.: 2'

With the exception of a few passages, this piece is well-suited for the bass trombone. The chromatic passage in the cadenza could be changed to a descending E♭ scale, and the groupings of seven and ten notes near the end could be easily altered to groups of four and six, respectively. The *Sérénade* contains one of the more pleasant melodies that can be found in this repertoire.

———. *Morceau de concours* [Contest Piece]. LED, n.d. 189 meas.; 6'35"; C(F)-a♭'; 6*; G; cadenzas. bar or b saxhn, pf Recording: 48.

"À l'artiste et Ami J. Balay, ex-soliste de la Musique de la Garde et de l'Opéra"

Lent: C, cads.: ♩ = 69: 15 meas.: 1'
Lent: C : ♩ ≈ 66: 25 meas.: 1'30"
Poco più vivo: C, cad.: 16 meas.: 2'
Moderato: $\frac{3}{4}$: ♩ = 80: 4 meas.: 10"
Allegro: ♩ = 200-208: 118 meas.: 1'45"
Più vivo: 11 meas.: 10"

Like Barat's *Introduction et Sérénade*, this work can be edited for bass trombone, although it is a little less accessible. There are more chromatic passages, and the part is in B♭ treble clef. The *Morceau* is written in two major sections of which the first is lyrical and the second is a lively $\frac{3}{4}$ with plenty of technical challenges.

†———. *Réminiscences de Navarre*. LED, 1950. 129 meas.; 4'55"; F'-g'; 7*; cadenza, trill. tba/b saxhn, pf

"À mon Ami Paul Bernard, Professeur au Conservatoire National de Musique"

Andante: C : ♩ = 66: 18 meas.: 1'05"
Plus vite: C : 12 meas.: 40"
1° Tempo: C, cad.: 10 meas.: 1'15"
Allegro: 2/4, 3/4 : ♩ = 138: 89 meas.: 1'55"

Unlike other works by Barat, *Réminiscences* will need no editing for performance on bass trombone. The theme makes use of the overtone series in a sort of horn call. Because of this, triads are used frequently. Many triplet patterns will challenge good college-level players.

Barboteu, Georges (b. 1924). *Divertissement.* CHO, 1975. 3'30" (3'30"); A'-g; 7. Recording: 4. solo tba, 2 trpts, hn, trbn

"Pour mon ami E. Raynaud"

Allegro moderato: 2/4 : 166 meas. (R)

This piece is a technical display for the tuba. Most of the material is either scalar or chromatic, and there is very little legato playing from the entire group. This is an entertaining piece with much repetition; its light character makes it appropriate as a closing number on recitals. Only the first eight measures are repeated; the tempo needed to achieve the indicated performance time is ♩ = 100.

†——. *Prélude et cadence.* CHO, 1977. 5'15" (5'50"); E'-c"; 7; GB; cadenza, flutter tongue, trills. b saxhn/tba (C or F)/b trbn, pf

"À mon Ami Paul Bernard, professeur au Conservatoire National Supérieur de Musique"

Prelude: Lent: 2/4, 4/4 : ♪ = 80: 38 meas.: 3'40"
Cadence: 59 quarters: ♩ ≈ 40: 1'35"

Although the tempo remains constant, much variety is created through the alteration of time values. The piano part has several animated interludes but for the most part sustains tone clusters under the soloist.

A note from the composer included in the solo part is translated, "For the 'bass trombone' version the trills are omitted, the notes placed at the higher octave are good." A mistake exists in both solo parts: in the tuba/bass trombone part, the e♮' in the second system from the bottom should read a c" and the next note is an optional f'; in the saxhorn part, the written b♭' should read a d" with the next note being an optional g' (compare the parts to the piano score).

This was the Paris Conservatory contest piece for 1977.

†——. *"Romantic flash."* CHO, 1984. 181 meas.; 5'55" (7'); F'-b'; 7; TB; cadenza, cup mute, flutter tongue, glissando. b trbn, pf

"À mon ami Guy Destanque"

Maestoso: 2/4, 3/4, C : ♩ = 72: 40 meas.: 2'15"
Plus allant: 2/4, 3/4, C, cad.: 23 meas.: ♩ = 80: 1'10"
♪ = 76: 2/8, C : 10 meas.: 1'
Allegro vivo: 6/8 : ♩. = 138-144: 108 meas.: 1'30"

Written in three sections of contrasting styles, this work provides the soloist with a moderate amount of variety. There is a considerable amount of disjunct motion which takes the soloist from one range extreme to the other with little preparation. The meter changes are quite straightforward, and the piano cues have been prepared well. The indication *"Flatt."* was left out of the solo part on the third beat of the measure before "B."

This was the Paris Conservatory contest piece for 1984.

Bariller, Robert (b. 1918). *L'enterrement de Saint-Jean* [The Funeral of Saint John]. LED, 1960. 4'5" (5'); A'(A)-f'; 1-2*. tba/b trbn/ b saxhn, pf

"À Paul Bernard, très amicalement"

Tempo di Marcia funebre: C : 29 meas.: 1'55"
Un poco più vivo, ma quasi maestoso e marcato: $\frac{2}{4}$: 25 meas.: 45"
Coma prima: C, $\frac{6}{4}$: 21 meas.: 1'25"

If the performer decides to perform this work with the publisher's suggested duration, the tempos would be ♩ = 50 for the main tempo and ♩ = 54 for the più vivo tempo. This would be very demanding in endurance for nearly any performer; a more accessible selection would be ♩ = 60 (66 for più vivo). With the exception of the last note (A'), the tessitura is entirely in the middle range, with an A (great) being the next lowest note. The piano part includes the excerpt of the drama by Alfred de Musset (1810-1857) (*Fantasio*, Act I, Scene II) which inspired the composer to create this work. (It is interesting to note that Musset had an intermittent love affair with the novelist George Sand from 1833-1835.) The excerpt is translated below.

(A funeral passes...)

Fantasio
Hey! Brave men, who are you interring there? It is not the hour to bury properly.

The Porters
We are interring Saint John.

Fantasio
Saint John is dead? The king's fool is dead? Who has taken his place? The minister of justice?

The Porters
His place is vacant, you can take it if you want.

———. *Hans de Schnokeloch*. LED, 1961. 145 meas. (R); 5'5" (5'); C♯-a'; 2* [4-5]; glissandos. b trbn/tba/b saxhn/(t trbn), pf

"À Paul Bernard, En hommage à son magnifique effort en faveur du Trombone-basse mixte dont il souligne, dans son excellente méthode, les advantages indiscutables"

Allegro moderato e con spirito: $\frac{2}{4}$, $\frac{3}{4}$: 30 meas.: 40"
Meno: $\frac{5}{8}$, $\frac{2}{4}$, $\frac{3}{4}$: 21 meas.: 35"
Presto (doppio movimento): $\frac{2}{4}$: 4 meas.(R to beg.): 5"

Allegro maestoso: 2/4, 3/4, 5/4, 6/4, ¢ : 31 meas.: 1'5"
Tempo 1° subito: 2/4, 3/4 : 30 meas.: 40"
Meno: 5/8, 2/4, 3/4 : 21 meas.: 35"
Scherzo (doppio movimento): 2/4 : 8 meas.: 5"

The level of difficulty assigned by the publisher is probably a mistake. Considering the range, meter shifts, and facility of technique required, this piece warrants at least a four to five rating. Although not indicated in the title, the composer notes in the piano score that this piece is equally playable on the tenor trombone; indications are made throughout for octave shifts when the part is impractical for the tenor trombone. The glissando in the last measure of the fourth system of the solo part is realized both in ascent and descent (also in the last measure of the seventh system on page two). A note from the composer at the beginning of the piano score is translated below.

> The principal theme of this piece is borrowed from a very popular chanson from Alsace. The hero, Hans, is at once the type of the mock middle-class comic and cabaret artist, while at the same time he portrays the eternal malcontent. The chanson also ventures to maintain that he has everything he wants, but he does not want what he has; that he does not believe what he says and he does not say what he thinks; and that he goes where he wants and that he is not pleased where he stays. My music is less disagreeable.

†**Barraine,** [Jacqueline] **Elsa** (b. 1910). *Andante et allegro.* SAL, 1958. 131 meas.; 3'40"; B♭'-b♭'; 7; TB; cadenza. b saxhn, pf

"À Paul Bernard, Professeur au Conservatoire National Supérieur"

Modéré molto sostenuto espressivo et rubato: 2/8, 5/8, 2/4, 3/4, C : 55 meas.: 1'40"
Allegro molto giocoso: 2/8, 3/8, 4/8, 5/8, 2/4, 3/4, C, 5/4 : 76 meas.: 2'

The "Andante" is quite lyrical and is generally more disjunct than the "Allegro." Numerous chromatic alterations exist in the "Allegro," and that combined with reading a transposed B♭ bass clef part (no part in C exists) in the key of G♭ Major (concert E Major) is particularly difficult. A transcription of the solo part would probably be in order, and there should be few technical problems for its performance on bass trombone.

This was the Paris Conservatory contest piece for 1958.

†——. *Chiens de paille* [Straw Dogs]. JOB, 1966. 79 meas.; 6'35" (7'); G'(C)-b♭'; 8; complex meters, glissandos, unmetered sections. tba/t or b trbn/bn/Ondes Martenot, pf

"à la mémoire d'A.W.Y."

Modéré: 2/8, 3/8, 5/8, 7/8, 8/8, 9/8, 10/8, 13/8 : ♪ = 88: 20 meas.: 1'25"
Plus lent: 4/8, 7/8 : ♪ = 72: 10 meas.: 50"
Un peu plus animé: 3/16, 5/16, 6/16, 7/16, 8/16, 9/16, 10/16, 11/16 : 29 meas.: 1'30"
Librement: n.m.: 8 meas.: 1'15"
Un peu plus lent qu'au début: 5/8, 6/8, 7/8, 9/8, 10/8, 11/8 : ♪ = 60: 12 meas.: 1'35"

A brief passage from the composer is translated below:

> In ancient China, one used to put straw dogs in front of funeral processions to seize evil spirits on the passage. They were then burned, and the spirit of the dead person was able to fly up to heaven.

The difficulty in this work comes from maintaining concentration while navigating through meter changes that occur nearly every measure. The slower passages tend to be disjunct, and the faster ones are either scalar, chromatic, or a mixture of both. Ensemble between the soloist and pianist does not appear to be as difficult as in similar works. Endurance may be a problem because of a general lack of rests.

This was the Paris Conservatory contest piece for tuba in 1966.

Beaucamp, Albert [Maurice] (b. 1921). *Cortège* [Procession]. LED, 1953. 2'25"; C-g'; 1-2* [3]; unaccompanied section. tba/db/b saxhn/ b trbn, pf

"à Armand François"

Grave: $\frac{2}{4}$: ♩ = 48: 57 meas.

The basic style of this piece is legato with a solemn quality. It would serve well to develop a sense of phrasing in a very slow work. With the consideration of endurance and range, the degree of difficulty should be raised to three.

Beethoven, Ludwig van (1770-1827). *Danse villageoise* [Rustic Dance]. BILL, 1989. Adapted by André Goudenhooft, piano realization by Augustin Maillard. 2'15" (3'); C-c'; 2-4. b trbn/tba, pf

Standard version: Allegro moderato: $\frac{3}{4}$: ♩ = 138-144: 24 meas. (2R) + 32 meas.

Simplified version: Allegro moderato: $\frac{3}{4}$: ♩ = 138-144: 24 meas. (2R) + 16 meas. (R)

This work was extracted from *Thèmes variés* for violin. When taken at the indicated tempo, this work may cause some technical problems for the young player. The multiple difficulty level was assessed because there are standard and simplified parts. Only the technical passages have been simplified, although the range remains the same. Even in the standard part, there are plenty of ossias. Those indications, combined with numerous piano cues, make the part appear cluttered. The simplified version has a mistake in the last two measures. The first and second ending signs have been omitted by mistake.

This edition was prepared by André Goudenhooft, currently bass trombonist with *l'Orchestre National de France*. This adaptation is an extension of Mr. Goudenhooft's use of earlier works in order to develop musical feeling as well as technique.

†**Bernaud, Alain**. *Humoresque*. ESC, 1964. 330 meas.; 9'40" (9'10"); F'-b'; 9; cadenza, complex meters, double and triple tonguing, unaccompanied sections. tba/b saxhn, pf

"à Paul Bernard, Professeur au Conservatoire de Paris"

Pomposo: $\frac{3}{8}$, $\frac{7}{8}$, $\frac{4}{4}$, $\frac{7}{4}$, $\frac{3}{2}$: ♩ ≈ 72: 18 meas.: 1'5"

Poco più mosso: $\frac{4}{4}$: ♩ = 104-108: 8 meas.: 20"

Molto ritmico: 3/16, 5/16, 6/16, 7/16, 9/16, 11/16, 15/16, 2/8, 3/8, 5/8, 1/4, 2/4, 3/4, 4/4, 5/4, 6/4, 7/4, 9/4, cad.: 291 meas.: 7'30"
Andantino: 7/8, 4/4, 5/4 : 13 meas.: 45"

The "Pomposo" serves as an introduction to this light-hearted work. The piano and solo parts serve equal roles at the beginning, but from the "Molto ritmico" to the end, the piano is relegated to harmonic and rhythmic support. The complex meter changes are somewhat repetitious, making them more approachable than in similar works. Nearly every facet of style and technique is addressed, and the extended cadenza is highly virtuosic. There are few rests, and, considering that the entire range is used almost all the time, endurance may be a serious problem. There are many flashy technical passages that are not very idiomatic for the bass trombone, and the time required to master their execution could hinder the preparation of other works on the same recital. If this piece were to be programmed, editing should be seriously considered.

Beugniot, Jean-Pierre (b. 1935). *Légende.* BILL, 1981. 80 meas.; 2'25" (2'15"); E-f'; 3. b saxhn/tba/b trbn, pf

Large et décidé: 2/4, 3/4 : ♩ = 88: 14 meas.: 20"
Allant: 2/4 : ♩ = 100: 7 meas.: 10"
♩ = 80: 2/4, 3/4 : 17 meas.: 30"
Plus lent: 3/4 : ♩ = 66: 15 meas.: 40"
Plus animé: 3/4 : 8 meas.: 20"
♩ = 108-112: 2/4 : 10½ meas.: 10"
Large: 2/4 : ♩ = 60: 4½ meas.: 10"
Vif: 2/4 : ♩ = 120: 4 meas.: 5"

This short piece has plenty of variety with its frequent style and tempo changes. There are enough elements here to challenge and keep the interest of advanced junior high students. Because of its range, this piece would also be suitable for tenor trombone.

†**Bigot, Eugène** [Victor] (1888-1965). *Carillon et bourdon* [Carillon and Great Bell]. LED, 1951. 100 meas.; 3'45" (4'); E'-a♭'; 7*. tba/b saxhn, pf

"à Monsieur Paul Bernard, Professeur au Conservatoire National de Musique"

Allegro moderato: 2/4, 3/4, C, 5/4, 9/4, 3/2 : ♩ = 112: 52 meas.: 1'55"
Meno mosso: 3/4, C : ♩ = 100: 21 meas.: 50"
I° Tempo: C, 6/4 : ♩ = 112: 27 meas.: 1'

As the title suggests, this work imitates the character and style of a carillon through the sustained pedal points (mostly in the piano) and constant quarter-note movement throughout. Some triplet and sixteenth-note passages are tricky, but manageable on the bass trombone.

Bigot, Pierre. *Cortège* [Procession]. COM, 1983. 2' (2'); F(B♭)-c'; D2*. tba/b saxhn, pf

Maestoso: C : 32 meas.

This brief piece is in ABA form, and there is no style contrast between sections. Few editorial markings are made, but the general feel suggests either two- or four-bar phrases. Although the range would suggest that this piece could be performed on a tenor trombone, several passages could be facilitated by an F valve. The tempo to achieve the indicated performance time is ♩ = 64.

†**Bitsch, Marcel** (b. 1921). *Impromptu.* LED, 1957. 95 meas.; 3'50" (4'15"); F'-b♭'; 7*; TB; a piacere section, unaccompanied sections. b saxhn/tba/b trbn, pf

"à Paul Bernard, Professeur au Conservatoire National de Musique"
A piacere: 1 meas.: 55"
Andante quasi adagio: C, 5/4 : ♩ = 54: 20 meas.: 1'30"
Vivo: 5/8 : ♩ = 132: 55 meas.: 1'5"
Moderato: 2/4, 3/4 : ♩ = 108: 19 meas.: 20"

Although the beginning is marked "a piacere," the composer suggests numerous dynamic shadings to be observed by the performer (usually these, too, are to be used at the performer's discretion); the piano part consists of a series of sustaining chords until the "Andante." The technical passages in the moderato section are difficult but not so difficult to require editing for the bass trombone. *Impromptu* combines a good variety of styles in a short piece and has plenty to offer to advanced players.

†———. *Intermezzo.* LED, 1968. 156 meas.; 5' (5'); G'-b♭'; 8-9*; GB; cadenza. tba/b saxhn, pf

"À Paul Bernard, Professeur au Conservatoire National Supérieur de Musique"

Andante sostenuto: 2/4, cad.: ♩ = 60: 32 meas.: 1'50"
Allegro moderato: 2/4 : ♩ = 76: 46 meas.:1'15"
Poco a poco accelerando: 3/8, 2/4 : 22 meas.: 25"
a Tempo: 2/4, 3/4 : ♩ = 76: 40 meas.: 1'5"
a Tempo accel. poco a poco: 2/4 : 16 meas.: 25"

Written in two main sections, this piece is intended more for valved instruments than a bass trombone, although it is approachable by an advanced bass trombonist. The first section includes a lyrical melody in a disjunct style that requires considerable flexibility (there are two slurs of a minor fourteenth!). The second section is more lively, and two accelerandos can become unmanageable if not executed properly.

†**Boizard, Gilles**. *Diptyque: "Aux statues de Bomarzo."* EDMT, 1967. 134 meas.; 6'10"; G'-b♭'; 8; complex meters, flutter tongue, glissandos, quasi cadenza, trills, unaccompanied sections. b trbn, pf

I. Andante: C : ♩ = 58: 11 meas.: 45"
brutale: ♩ = 72: 9 meas.: 30"
Tempo 1°: 2/4, C : ♩ = 58: 13 meas.: 50"
♩ = 𝅗𝅥 del Tempo précédente: C : ♩ = 44: 3 meas.: 15"
Tempo 1°: C : ♩ = 58: 6 meas.: 25"
♩ = 72: 12 meas.: 40"
Movement I = 54 meas.: 3'25"

II. Presto: $\frac{5}{8}$, $\frac{6}{8}$, $\frac{7}{8}$, $\frac{8}{8}$, $\frac{9}{8}$, $\frac{10}{8}$, $\frac{11}{8}$, $\frac{12}{8}$, $\frac{13}{8}$: 14 meas.: 25"
Allegro: $\frac{3}{4}$, $\frac{4}{4}$: triolet un peu plus rapide que trois ♪'s du Movement précédent [triplet a little faster than three ♪'s of the previous section]: 5 meas.: 15"
Presto: $\frac{5}{8}$, $\frac{6}{8}$, $\frac{7}{8}$, $\frac{8}{8}$, $\frac{9}{8}$: 10 meas.: 20"
Allegro: $\frac{4}{4}$: 5 meas.: 10"
Presto (non troppo): $\frac{4}{8}$, $\frac{5}{8}$, $\frac{6}{8}$, $\frac{7}{8}$, $\frac{8}{8}$: 14 meas.: 20"
Allegro: $\frac{3}{4}$, $\frac{4}{4}$, $\frac{5}{4}$: 13 meas.: 30"
Allegro giusto: $\frac{4}{4}$: 3 meas.: 10"
quasi cadenza (Presto): $\frac{3}{8}$, $\frac{5}{8}$, $\frac{7}{8}$, $\frac{9}{8}$, $\frac{11}{8}$, $\frac{13}{8}$, $\frac{15}{8}$, $\frac{4}{4}$: 11 meas.: 25"
Allegro deciso: $\frac{4}{4}$: 5 meas.: 10"
Movement II = 80 meas.: 2'45"

The first movement contains a great deal of disjunct motion and complex rhythms for the soloist. Two slower sections allow for a smoother playing style, but still much rhythmic variety continues in the piano. There is an "attaccare" leading to the second movement. The second movement quickly changes moods and styles, and there is more disjunct motion for the soloist; at one point, the soloist must span three octaves in the span of nine eighth notes (Presto tempo). The $\frac{5}{8}$ meter should read "$\frac{5}{4}$" in the 3d meas., 5th sys., p. 3 of the bass trombone part.

This was the Paris Conservatory contest piece for 1967.

Boutry, Roger (b. 1932). *Pièce brève* [Short Piece] SAL.

†———. *Tubacchanale* [Tuba Revel]. LED, 1956. 257 meas.; 7'20"; E'-(a')b'; 8*; cadenzas. tba/b saxhn, pf

"À mon ami Paul Bernard, Professeur au Conservatoire National de Musique"

(Introduction.) Allegro moderato: $\frac{3}{4}$, $\frac{5}{4}$, ¢, cad.: 𝅗𝅥 ≈ 76: 29 meas.:1'10"
Intermezzo. Allegretto scherzando: $\frac{3}{4}$: ♩ = 138-144: 37 meas.: 45"
Andante: $\frac{3}{4}$: ♩ = 63: 56 meas.: 2'40"
Allegro: $\frac{3}{8}$, $\frac{5}{8}$, $\frac{7}{8}$, $\frac{2}{4}$, $\frac{3}{4}$, cad.: ♩ ≈ 144: 105 meas.: 2'10"
a Tempo vivace: ¢ : 𝅗𝅥 = 108: 30 meas.: 35"
Intermezzo = 228 meas.: 6'10"

One source suggests that a bacchanal is an orgy or a noisy, uproarious dance. Whatever the case, this piece is lively throughout, with a sufficient amount of stylistic contrast. For effective performance on bass trombone, the soloist should adjust some of the tempos down slightly; many passages take advantage of the valved-instruments' ability to play rapid slurred passages without articulating each note. There are two optional cuts; the second cut eliminates several extended chromatic passages.

———. *Tubaroque*. LED, 1955. 135 meas.; 3'30"; A'-g'(a♭'); 4-5*. tba/b saxhn/b trbn, pf/orch

"à mon ami Paul Bernard"

Introduction: C : 4 meas.: ♩ = 72: 15"
Movement de Valse lente: $\frac{3}{4}$: ♩ = 104: 31 meas.: 55"
Allegretto: $\frac{3}{8}$, $\frac{3}{4}$: ♩ = 112: 65 meas.: 1'20"
Moderato: $\frac{3}{4}$, C : ♩ = 76: 10 meas.: 30"
Allegro: $\frac{3}{4}$, C : 𝅗𝅥 = ♩ précédente: 25 meas.: 30"

Although the title might infer otherwise, there are no direct musical references to the Baroque era. This piece is in four independent sections and behaves much like a fantasy. There are no surprises, and each section leads well into the next. The moderato has several difficult grace notes to execute, and the last allegro contains a fair amount of syncopation. An orchestral accompaniment is available on rental from LED. The instrumentation includes: fl, ob, bn, hn, trpt, timp, strgs.

Bozza, Eugène [Joseph] (b. 1905). *Allegro et finale*. LED, 1953. 142 meas.; 5'; E-a'(b'); 5*; GB; cadenza, extended unaccompanied sections. db/tba/b saxhn/b trbn, pf

Allegro deciso: $\frac{3}{4}$: 30 meas.: 50"
Moderato: $\frac{3}{4}$: 13 meas.: 25"
Un peu moins vite: $\frac{3}{4}$: 16 meas.: 30"
Andantino: $\frac{6}{8}$: 24 meas.: 1'25"
Allegro: cad. ($\frac{2}{4}$, $\frac{3}{4}$): 18 meas.: 30"
Moderato: $\frac{3}{4}$: ♩ = 72: 18 meas.: 45"
Allegro deciso: $\frac{3}{4}$: 23 meas.: 35"

A multi-section work with plenty of variety, *Allegro et finale* is one of finest mid-level compositions in this body. The cadenza and final section are closely based on the opening section, and the others provide good contrast. Because of the quality of this work and feasibility for performance, many tenor trombonists have added it to their libraries. In the solo part, the indication "Un peu moins vite" was left out in the 6th meas., 7th sys., p. 1; "rit." was left out in the 7th meas., 9th sys., p.1 (meas. before "Andantino"); and "Più allegro" should be indicated 4 meas. from the end.

——. *Concertino*. LED, 1967. 345 meas.; 9'25" (17'); F'-a♭'/g♯'; 7*; cadenzas. tba/b saxhn, orch/pf

I. Allegro vivo: $\frac{2}{4}$, $\frac{3}{4}$, cad.: 130 meas.: 3'30"
II. (avec le caractère d'une improvisation) [with the character of an improvisation]: cad.: 55"
Andante ma non troppo: $\frac{2}{4}$: 55 meas.: 2'20"
Movement II = 56 meas.: 3'15"
III. Allegro vivo: $\frac{6}{8}$, $\frac{2}{4}$, cad.: ♩. = 160: 120 meas.: 2'5"
Moderato: $\frac{6}{8}$, $\frac{9}{8}$, $\frac{2}{4}$: 38 meas.: 35"
Movement III = 159 meas.: 2'40"

In the first movement, the solo makes much use of chromatic material and a few disjunct patterns. The "Allegro" portion of the cadenza is reminiscent of several of Bozza's other works, and the last six measures appears to be a shortened version of the ending to his *New Orleans* (1962). It is interesting to note that the second movement is, in its entirety, only a slight alteration of the last "a piacere" and

"Andante ma non troppo" sections of *New Orleans*. The final movement has a more playful tone, with many moving triplets for the soloist. The cadenza continues in the same style, and contains some grace notes which may be difficult to execute effectively. Although intended for tuba or bass saxhorn, the bass trombonist could perform this work with only minor editing of some low chromatic passages in the first movement. This work also has an orchestral accompaniment available on rental from LED.

†———. *New Orleans*. LED, 1962. 142 meas.; 5'45"; F'-a'; 7*; TB; glissandos, unmetered sections. b saxhn/tba/b trbn, pf

"À monsieur Paul Bernard, Professeur au Conservatoire National Supérieur de Musique"

4/4, n.m.: ♩ = 60: 13 meas.: 2'15"
Andante ma non troppo: 3/4 : ♩ = 72: 42 meas.: 1'45"
Allegro giocoso: 2/4 : 78 meas.: 1'35"
Moderato: 2/4 : 9 meas.: 10"

Written in two major sections, this piece is characteristic of Bozza's compositional style. The first section essentially begins with an extended cadenza that is accompanied by occasional chords in the piano. The accompaniment for the andante is reminiscent of the style and character found in his *Ballade, Op. 62* (1944) for tenor trombone. The second section employs a syncopated figure that perhaps reveals the influence of jazz on the work.

———. *Prélude et allegro*. LED, 1953. 99 meas.; 5'25"; (A')E-a'; 5* [6]; cadenza. Recording: 19. db/tba/b saxhn/b trbn, pf

"à Monsieur Moulard, Professeur de Contrebasse au Conservatoire National de Valenciennes"

Moderato (Calme): 4/4 : 21 meas.: 1'10"
Allegro moderato: 4/4 : 18 meas.:40"
Un peu plus vite: 4/4 : 28 meas.: 55"
Tempo I° [Allegro]: 2/4, 4/4, cad.: 32 meas.:2'40"

The melodic material at the beginning is disjunct and exploits the interval of a perfect fourth. The allegro moderato opens with a jaunty theme that is not unlike the main theme of his *Allegro et finale* published in the same year. This piece contains a technical workout for the soloist, as well as some high sustained passages. The technical considerations alone should justify a degree of difficulty of "six" for trombonists. Because of the written range and tessitura, this piece would also be feasible for performance on tenor trombone.

———. *Thème varié* [Varied Theme]. LED, 1957. 92 meas.; 4' (4'); G'-(f')g'; 5* [6]; cadenza. tba/b saxhn/b trbn, pf

Thème: Allegretto pomposo: 3/8 : ♪ = 112: 18 meas.: 30"
Var. 1: Tempo I°: 3/8 : 16 meas.: 25"
Var. 2: Moderato: 3/8 : ♪ = 100: 18 meas.: 30"
Var. 3: Grave: 3/2 : 𝅗𝅥 = 80: 16 meas.: 35"
Var. 4: Allegro maestoso: 3/4, 4/4 : ♩ = 96: 16 meas.: 30"

(Var. 5): Lent: 3/4, cad.: ♩ = 76: 5 meas.: 1'25"
Allegro vivo: 3/4 : 3 meas.: 5"

Although this is probably not intentional, the main theme of this work brings to mind old sea chanteys or similar folk songs, because of the pompous style and relatively slow three feel. Each of the four accompanied variations should be interpreted independently, with careful consideration for style. The cadenza, essentially a fifth variation, allows the performer to exploit his brilliant style throughout the range of the solo instrument. The tessitura is generally low; two slurred passages, both being chromatic and covering the span of two octaves, will challenge players of all performance levels to maintiain continuity. The technical considerations alone should justify a degree of difficulty of "six" for bass trombonists.

Brouquières, Jean. *Au temps de la cour* [At the Time of the Heart]. MAR, 1982. 66 meas.; 2'5"; F-b♭; P*. b saxhn/tba, pf

Moderato: 3/4 : ♩ = 88: 54 meas. (R)

Written in ABA form in the key of B♭, this piece remains in one style throughout, although the B section modulates to E♭. There are many clear editorial markings, and this piece would also be suitable for performance on tenor trombone. The first eight measures are repeated.

——. *Tubaria.* MAR, 1983. 2'25" (2'15"); F-f'; P*. tba/b saxhn, pf

"À Jean-Paul Dambacher, amicalement. J.B."

Moderato: 3/4 : ♩ = 76: 26 meas.: 1'
Poco più vivo: 3/4 : ♩ = 96: 20 meas.: 40"
I° Tempo: 3/4 : ♩ = 76: 20 meas.: 45"

This piece is written in ABA form, and it is in the key of F Major. The editorial markings are clear, and the style changes between sections are easy to discern. Because of its range, this piece would also be suitable for performance on tenor trombone. It won the *Concours de Composition 1983 de la Confédération Musicale de France, Prix Robert Martin.*

†**Brown, Charles** [Louis Georges] (b.1898). *Récitatif, lied et final.* LED, 1961. 238 meas.; 6'55" (7'); E'(C)-(a')b♭'; 8*; TB; unaccompanied sections. b saxhn/tba/b trbn, pf

"À mon ami Paul Bernard, Professeur au Conservatoire National Supérieur de Musique"

Lent: 2/4, 4/4 : ♩ = 60: 27 meas.: 1'45"
♩ = 80: 2/4 : 103 meas.: 2'35"
♩ = 120: 6/8, 2/4, 3/4, 4/4, 5/4 : 86 meas.: 1'40"
Lent: 4/4 : ♩ = 60: 6 meas.: 25"
Allegro: 2/4, 3/4, 4/4, 5/4 : ♩ = 120: 16 meas.: 30"

As the title suggests, this piece is written in three main sections, although a brief reminiscence of the *recitatif* interrupts the *final.* While each section exhibits a particular style, the entire work contains very disjunct writing, and the *final* can become unmanageable if played too quickly. The grace notes will need much practice to be executed properly. A very poor editing job was done on both solo parts; there are too many errors to include in this essay. The performer would be well advised to carefully compare the solo part to the piano score from beginning to end.

†**Cals, Michel**. *Pièce brève* [Short Piece]. LED, 1976. 201 meas.; 7'15" (6'30"); E'-g'; 8*; complex meters, flutter tongue, glissandos, *sourdine sèche* [fiber straight mute], plunger, proportional notation, unmetered sections. b trbn, pf

Lento: 2/4, 4/4, 5/4, n.m.: ♩ = 60: 15 meas.: 2'15"
♩ = 72: 3/8, 5/8, 2/4, 3/4, 4/4, 5/4, n.m.: 19 meas.: 1'20"
Allegro: (33/8), 3/4, 5/4, ¢, 3/2 : 𝅗𝅥 = 112: 69 meas.: 1'20"
𝅗𝅥 = 144: 5/4, ¢, 3/2 : 33 meas.: 30"
Lento: 3/4, 4/4 : 13 meas.: 50"
Tempo [𝅗𝅥 = 112]: 7/8, 3/4, 5/4, ¢, 3/2 : 52 meas.: 1'

This piece explores several modern performance techniques that have been used more frequently in recent years. It employs an ABAB form with a slow, proportionally-written introduction. The first section begins with a melody that is highly rhythmic and uses many half and whole steps. The B sections contain a highly-syncopated rhythm and many extreme dynamics (e.g, *fff* on an E'!). The second A section is based on the "♩ = 72" portion of the first A section. Some practice will be needed to coordinate the plunger work. Most of the accompaniment is either in tone clusters, a single running line, or in octaves. The indication "T° 𝅗𝅥 = 112" was left out of the solo part in the 3d meas., 1st sys., last page.

†**Carles, Marc** (b. 1933). *Introduction et toccata*. LED, 1961. 243 meas.; 6'20" (6'25"); B'-a'; 8*; complex meters. b trbn/tba/b saxhn, pf

"à Paul Bernard, Professeur au Conservatoire National Supérieur de Musique"

Maestoso: 2/4, 3/4, 4/4, 5/4 : ♩ ≈ 58: 23 meas.: 1'30"
Allegro marcato: 2/4, 3/4, 4/4, 2/2 : ♩ = 176: 90 meas.: 2'
Poco più lento: 4/4, 5/4 : 17 meas.: 25"
Tempo [♩ = 176]: 2/2 : 18 meas.: 25"
Lento quasi recitativo: 4/4, 5/4, 2/2 : ♩ = 60: 12 meas.: 30"
Vivo: 5/8, 6/8, 8/8, 9/8 : ♪ = ♪ de l'Allegro marcato: 83 meas.: 1'30"

The *Introduction* is a measured free passage in which the soloist plays a pattern that gets longer on each occurrence, and the piano moves only when the soloist sustains a half note or longer. The *Toccata* is in three main sections containing substantial counterpoint only in the first two. There is more disjunct motion in the *Toccata* than in the *Introduction*. In the bass trombone/tuba part, there is one beam too many in the 1st meas., 5th sys., p. 1.

†**Castérède, Jacques** (b. 1926). *Fantaisie concertante.* LED, 1960. 211 meas.; 7'5" (7'30"); B'-a'; 8*; cadenza, complex meters. Recordings: 18, 56, 67. b trbn/tba/b saxhn, pf

"à Paul Bernard, Professeur au Conservatoire National Supérieur de Musique"

Allegro ma non troppo: 3/8, 4/8, 5/8, 6/8, 7/8, 2/4, 3/4, 4/4 : ♩ = 104: 57 meas.: 1'50"
Più mosso: 5/8, 8/8, 3/4 : ♪ = triplet ♪ from previous tempo [♩ = 156]: 69 meas.: 2'15"
Calme e sostenuto: 6/8, 9/8, 2/4, 3/4, 4/4, 3/2 : ♩. = 66 (♪ constant): 42 meas.: 1'35"
a Tempo I°: 2/4, 4/4 : ♩ = 104: 8 meas.: 15"
Più mosso: 3/8, 5/8, 6/8, 7/8, 8/8, 9/8, 2/4, 3/4, 4/4 : ♩ = 112: 45 meas.: 1'10"

Fantaisie concertante is the most frequently performed work from this body of music. Written in three main sections, it is a one-movement work that explores nearly every facet of technique for the soloist. Characteristic of a fantasy, there are many accelerandos and ritardandos which are not annotated above. There are frequent modulations, many of which are chromatic, but the entire work is tonal. Both the solo and piano parts are virtuosic and require accomplished players.

†———. *Sonatine.* LED, 1963. 299 meas.; 6'40" (7'15"-7'20"); E'-a'; 7*; GB; unaccompanied sections. Recordings: 35, 66. tba/b saxhn, pf

"à Paul Bernard, Professeur au Conservatoire National Supérieur de Musique"

I. Défilé. Modéré, robuste et martial: 2/4 : ♩ = 108: 107 meas.: 2' (2')
II. Sérénade. 6/8 : ♩. = 50: 60 meas.: 2'25" (2'55")
III. Final. Allegro: 2/4, 3/4 : ♩ = 112: 18 meas.: 20"
Vivo: 2/3, 3/4, 6/8 : ♩. = 138: 31 meas.: 25"
Tempo I°: 2/4 : 5 meas.: 10"
Più tranquillo: 2/4 : ♩ = 104: 4 meas.: 10"
a Tempo allegro risoluto: 6/8, 9/8, 2/4 : ♩ = 120 (♩ = ♩.): 30 meas.: 30"
a Tempo: 2/4 : ♩ = 120: 9 meas.: 10"
Vivo: 6/8 : ♩. = 138: 24 meas.: 20"
Meno mosso: 6/8 : ♩. = 126: 11 meas.: 10"
Movement III = 132 meas.: 2'15"(2'10")

One of the most readily playable of the solos specifically written for a tuba, *Sonatine* is virtually equal in quality to his *Fantaisie concertante*, yet is quite different in character. Again, the writing is highly virtuosic for both soloist and accompanist. The "Défilé" is the most similar to the *Fantaisie*, but in a more pompous style. Much concentration is needed to execute the sudden octave shifts and clef changes. There are many accidentals, and keeping the sixteenth-note passages smooth and even is a challenge. The second movement contains perhaps one of the most beautiful melodies ever written for a low brass instrument. The soloist can truly take full advantage of the use of agogic accents and expressive playing throughout the entire range of the solo instrument. The "Final" is full of energy in a light-hearted character. The accidentals in the treble clef section are especially frightening. Two descending unaccompanied runs for the soloist, one at the end of the first mvt. and the other at the beginning of the last mvt., will require careful planning. The last note in meas. 3 of the solo part should be a "d" (vice "e").

†**Cecconi** [Botella], **Monic** [Gabrielle] (b. 1936). *Tuba-I.* RID, 1971. 64 meas.; 6'40" (≈ 7'); F'-g'; 7; feathered beaming, flutter tongue, half valve, non-standard meter indication, quarter tones, timed events, trills, unaccompanied sections, unmetered sections. tba, pf

Lent: $\frac{11}{8}$, $\frac{3}{4}$, $\frac{4}{4}$, $\frac{5}{4}$, $\frac{6}{4}$, $\frac{7}{4}$, $\frac{8}{4}$, $\frac{9}{4}$, n.m.: ♩ = 60: 23 meas.: 2'35"

Più mosso: ♩ = 100: $\frac{3}{4}$, $\frac{5}{4}$, $\frac{6}{4}$, n.m.: 30 meas.: 3'25"

Très lent comme au début: $\frac{4}{4}$, $\frac{7}{4}$: 3 meas.: 10"

Un peu plus lent: $\frac{1}{4}$, $\frac{2}{4}$, $\frac{3}{4}$, $\frac{4}{4}$, $\frac{6}{4}$, $\frac{8}{4}$: 8 meas.: 30"

Tuba-I is a good introduction to contemporary notation. There seems to be a tonal focus on F, and the interval of the tritone is used frequently. With the exception of the first and last minutes, the tessitura is entirely in or above the staff. The "Più mosso" contains an extended sustained section which can be taxing if all dynamic changes are observed. The piano part usually does not interfere with the solo part and often uses tone clusters. This work uses an interesting twist on the ABA form by having the soloist and pianist switch parts in the second A section.

This was the Paris Conservatory contest piece for tuba for 1971.

†**Challan, Henri** (b. 1910). *Intermezzo.* LED, 1970. 163 meas.; 6' (6'40"); A'-b'; 7*; GB; cadenza. tba/b saxhn, pf

Maestoso: $\frac{3}{4}$, **C** : ♩ = 54: 5 meas.: 20"
C : ♩ = 58: 4 meas.: 15"
C : ♩ = 66: 8 meas.: 30"
$\frac{2\frac{1}{2}}{4}$, **C** : (Plus animé) ♩ = 76: 3 meas.: 5"
Section 1 = 20 meas.: 1'10"

Allegro: $\frac{2}{4}$, $\frac{3}{4}$: ♩ = 132: 15 meas.: 15"
$\frac{2}{4}$: ♩ = 126: 14 meas.: 15"
$\frac{2}{4}$: ♩ = 120: 10 meas.: 10"
$\frac{3}{4}$, **C** : ♩ = 126: 14 meas.: 20"
$\frac{2}{4}$: ♩ = 116: 5 meas.: 5"
Section 2 = 58 meas.: 1'5"

(très expressif): $\frac{3}{4}$: ♪ = ♩ précédente: 9 meas.: 30"
$\frac{2}{4}$, $\frac{3}{4}$: ♩ = 66: 5 meas.: 15"
$\frac{3}{4}$: ♩ ≈ 96: 6 meas.: 10"
Section 3 = 20 meas.: 55"

Vif: $\frac{15}{8}$: ♩. = 126: 9 meas.: 20"
$\frac{9}{8}$, $\frac{12}{8}$, $\frac{15}{8}$, $\frac{18}{8}$: ♩. ≈ 120: 6 meas.: 15"
$\frac{9}{8}$, $\frac{12}{8}$, $\frac{15}{8}$: ♩. = 126: 16 meas.: 30"
Section 4 = 31 meas.: 1'5"

Cadence: ♩. ≈ 92: 10"
♩. ≈ 66: 25"

Bien rythmé: $\frac{3}{4}$, $\frac{3\frac{1}{2}}{4}$, C, $\frac{5}{4}$: 6 meas.: 15"
Vif: $\frac{2}{4}$: ♩ ≈ 160: 9 meas.: 5"
Cadenza = 16 meas.: 55"
(très expressif): $\frac{2}{4}$, $\frac{3}{4}$, C : 14 meas.: 45"
C : (a Tempo) ♩ = 63: 4 meas.: 15"
Section 5 = 18 meas.: 1'

Although much detail is indicated above, there is still plenty of tempo fluctuation not indicated, much like one would expect in a fantasy. In this multi-section *Intermezzo*, only the faster sections are contrapuntal. While the "très expressif" sections are essentially the same, the other sections are not related; the transitions are well prepared, and the lack of overall unity is not missed. Although the tessitura is not especially high, the lack of rests can make the work taxing and the higher passages may suffer.

Charles, Claude. *Cortège et danse* [Procession and Dance]. EDMT, 1973. 117 meas.; 4'; F-e♭'; 3; cadenza.

"Paul Bernard, Professeuer au Conservatoire National Supérieur de Musique de Paris"

Adagio: $\frac{2}{4}$, $\frac{3}{4}$, $\frac{4}{4}$: ♩ = 66: 23 meas.
Allegro: $\frac{3}{4}$: ♩ = 144: 94 meas.

†**Charpentier, Jacques** (b. 1933). *Prélude et allegro*. LED, 1959. 123 meas.; 5' (≈ 6'); E'-(b♭')c"; 7*; TB; cadenza, unmetered section. b saxhn/tba/db, pf

I. Prélude. Modéré: n.m.: 13 meas.: 1'
Allegro sostenuto: $\frac{4}{4}$: 23 meas.: 1'10"
II. Allegro. $\frac{2}{4}$, $\frac{3}{4}$, cad.: 87 meas.: 2'50"

The two movements of this piece provide for a good contrast of styles. Since the tempos have not been specified, the second movement can be very manageable for the bass trombonist when taken at a moderate tempo. This piece requires a moderate amount of facility in the lower register. In the solo part, the 1st meas., 2d sys., p. 1 should read "Adagio sostenuto" (vice "Allegro sostenuto").

Clérisse, Robert (b. 1899). *Chant d'amour* [Love Song]. BILL, n.d. 5'50"; D♭ (F)-g'; 5-6; trill. bar or b saxhn, pf

Modéré, sans lenteur: $\frac{3}{4}$: ♩ = 63: 122 meas.

The form of this piece is ABAB with a coda based on the A section, all sections being of similar style. There would be no problems for performance on bass trombone. The solo part is printed only in transposed B♭ bass clef.

——. *Idylle*. LED. 4*. b saxhn, pf

——. *Marine*. COM, 1962. 1'20"; C-g'; 4. tba/b saxhn, pf
Allegro risoluto: $\frac{2}{4}$: ♩ = 108: 70 meas.

Through-composed, this piece begins in d minor and ends in F Major. It works well for young bass trombonists, and the tessitura mostly remains in a comfortable range. There is one sixteenth-note passage that will require some careful coordination between the slide movement and tongue. The style indication at the beginning of the tuba part should be changed from "Allargando" to "Allegro risoluto."

——. *Pièce lyrique.* LED, 1957. 99 meas.; 5'20" (6'40"); B'(F)-(f')f#'; 4*; cadenza, trill. tba/db/b saxhn/b trbn, pf

"À mon ami D. Candelle, Soloiste des Concerts Colonne et de la Musique de l'Air"

Poco andante: $\frac{3}{4}$: 26 meas.: 1'5"
Tranquillo: $\frac{3}{4}$: 17 meas.: 45"
Più mosso: $\frac{3}{4}$, cad.: 7 meas.: 1'25"
Andantino: $\frac{2}{4}$, $\frac{3}{4}$: 37 meas.: 1'20"
Poco meno mosso: $\frac{3}{4}$: 6 meas.: 20"
Lento: $\frac{3}{4}$: 6 meas.: 25"

Though mostly conjunct, the melody contains several large jumps, some of which are greater than an octave. Written in ABA form, this piece has no surprises, and it is a good intermediate solo.

——. *Romance.* LED. 4*. b saxhn, pf

——. *Voce nobile* [Noble Voice]. LED, 1953. 59 meas.; 2'50"; C-f'; 3*; unaccompanied sections. tba/db/b saxhn/b trbn, pf

Moderato: $\frac{4}{4}$: ♩ = 84: 22 meas.: 1'5"
Poco animato: $\frac{4}{4}$: $17\frac{1}{2}$ meas.: 45"
Poco meno mosso: $\frac{4}{4}$: $7\frac{1}{2}$ meas.: 25"
I° Tempo: $\frac{4}{4}$: 12 meas.: 35"

This short piece, written in ABA form, uses a detached melody in d minor that returns in F Major. The soloist must maintain intensity and continuity of the line if it is to sound "noble." The B section contrasts, and the unaccompanied sections can be interpreted freely.

Corelli, Arcangelo (1653-1713). *Sonate, Op. 5, No. 7.* Adapted for bass trombone by Claude Chevaillier. ARP, 1984. 181 meas.; 10'; G'-c'; 5. b trbn, pf

Prelude. Vivace (non troppo): C : 24 meas. (R): 2'
Courante. Allegro: $\frac{3}{4}$: 74 meas. (R): 4'
Sarabande. Largo: $\frac{3}{4}$: 16 meas. (R): 1'30"
Gigue. Allegro: $\frac{6}{8}$: 69 meas. (R): 2'30"

While this is an Italian work originally for violin and continuo, this adaptation by Claude Chevaillier, currently Professor of Bass Trombone at the Paris Conservatory, is a valuable addition to the intermediate-level solos for bass trombone. Although the tessitura is rather low, this piece is quite playable. The editorial markings, although few, are good indications toward a musical performance. If all repeats are observed, endurance could become a problem because of a general lack of rests for the soloist. The piano part does not include the original figured bass. Persons interested in performing this work should probably consult an *Urtext* edition of the original and might consider using a continuo consisting of a viola da gamba or cello and harpsichord instead of a piano.

Creuze, Roland. *Eria*. BILL, 1985. 6' (6'30"); G♭'-(g')a'; 8; GTB; feathered beaming, flutter tongue, proportional notation. tba

"Créé par Fernand Lelong à Radio-France le 30 Mai 1980"

This piece consists of a series of several contrasting sections in which the basic pulse is given a specific tempo marking. There is more use of flutter tongue than in most any other work in the repertoire. Many of the indications are confusing, since no legend accompanies the solo. A squiggle indicates a slow, wide vibrato that becomes quicker and narrower throughout the duration of the note; a figure resembling a backwards-pointing arrow with a hollow tip seems to indicate an immediate crescendo that is sustained at the highest dynamic for a given length of time. The abbreviations "s.v.," "c.v.," and "n.v." are believed to represent *"senza vibrato," "con vibrato,"* and *"niente vibrato"* [barely audible vibrato], respectively. The use of both treble and tenor clefs is unnecessary, especially considering that the composer also wrote an a♭' in bass clef, and there is plenty of vertical space on the page.

Dalbavie, Marc-André. *Petit interlude*. Collection Fernand Lelong. BILL, 1992. (≈ 3'50"); C-g'; 7. unaccompanied b saxhn/tba

"Commande d'État, Ministère de la Culture, de la Communication, des Grandes Travaux et du Bicentenaire, Direction de la Musique et de la Danse"

Comme un écho: n.m.: ♩ = 60

As the style indication suggests, the entire piece is to performed "like an echo." This is accomplished by the repetition of staccato notes which usually begin with sforzandos and rapidly diminuendo until a new melodic fragment is introduced. The interval of the tritone is favored, and one never gets a sense of tonality. The piece is unified by beginning and ending with the repetition of the interval c-f♯. Musical interest is achieved at first by altering the rhythmic pulse from the beginning sixteenths to eighths, triplets, quintuplets, sextuplets, septtuplets, and thirty-second notes then later by the addition of trills. The high g' is achieved from a trill on f♯'. It would be a challenge to perform this solo effectively.

Damase, Jean-Michel (b. 1928). *Automne* [Autumn]. BILL, 1987. 2'15" (2'); c-c'; D. b saxhn/tba, pf

Moderato: **C** : ♩ = 72: 40 meas.

There are few expression markings indicated in this work, and the melodic material is rather uneventful. The piano part helps maintain interest with a syncopated rhythm that remains constant throughout.

——. *Bourrée*. BILL, 1987. 2'30" (2'30"); E♭-e♭'; 3. b saxhn/tba, pf

"À Fernand Lelong"

Allegro ma non troppo: $\frac{2}{4}$: 131 meas.: 2'30"

This work does not behave like most classical bourrées: it does not begin on an upbeat, does not use dactylic figures (— ˘ ˘), uses little syncopation, and is not in binary form. Instead, this *Bourrée* is written in ABA form, beginning in C Major. After a brief developmental section, the theme returns in e♭ minor and ends in C Major. There are no expression markings to dictate a particular style, and there are few dynamic indications throughout the work.

——. *Menuet éclaté* [Split Menuet]. BILL, 1987. 2'10" (2'20"); G-d'; P. b saxhn/tba, pf

Allegro moderato: $\frac{3}{4}$, $\frac{5}{4}$: ♩ = 124: 91 meas.

The title refers to the constant exchange of the melodic line between soloist and pianist. It is written in ABA form, although the style remains the same throughout. There is no indicated key signature, and there are numerous accidentals, but the tonal focus is centered around F Major. The changing meter is not so difficult that younger players cannot access this piece.

Daucé, Edouard. *Concertino*. COM, 1961. 80 meas.; 3'20"; G'-a'; 5. tba, pf

"à Monsieur J. Demailly"

Andantino con moto: C : 30 meas.: 1'20"
Largo: $\frac{3}{4}$: 18 meas.: 35"
I° Tempo: C : 32 meas.: 1'25"

This brief, one-movement *Concertino* is written in ABA form, and begins with an expressive melody in C Major. The "Largo" is developmental, and the soloist can exploit the romantic quality with his expressiveness. The main theme returns up an octave in a more marked style to a new accompaniment. The coda (the last 16 meas.) employs a gradual accelerando to the end.

Defaye, Jean-Michel (b. 1932). *Deux [2] danses*. Adapted for bass trombone by Donald Knaub. LED, 1954 & 1977. 211 meas.; 8'25" (8'); F'-b♭'; 8*; cadenza, cup mute. Recording: 15. b trbn, pf

I. Danse sacrée [Ritual Dance]. Lent: $\frac{4}{4}$, cad.: ♩ = 60: 76 meas.: 6'20"
II. Danse profane [Secular Dance]. Mouvement de Samba: $\frac{2}{2}$: 135 meas.: 2'5"

This outstanding adaptation for bass trombone made by Donald Knaub has become so popular, in fact, that it is nearly the most frequently performed French solo for bass trombone. The piano score only reflects the original tenor trombone solo part. The *Danse sacrée* uses more tenor clef than most other French works. (See also entry in Chapter 4).

——. *Morceau de concours I.* LED, 1990. 2'5" (≈ 2'10"); F♯-d'; 4. tba, pf

♩ ≈ 120: $\frac{4}{4}$: 63 meas.: 2'5"

This one-movement work is written in a lyrical style. There are only two dynamic markings in the piece (*p* and *pp*), so there is much room for expression and interpretation. The piano part is very simple, consisting chiefly of two-note chords in the left hand and an eighth dotted-quarter rhythm on a single line in the right.

——. *Morceau de concours II.* LED, 1990. 2'15" (≈ 2'20"); C-g'; 5. tba, pf

♩ = 104-108: $\frac{2}{4}$, $\frac{4}{4}$: 61 meas.: 2'20"

This one-movement work is written in two major sections and a coda, all of which share the same tempo. The first section is lively, and the first seven measures are in unison with the piano. There is a moderate amount of syncopation, and there are many accidentals. The second section is more lyrical, despite a more disjunct melody. The piano part is relegated to harmonic and rhythmic support.

——. *Morceau de concours III.* LED, 1990. 97 meas.; 4'55" (≈ 4'50"); E♭'-c"; 8; cadenza, feathered beaming. tba, pf

♩ = 168: $\frac{4}{4}$, n.m.: 44 meas.: 1'15"
Lento: $\frac{4}{4}$: ♩ = 66: 24 meas.: 1'25"
Tempo I meno mosso: $\frac{4}{4}$, cad.: 27 meas.: 2'5"
Lento: $\frac{4}{4}$: 2 meas.: 10"

The melodic interval of a half step is used frequently, especially in the outer sections. The middle section contains some long phrases and in one instance a disjunct passage covering two octaves within five eighth-notes' time. The final section contains many slurred sixteenth-note passages, and would be difficult for the bass trombonist if the tempo were not adjusted. The piano part is relegated to harmonic and rhythmic support. A special note: accidentals affect only the octave in which they occur (only a problem in the middle section and the cadenza).

——. *Suite marine.* LED, 1989. 261 meas.; 6'40" (7'5"); E♭-e♭'; 6. tba, pf

1. L'otarie [The Sea Lion]. ♩ = 120: $\frac{3}{4}$, $\frac{4}{4}$: 48 meas.: 1'35" (1'35")
2. Le cachalot [The Sperm Whale]. ♩ = 76: $\frac{4}{4}$: 28 meas.: 1'30" (1'30")
3. Le requin [The Shark]. ♩ = 132-138: $\frac{2}{4}$, $\frac{3}{4}$, $\frac{4}{4}$: 46 meas.: 1'20" (1'20")
4. L'éléphant de mer [The Elephant Seal]. ♩ ≈ 108: $\frac{4}{4}$: 27 meas.: 1' (1'20")
5. Le baleineau [The Whale Calf]. ♩ = 126: $\frac{3}{4}$, $\frac{4}{4}$: 28 meas.: 55" (53")
6. Le dauphin [The Dolphin]. 𝅗𝅥. = 63: $\frac{3}{4}$: 84 meas.: 1'20" (1'20")

Each movement in this suite has a programmatic theme, and all are enjoyable to perform. The convenience of separate movements would allow for the use of only a few for a shortened suite. There are no major technical problems throughout, and the tessitura is moderate. Each movement takes only one page of the solo part. Although the composer is specific with expression markings, there are few written tempo fluctuations, thus allowing some extra room for interpretation.

Delgiudice, Michel (b. 1924). *Abuto.* LED, 1982. 3'10" (≈ 3'30"); (D)F-d'; D2-P1*. tba/b saxhn, pf

Moderato: C : ♩ = 84: 67 meas.

This piece is in ABA' form, and it modulates from B♭ Major to g minor and back. There are more expression markings than in similarly graded works, and the range may be a little ambitious for this grade level. Almost all motion is either by diatonic movement or by arpeggiation. This piece is written very well.

——. *Ali-Baba.* BILL, 1977. 2'55"; B♭-d'; 1-2. b saxhn (B♭ or C)/tba/ b trbn, pf

Moderato: C : ♩ = 80-84: 59 meas.: 2'55"

This piece won the *Prix de Composition de la Confédération Musicale de France* in 1977. Although the range may be a little ambitious for most beginning tuba students, the work is well-suited for a beginner on the bass trombone.

——. *L'antre de Polypheme* [The Lair of Polyphemus]. MAR, 1981. 110 meas.; 3'25" (≈ 4'20"); C-f; P2*. b saxhn/tba, pf

1. Andante. ♩ = 84: C : 40 meas.: 1'55" (2'20")
2. Les astuces d'Ulysse [The Tricks of Ulysses].
   Allegretto: 2/4 : ♩ = 96: 70 meas.: 1'30" (≈ 2')

This is the last and most difficult work in a series for young players by this publisher. Much care seems to have been taken in the preparation of the parts because they have been meticulously scrutinized and there is plenty of vertical space between staves. The first movement is in A♭ Major, and the second in f minor; both are in ABA form with the return being performed up one octave. Most of the movement is diatonic, and there are plenty of rests throughout. This piece is very suitable for young bass trombonists.

——. *Danse de l'éléphant.* MAR, 1981. 2' (≈ 2'30"); E♭-c'; D2*. b saxhn/ tba, pf

Andante: ♩ = 88-92: 3/4 : 60 meas.

This is the second in a series of four works for young tuba players. The editing is first-rate, and there are just enough expression markings. The piece is in E♭ Major, and most of the movement is diatonic, except for a descending arpeggio in quarter notes from b♭'-E♭ at the end.

——. *Le petit baobab.* MAR, 1981. 2'40" (≈ 3'); F-b♭; D1*. b saxhn/ tba, pf

Andante: C : ♩ ≈ 84: 56 meas.

This is the first and easiest in a series for young tubists. Written in ABA form, the soloist states the theme at the beginning and answers the piano in a small fugato on the return. There are some sequential patterns exchanged between parts, and all the downward scalar passages are unaccompanied. There is much music here for the beginner; it would also serve well for young trombonists. Its range does not prohibit its performance on a tenor trombone.

——. *Le petit mammouth.* MAR, 1981. 1'55" (≈ 2'30"); G-d'; P1*. b saxhn/tba, pf

Moderato: $\frac{6}{8}$: ♩. = 72-76: 72 meas.

The third in a series for young tubists, this piece uses more arpeggiated movement than others in this series. It is written in g minor, and there are a reasonable number of expression markings.

——. *Dix [10] petits textes.* ESC, 1954. 241 meas.; 8'20"; G'-g♯'; 8; complex meters. tba/b or cb saxhn, pf

"à Monsieur P. Bernard, Professeur au Conservatoire National de Paris"

I. Moderato: $\frac{2}{4}$, $\frac{3}{4}$, C : 25 meas.: 1'
II. Andante: $\frac{9}{8}$, $\frac{12}{8}$: 23 meas.: 1'
III. Moderato: $\frac{3}{4}$: 25 meas.: 50"
IV. Andante: $\frac{3}{4}$: 26 meas.: 1'5"
V. Mouvement de Java: $\frac{2}{4}$, $\frac{3}{4}$, C : 26 meas.: 40"
VI. Moderato: $\frac{2}{4}$: 28 meas.: 35"
VII. Moderato: C : 14 meas.: 35"
VIII. Andante sostenuto: $\frac{6}{8}$: 27 meas.: 55"
IX. Moderato: $\frac{6}{8}$, $\frac{12}{8}$, $\frac{2}{4}$, $\frac{2}{4}$ + $\frac{1}{8}$, $\frac{3}{4}$, C + $\frac{1}{8}$: 25 meas.: 1'
X. Assez vite: $\frac{1}{8}$, $\frac{2}{8}$, $\frac{3}{8}$, $\frac{4}{8}$, $\frac{5}{8}$, $\frac{6}{8}$, $\frac{7}{8}$, $\frac{8}{8}$: 22 meas.: 40"

Each movement in this suite carries its own particular style, and thus it may be reduced to only a few movements for performance, if desired. Though they are written in standard keys, there is still a considerable amount of disjunct motion, and large leaps of two or three octaves are not uncommon. Although some extended low phrases require careful breath control, there are no major problems that would prevent its performance on bass trombone.

Depelsenaire, Jean-Marie (b. 1914). *Funambules* [Tight-Rope Walkers]. EDMT, 1961. 3'; A-g'; 3.

Moderato: $\frac{2}{4}$: 100 meas.

——. *Jeux chromatiques* [Chromatic Games]. BILL, 1960. 143 meas.; 3'40"; E-g'; 6; unaccompanied sections. trbn/tba, pf

"À Monsieur Moulard, professeur au Conservatoire de Valenciennes"

Moderato: C : 55 meas.: 2'10"
Allegretto: $\frac{2}{4}$: 58 meas.: 1'
♩ = ♩.: $\frac{6}{8}$: 30 meas.: 30"

The "Moderato" begins with a brief piano introduction, and the soloist is then given an extended unaccompanied passage that should be interpreted like a cadenza. Most of the material is chromatic, but the "Allegretto" is more tonal. The underlying tonality is c minor throughout. All the *brillante* passages in the "Allegretto" are unaccompanied.

†**Désenclos, Alfred** (1912-1971). *Suite brève dans le goût classique* [Short Suite in the Classical Style]. LED, 1965. 183 meas.; 8'10" (11'); G'-c"; 8*. tba, pf

"à Paul Bernard, Professeur au Conservatoire National Supérieur de Musique"

I. Prélude. Moderato: 3/4, C, 5/4 : 33 meas.: 1'45"
II. Fuguette. Allegro ma non troppo: C : 47 meas.: 1'40"
III. Aria. Andante: 12/8 : 37 meas.: 2'5"
IV. Finale. Allegro risoluto: 12/8 : 66 meas.: 2'40"

Although originally written for French tuba, this piece works well on the bass trombone because of its range. The tessitura is mostly in the middle register, but becomes high toward the end of the *Finale*; this combined with the general lack of rests may cause endurance problems. The numerous sixteenth and triplet passages will require much concentration to avoid becoming overly tense. This is a very demanding work if played in its entirety.

Desportes, Yvonne [Berthe Melitta] (b. 1907). *Un souffle profond* [A Deep Breath]. BILL, 1981. 186 meas.; 6'20" (6'); F'-a♭'; 5-6; cadenza, glissandos, trills, triple tonguing. b trbn/tba, pf

Assez lent: C : ♩ = 63: 9 meas.: 35"
C : ♩ = 72: 29 meas.: 1'35"
Section 1 = 38 meas.: 2'10"
Allegro: C : ♩ = 144: 27 meas.: 45"
Largo espressivo: 6/8, 9/8 : ♩. = 46: 20 meas.: 55"
6/8 : (un poco più mosso): 18 meas.: 40"
Section 3 = 38 meas.: 1'35"
Allegro: 2/4, cad.: ♩ = 92: 83 meas.: 1'50"

Written in four different sections, this piece takes advantage of one of the most prominent characteristic techniques of the trombone—the glissando. Each section challenges a particular facet of technique and style; the cadenza gets its motivic material from the first section. Many quick glissandos from first to seventh position should be practiced carefully. All glissandos are descending. The solo and piano serve essentially equal roles.

†**Devos, Gérard** (b. 1927). *Deux [2] mouvements contrastés.* LED, 1960. 135 meas.; 5'25" (6'50"); D'(A')-b♭'; 7*; cadenza, complex meters, trills. tba/b trbn/b saxhn, pf

Calme, legato et sans nuance: 4/2, 3/1 : ♩ = 84: 19 meas.: 1'50"
Allegro giocoso: 5/8, 7/8, 1/4, 2/4, 3/4, 4/4, 3/4 + 3/8, cad.: 106 meas.: 3'35"

The first movement consists entirely of slurred eighth and quarter notes, and the phrases are quite long. While scalar passages predominate, there are some occasional slurs of a sixth or larger; there is one intervallic leap of three octaves and a major second in the space of a quarter note, though it is not slurred. The second movement is attacca and begins with a jaunty theme. There is much more disjunct motion in this movement. This work is very demanding because of its challenges in the areas of concentration, breath control, overall range, and a general lack of rests.

†**Dondeyne, Désiré** (b. 1921). *Divertimento*. LF, 1978. 365 meas.; 11'45", with cut 9'55" (13', with cut 11'); (E')F'-f#'; 8; cadenza, trills. tba (C or F)/b saxhn, pf

"à Francois Poullot, Tuba solo de la Musique de la Garde Républicaine de Paris"

Allegro: ¢ : 𝅗𝅥 = 104-108: 79 meas.: 1'30"
Andante: 4/4 : ♩ = 60: 28 meas.: 1'50"
a Tempo I°: ¢ : 𝅗𝅥 = 104-108: 40 meas.: 45"
L'Istesso Tempo: 2/4, 3/4, cad.: 𝅗𝅥 = ♩.: 67 meas.: 2'15"
Più moderato: 2/4, 3/4 : ♩ = 96: 54 meas.: 1'35"
Lent: 2/4, 4/4 : ♩ = 54: 38 meas.: 2'45"
I° Tempo Allegro: ¢ : 𝅗𝅥 = 104-108: 59 meas.: 1'5"

This piece behaves much like a concerto in one movement. An optional cut deletes the "Andante." This piece is constructed well, contains many flashy passages, and it would be worthy to pursue its performance with a large ensemble.

There are two versions of ensemble accompaniment. The orchestration for the "Symphonic Orchestra" version includes: 2 fls, 2 obs, 2 cls, 2bns, 2 hns, 2 trpts, 3trbns, timbales, hp, and strings. The "Wind Ensemble" version includes: 2 fls, 2 obs, 2 bns, 2 solo cls, 2 1st cls, 2 2d cls, 2 b cls, 2 a saxphns, 2 t saxphns, 2 bar saxphns, 2 hns, 2 trpts, 3 trbns, cb saxhn (in absence of db), db, and timbales. The scores and parts are available from the publisher. The first performance with orchestra was on 11 March 1979 at Le Havre.

This was the Paris Conservatory contest piece for 1978.

——. *Cinc [5] études (avec accompagnement de piano)*. BILL.

——. *Cinc [5] "pièces courtes": Pour jeune tubistes*. BILL, 1987. 137 meas.; 5'25" (≈ 10'); (G')C-c'; 3. tba/b saxhn, pf

"à Fernand Lelong, Professeur au C.N.S.M. de Paris"

I. Andante expressivo: 9/8 : 33 meas.: 1'25" (2')
II. Tempo di marcia: 2/4 : 25 meas.: 30" (30")
III. Modéré: 3/4 : 18 meas.: 45" (1')
IV. Allegretto: C : 22 meas.: 1' (1'45")
V. Andante (sans lenteur): 3/4 : 39 meas.: 1'45" (2')

Each piece is tonal, and yet each contains at least one digression from the underlying tonality. These are excellent for younger players to develop a sense of intonation through quick harmonic movements. There are plenty of ossia passages, and each piece is rather short. Although originally for tuba or bass saxhorn, these pieces would work well for students who switch to the bass trombone early in high school. This is a delightful collection that would probably appeal to any audience.

†———. *Sonatine in C.* EDMT, 1967. 170 meas.; 7'30"; D'(G')-a'; 7; cadenza. b saxhn, pf

Allegro moderato: $\frac{3}{8}$, $\frac{7}{8}$, $\frac{2}{4}$, $\frac{3}{4}$, C : ♩ = 80-84: 55 meas.: 1'50"
  Più lento: C : 6 meas.: 20"
Andante: $\frac{3}{4}$: ♪ =66-72: 23 meas.: 2'
  Poco più mosso: $\frac{3}{4}$: ♪ =84 (♩ =42): 10 meas.: 45"
  Tempo I°: $\frac{2}{4}$, $\frac{3}{4}$, cad.: ♪ = 66-72: 12 meas.: 1'30"
Allegro vivo: $\frac{6}{8}$, $\frac{9}{8}$, $\frac{3}{4}$: ♩. = 116-120: 64 meas.: 1'5"

Written in three major sections in one continuous movement, this piece is a fine showcase for the bass saxhorn. The outer sections tend to be technically oriented with several awkward rhythms in the first section. The middle section is a beautiful expressive melody which could be taxing at the indicated tempo because the tessitura is generally above the staff. This piece is worthy of consideration; however, the part must be transposed. The measure indication "160" is marked one measure too early in both the solo and piano parts.

This was the Paris Conservatory contest piece for 1967.

†———. *Tubissimo.* BILL, 1983. 112 meas.; 4'45" (6'30"); F'(A')-e'(g'); 7; unaccompanied sections, unmetered section. tba/b saxhn, pf

"à Fernand Lelong"

Modéré: n.m.: 14 meas.: 1'50"
Andante: $\frac{4}{8}$: ♪ = 60: 24 meas.: 1'35"
Allegro: $\frac{2}{4}$, $\frac{3}{4}$: ♩ = 116: 38 meas.: 40"
Tempo Allegro: $\frac{6}{8}$: ♩. = 120: 18 meas.: 20"
Is Tesso Tempo Brilliante: $\frac{2}{4}$: 18 meas.: 20"

Written in five brief sections, *Tubissimo* contains a sample of many styles and techniques. The piano and soloist exchange statements in a free section at the beginning. The tempos of the fourth and fifth sections should probably be adjusted for the bass trombonist.

This was the Paris Conservatory contest piece for 1983.

Dubois, Pierre Max (b. 1930). *Cornemuse* [Bagpipes]. LED, 1961. 3'25" (3'30"); E-a'; 5*. tba/b trbn/b saxhn/db, pf

Allegro ben moderato: $\frac{4}{4}$: 88 meas.: 3'25"

The first ten and last eleven measures of the piece are a series of high (g')'s; at the beginning, the dynamic is a constant piano, but at the end, it is a steady diminuendo from forte to pianississimo decrescendo! Needless to say, this work is very taxing before the main part is even considered. The tessitura generally lies high. Because of its range, this work could easily be performed on a tenor trombone. Meas. 3 of the solo part is missing one ledger line.

———. *Fantaisie.* CHO, 1965. 162 meas.; 5'25"; F'-c"; 7; GB; glissando, trills, unaccompanied sections. b saxhn/tba/b trbn, pf

"À Monsieur Paul Bernard"

I. Marche Anglo-Saxhorn. Allegro giusto: 4/4 : 57 meas.: 2'
II. Sicilienne inachevée. Andante: 6/8 : 45 meas.: 1'20"
III. Tango. Allegro marcato: 4/4 : 60 meas.: 2'5"

The first movement is a lively march with several tricky unaccompanied sixteenth-note passages, most of which are either scalar, chromatic, or a combination. The use of syncopation is quite common. The "Sicilienne inachevée" is written in g♯ minor, and, as the movement's name suggests, the theme is not always completed. The "Tango" contains many rapid, slurred sixteenth-note passages, but are manageable on bass trombone; however, the trills should probably be omitted when performing it on bass trombone.

———. *Histories de tuba.*

Vol. 1. *Plantez les gars!* [Plant them Boys!] BILL, 1984. 45 meas.; 2'15"; F-(d')f'; 2; cadenza, unaccompanied section. b saxhn/t tba/b tba, pf

Introduction: cad. (4/4): 13 meas.: 35"
Maestoso: 4/4 : ♩ = 76: 32 meas.: 1'40"

This volume exploits the maestoso character of the solo instrument well. The cadenza is well-written, and serves as a good introduction for younger students.

Vol. 2. *Le petit cinéma* [The Little Theater]. BILL, 1984. 96 meas.; 2'15"; A'-f'; 4; cadenza, unaccompanied sections. b saxhn/t tba/b tba, pf

Andantino: 2/4, cad.: ♩ = 80-88: 40 meas.: 50"
Détendu [relaxed]: 2/4 : 39 meas.: 1'
Tempo primo: 2/4 : 17 meas.: 25"

A brief, unaccompanied, six-measure introduction sets the mood for the piece. It is written in ABA form; the main theme is lively but lyrical. The solo part includes a variation of this theme on return to the second A section. There are some disjunct passages throughout, and the cadenza is appropriate for the intended level.

Vol. 3. *Le grand cinéma* [The Big Theater]. BILL, 1984. 146 meas. (R); 4'30"; G♯'/A♭'-(f♯')g'; 6; cadenza. b saxhn/t tba/b tba, pf

Lentement: cad.: 30"
Andante: 4/4 : ♩ = 72: 30 meas.: 1'40"
Scherzando: 3/8 : ♩. = 60: 115 meas. (R): 2'20"

The opening quasi cadenza is manageable, and serves as a good introduction to the piece; the last F and D in the cadenza should probably be marked with naturals for clarity. The "Andante" contains some low sustained passages, and good breath control and phrasing are essential. The "Scherzando" is lively and has a moderate amount of disjunct motion. The quintuplet is difficult to place correctly. Twenty-six measures are repeated.

Vol. 4. *Concert opéra.* BILL, 1988. 245 meas.; 9'5" (9'); G'-g♯'; 7; cadenza, glissandos, double and triple tonguing, flutter tongue, trills, unaccompanied sections. b saxhn/b tba, pf

1. *«V» comme Verdi* ["V" Like Verdi].
   Lent: cad. ($\frac{3}{4}$): 45"
   Andante: $\frac{3}{4}$: ♩ = 76: 112 meas.: 4'25"
   Movement 1 = 113 meas.: 5'10" (5')

2. *«O» comme Offenbach* ["O" Like Offenbach].
   Giocoso: $\frac{4}{4}$ (¢): ♩ = 132: 43 meas.: 1'20"
   ♩ = ♩.: $\frac{3}{4}$: 46 meas.: 1'5"
   $\frac{4}{4}$, cad.: 42 meas.: 1'30"
   Movement 2 = 132 meas.: 3'55" (4')

Mvt. 1 is written like an aria, and it should be interpreted as such. There is much room for expression and tempo fluctuation, with many unaccompanied sections. The accompaniment provides only minimal harmonic and rhythmic support. Mvt. 2 is written in ABA form, and the final section after the cadenza is a continual accelerando to the end that must be gauged carefully.

†———. *Piccolo suite.* LED, 1957. 188 meas.; 6'20" (6'30"); F'-a♯'; 8*; unaccompanied sections. tba/b saxhn/b trbn, pf/(orch (Mvt. 3))

"À Monsieur Paul Bernard, Professeur au Conservatoire"

I. Prélude. Allegro pomposo: $\frac{2}{4}$, $\frac{3}{4}$, $\frac{4}{4}$: 41 meas.: 1'30"
II. Air. Poco andante: $\frac{4}{4}$: 49 meas.: 3'
III. Polka. Allegretto: $\frac{2}{4}$: 98 meas.: 1'50"

The "Prélude" is in ABA form, and it contains many quick tonal shifts. There are many exposed sixteenth-note passages, so the tempo should be chosen wisely. The "Air" contains a few passages that require a considerable amount of air and a few slurred melodic intervals of a major ninth. While the main melodic material of the "Polka" is either chromatic or scalar, there are a few abrupt leaps, including two of a minor twenty-first (two octaves and a minor seventh). Again, the tempo must be carefully chosen and adhered to by the bass trombonist. This movement has a chamber orchestra accompaniment available for rent. The orchestration includes: fl, cl, ob, hn, timp, perc, strgs.

†———. *Si trombone m'était conté* [If the Trombone Had Told Me]. ESC, 1975. 130 meas.; 5'35" (6'); F'-b♭'; 6; complex meters, unaccompanied sections. b trbn, pf

"À mon cher ami Paul Bernard"

I. Chanson triste [Sad Song]. Adagio: $\frac{3}{16}$, $\frac{2}{4}$: ♪ = 54: 44 meas.: 3'5"

II. Tambourin. Allegretto: $\frac{2}{4}$, $\frac{3}{4}$: ♩ = 69: 86 meas.: 2'30"

One of the very few contest solos written exclusively for bass trombone, this piece seems more accessible to intermediate bass trombonists than other works. There are many diatonic thirty-second-note passages in the first movement, but the tempo is quite slow. There is more chromatic solo movement in the "Tambourin," and a sixteenth-note pulse is maintained throughout; two descending chromatic scales are unaccompanied. This is an excellent intermediate work, and it makes a fine exercise for slide coordination and intonation.

†**Durand-Audard, Pierre** [Max] (b. 1930). *Dialogue*. LED, 1970. 104 meas.; 6'20" (7'20"); G♯'-a'; 9*; GB; complex meters, flutter tongue, quasi-cadenza passages, trill, unaccompanied sections. b trbn/tba/ b saxhn, pf

"à Monsieur Paul Bernard, Professeur au Conservatoire National Supérieur de Musique"

Largo assai: 4(/4), 5/4 : ♩ = 36: 8 meas.: 55"
Poco animato: 2/4, 3/4, 4(/4), 5/4, 6/4 : ♩ ≈ 58: 42 meas.: 2'40"
Allegro: 7/16, 8/16, 9/16, 10/16, 11/16, 12/16, 13/16, 14/16, 15/16, 9/8 : ♪. = 80: 48 meas.: 2'20"
Andante: 4(/4) : ♩ = 58: 2 meas.: 10"
Tempo: 12/16, 15/16 : ♪. = 80: 3 meas.: 10"
♩ = 36: 4(/4) : 1 meas.: 5"

Written in two major sections, *Dialogue* focuses on the use of the middle to low registers. The first section functions as an extended cadenza with occasional accompanied sections, and there is plenty of room for freedom of expression and interpretation on the part of the soloist. The "Allegro" is a moderately-paced dance of sorts, and, aside from the constant changing meter, there are few technical problems for the soloist. The ∿∿∿∿ has been left off the four notes in the third and fourth measures of "9" and should be added for clarity. In general, there are more complex meters in this piece than in others, and the constant changing of meters compounds the situation; much concentration will be needed to successfully negotiate this maze of meters.

†———. *Tournevalse* [Turning Waltz]. BILL, 1978. 94 meas.; 6'15" (6'30"); F'-(g')b♭'; 7; non-standard meter indication, quasi cadenzas. b saxhn/tba/b trbn, pf

"à Monsieur Paul Bernard, Professeur au Conservatoire"

Andantino con moto: n.m.: 45"
Scherzando vivace: n.m.(5/8, 6/8, 7/8, 8/8, 9/8, 10/8, 11/8, 12/8, 15/8, 17/8, 18/8, 25/8, 27/8), cad.: ♩. = 84: 83 meas. (R): 4'20"
Tempo I°: n.m.: 40"
Largo: 3/4, 4(/4) : ♩ = 52: 9 meas.: 30"

The waltz-like main section is surrounded by two quasi cadenza sections, and the "Largo" serves as a coda. The unifying pattern "a, g♯, b♮" occurs throughout the entire work, although it may be displaced by an octave or some other interval. In general, the measures have no meter indicated, and the rests have one numeral to show the number of eighths in that measure. The measures are subdivided into groups of two and three, but are displaced in nearly every measure. The performer would be wise to indicate these groupings of two and three with "|" and "Δ" (or some other system) throughout the "Scherzando," respectively. Twenty-six measures are repeated. In the tuba/bass trombone part, the key signatures have been displaced up one space in the bass clef staff, with the exception of the first two systems of p. 1 and the first system of both p. 2 and p. 3, which are placed correctly.

Faillenot, Maurice. *Introduction et rigaudon*. BILL, 1985. 68 meas.; 1'35" (2'); G-(e')g'; 3. t saxphn/bar saxhn/b saxhn/tba, pf

Lento: 3/4 : ♩ = 60: 12 meas.: 20"
Allegretto non troppo: 2/4 : ♩ = 92: 56 meas.: 1'15"

This "Introduction" begins in c minor and affords the soloist with a fair amount of expressive material. The "Allegro non troppo" is in C Major, and, unlike most rigadoons, the melody begins on the downbeat and has only has one reprise, making it an ABA form. Nevertheless, the tune is quite dance-like and would be enjoyable for younger players. Because of the range, this piece could also be played on a tenor trombone.

Fayeulle, Roger. *Bravaccio*. LED, 1958. 154 meas.; 5'10" (5'30"); A'-(f')a'; 7*; trills. tba/b saxhn/b trbn, pf

"à B. Mari, Tuba Solo de l'orchestre du Théatre National de l'Opera"

(Introduction).
Maestoso declamando: 3/4, C : ♩ ≈ 54: 12 meas.: 55"
Più mosso: 2/4, 4/4 : 7 meas.: 30"
Tranquillo: 2/4, 3/4 : ♩ = 66: 5 meas.: 15"
Poco animato: 2/4, 4/4 : 4 meas.: 10"
Allegretto pomposo: ¢ : 𝅗𝅥 = 80: 28 meas.: 40"
Molto moderato: 4/4 : ♩ = 60: 6 meas.: 15"
Introduction = 62 meas.: 2'45"

Air bravache [Blustery Wind].
Allegro risoluto: 3/4 : ♩ = 120: 16 meas.: 25"
Molto più lento: 2/4, 3/4 : ♩ = 72: 4 meas.: 10"
a Tempo: 2/4, 3/4 : 29 meas.: 45"
Più moderato: 3/4 : 5 meas.: 10"
a Tempo più vivo: 2/4, 3/4 : ♩ = 132: 8 meas.: 10"
Animando: 2/4, 3/4 : ♩ = 144: 16 meas.: 20"
Vivo: 3/4 : ♩ = 160: 8 meas.: 10"
Lento: n.m.: 1 meas.: 10"
Presto: 2/4 : 5 meas.: 5"
Air bravache = 92 meas.: 2'25"

There is much room for expression and interpretation in this piece that behaves like an extended aria. The brief "Molto moderato" section in the introduction includes an excerpt from Brander's recitative from Hector Berlioz's *Damnation of Faust*. The piano part is relegated to rhythmic and harmonic support. Two optional cuts are suggested by the composer.

Franck, Maurice (b. 1892). *Prélude, arioso et rondo*. EDMT, 1969. 141 meas.; 7'; A♭'-b♭'; 8; complex meters, glissando. (b) saxhn/b trbn/tba, pf

"À Paul Bernard, Professeur de Conservatorie National Supérieur de Musique"

Avec emphase: C : ♩ ≈ 60: 16 meas.: 1'
Allegro: 2/4, C : ♩ = 100: 7 meas.: 10"
Adagio: 4/8, 6/8, 7/8, 9/8, 12/8 : ♪ = 63: 11 meas.: 1'25"

Più vivo et en accélérant: 3/4, C : 3 meas.: 10"
Allegro: 2/4, 3/4, C : ♩ = 96: 6 meas.: 10"
Tempo I°: 6/8, 12/8 : 3 meas.: 10"
Allegro: 5/16, 5/8, 7/8 : ♪ = 152: 42 meas.: 1'35"
Très calme: 4/8, 6/8, 7/8, 9/8, 12/8 : 29 meas.: 1'55"
Più vivo: 3/8, 4/8, 5/8 : ♪ = 208: 24 meas.: 25"

This is a major work of varying styles and moods. Though there is nothing here most advanced bass trombonists cannot play, much concentration is needed to execute the many slurred sixteenth- and thirty-second-note passages effectively. The "Avec emphase" section is a quasi cadenza over a tremolo piano part with small interludes by the piano. The style, dynamics, and direction of the solo part are meticulously indicated.

This was the Paris Conservatory contest piece for 1969.

Gabaye, Pierre (b. 1930). *Tubabillage* [Tuba Prattle]. LED, 1959. 168 meas.; 3'15" (3'10"); C-e'; 4-5*. tba/db/b saxhn/b trbn, pf

Allegro: 2/4, 3/4, 4/4, 5/4 : ♩ = 138: 19 meas.: 30"
♪ = ♪: 6/8 : 73 meas.: 1'35"
♩. = ♩: 12/8, 4/4 : 12 meas.: 30"
Poco più vivo: 6/8, 12/8 : 28 meas.: 64 meas.: 40"

This piece seems to be a theme and variations on a spirited opening theme. This is a good intermediate work with no surprises.

†**Gartenlaub, Odette** (b. 1922). *Essai*. RID, 1970. 173 meas.; 5'10" (6'30"); F'-g♯'; 6; complex meters, glissandos. b saxhn/tba/b trbn, pf

"À Monsieur Paul Bernard"

Marcato: 3/4, C, 5/4 : ♩ = 100: 44 meas.: 1'40"
Presto: 2/8, 3/8, 4/8, 5/8, 4/4 (♩ = ♩. préc.): ♪ = 200: 80 meas.: 1'25"
Andantino: 3/4, C : ♩ = 80: 49 meas.: 2'5"

Each section of this work is independent in style and musical content. The opening motive at the beginning is varied but remains recognizable throughout the "Moderato." The "Presto" is disjunct and contains many tricky chromatic alterations. The "Andantino" is very smooth and flowing, and it tends to favor the interval of a tritone.

This was the Paris Conservatory contest piece for 1970.

Gotkovsky, Ida (b. 1933). *Lied*. MAR, 1983. 1'10" ; F♯-f♯'; 4. b trbn, pf

Cantabile: 2/4 : ♪ = 69: 20 meas.: 1'10"

Written in E Major, this piece is quite expressive and displays the unique timbre of the bass trombone well. It is through-composed, and the range would permit its performance on a tenor trombone. There is one slurred melodic leap of a minor tenth.

†———. *Suite*. SAL, 1959. (6'30"); F'-b♭'; 7; cadenza. tba, pf

"à Monsieur Paul Bernard, Professeur au Conservatoire National Supérieur de Musique de Paris"

Introduction. Marcato: $\frac{3}{4}$: ♩ = 92: 36 meas.: 1'10"
Andante. Sostenuto molto legato: C : ♩ = 66: 35 meas.: 2'5"
Final. Léger, vif: $\frac{2}{4}$: ♩ ≈ 128-132: 206 meas.: 3'

There are a few tricky rhythmic patterns in the first movement, some large slurred intervals in the second, and many arpeggiated sixteenth notes and some slurred major ninths in the last. This is a fine composition that can be easily adapted for bass trombone.

This was the Paris Conservatory contest piece for 1959.

Goudenhooft, André, ed. *Hommage à V. F. Verrimst: D'après son 2ᵉ morceau de concours pour contrebasse et piano* [Homage to V. F. Verrimst: After His Second Contest Piece for Contrabass and Piano]. BILL, 1986. 175 meas.; 4'45" (≈ 6'); F'-g'; 8; trill. b trbn, pf

Allegro vivace con fuoco: ¢ : 𝅗𝅥 = 96: 20 meas.: 25"
Maestoso: C : 20 meas.: 1'10"
Andante cantabile: $\frac{6}{8}$: ♩. = 63: 39 meas.: 1'15"
Allegro fieramente: $\frac{2}{4}$: ♩ = 100: 96 meas.: 1'55"

As might be inferred from the title, this piece is not very idiomatic for bass trombone. If performed in its entirety, this piece will fully challenge the performer's concentration and endurance. To play the final "Allegro fieramente" section at the indicated tempo will require a superior player; the numerous ornaments will need much attention, and some triple tonguing may be required for one passage. The piano part is moderately difficult.

†**Henry, Jean-Claude** (b. 1934). *Mouvement*. LED, 1972. 78 meas.; 5'50"(≈ 5'45"); F'-b'; 8*; cadenza, complex meters, mute, unmetered sections. tba/b saxhn/b trbn, pf

"à Paul Bernard"

Modéré, expressif: $\frac{6}{8}$, $\frac{8}{8}$, $\frac{10}{8}$, $\frac{32}{8}$: ♪ = 144: 18 meas.: 1'5"
Allant: $\frac{8}{8}$, $\frac{9}{8}$, $\frac{10}{8}$, $\frac{11}{8}$, $\frac{15}{8}$, $\frac{3}{4}$, $\frac{4}{4}$, $\frac{5}{4}$, $\frac{6}{4}$: ♩ = 120 (sans traîner) [do not drag]: 21 meas.: 45"
Vif: $\frac{8}{8}$, $\frac{9}{8}$, $\frac{15}{8}$: ♪ = 208: 5 meas.: 15"
Lent, très expressif: $\frac{7}{8}$, $\frac{8}{8}$, $\frac{10}{8}$, $\frac{11}{8}$, $\frac{12}{8}$: ♪ = 69: 9 meas.: 1'10"
Rubato, expressif: cad.: ♪ = 104-192: 45"
♪ = 80: $\frac{12}{8}$: 1 meas.: 10"
Sans lenteur, avec souplesse: $\frac{8}{8}$, $\frac{10}{8}$, $\frac{12}{8}$, $\frac{17}{8}$, $\frac{19}{8}$, $\frac{20}{8}$: ♪ = 176: 7 meas.: 35"
Plus vif: $\frac{5}{8}$, $\frac{6}{8}$, $\frac{7}{8}$, $\frac{8}{8}$, $\frac{10}{8}$, n.m.($\frac{25}{16}$): ♪ = 144: 11 meas.: 35"
a Tempo: n.m.($\frac{24}{8}$): ♪ = 200: 1 meas.: 5"
♩ = 144: n.m.: 4 meas.: 25"

This piece requires a great deal of stamina on behalf of the soloist. In the numerous sections, the soloist is required to constantly play at both range extremes, determine proper phrasing, and maintain constant awareness of the current meter. There is a lot of high register playing and a general lack of rests that make this piece very taxing.

†**Holstein, Jean Paul**. *Triade*. CHO, 1973. 196 meas.; 6'35"; C-g♯'/a♭'; 7; GB; beams extended from note heads, compound meters, feathered beams, mute, timed events, unaccompanied sections. tba, pf

"à Monsieur Paul Bernard, Professeur au Conservatoire National Supérieur de Musique de Paris"

1. Lied. (♩ = 60): 2/4 : 53 meas.: 1'25"
   Plus lent: 2/4 : ♩ ≈ 48: 7 meas.: 20"
   Plus vite: 2/4 : ♩ = 80: 6 meas.: 10"
   Tempo I°: 2/4 : ♩ = 60: 16 meas.: 20"
   Lied = 82 meas.: 2'15" (2'30")
2. Joute [Joust]. (n.m.): 40"
   (♩ = 120): **C** : 14 meas.: 40"
   (n.m.): 45"
   Chanté: n.m.: ♩ = 60: 20"
   Joute = 17 meas.: 2'25" (2'30")
3. Danse. (♩ = 160): 3/4, 4/4 : 97 meas.: 1'55"

The first movement is like an aria and is quite free. Occasional tone clusters in the piano are used to indicate its presence, but it always remains subdued. "Joute" is the only movement that uses contemporary notation; the runs at the beginning can be interpreted as four passes in a joust. A simple syncopated melody is contained in the brief metered section. "Danse" is in ABA form, and the piano and soloist share an essentially equal role.

Jolas, Betsy (b. 1926). *Trois [3] duos*. LED, 1985. 111 meas.; 5'5" (5'40"); C'-g'; 8*; complex meters, feathered beaming, multiphonics, unmetered sections. tba, pf

"pour les quatre-vingts ans de Francis Bott"

I. Secrètement instable [Internally Unstable]: 4/4 : ♩ ≈ 48: 3 meas.: 15"
   Tempo più mosso: 4/4 : ♩ ≈ 60: 2 meas.: 10"
   Tempo I°: ♪ = 96: 5/8, 3/4, 4/4 : 5 meas.: 20"
   Più mosso: 2/4, 3/4, 4/4, 5/4 : ♩ ≈ 60: 12 meas.: 45"
   Tempo I°: 4/4, 5/4, n.m.: ♩ ≈ 48: 5 meas.: 30"
   Tempo più mosso: 3/4, 4/4, 5/4, n.m.: ♩ ≈ 69: 4 meas.: 15"
   Mvt. I = 31 meas.: 2'15" (2'30")
II. Étrangement vif [Extraordinarily Fast]: 5/16, 6/16, 7/16, 9/16, 10/16, 3/8, 4/8, 3/4 :
   ♪. ≈ 160: 26 meas.: 25"
   Meno mosso: 2/8 : ♪ ≈ 120: 5 meas.: 5"
   Modéré: 2/8, 3/8 : ♪ ≈ 88: 12 meas.: 10"
   Tempo I°: 5/16, 6/16, 9/16 : ♪. = ♪ ≈ 160: 14 meas.: 10"
   Mvt. II = 57 meas.: 50" (1'10")
III. Lourdement agité [Heavily Agitated]: 2/4, 3/4, 4/4, 5/4 :
   ♩ ≈ 42: 23 meas.: 2' (2')

This is one of a very few works whose style indications at the beginnings of movements are so precise. This, combined with fine editing, make this piece easier to interpret than other similar works. Although specified only for tuba, this work is very feasible for performance on bass trombone. The single multiphonic has a rather novel effect. There are a few tricky complex rhythms and meters in the second movement, and the timing of the feathered beaming will need to be carefully planned. This is an excellent work.

Joubert, Claude Henry. *Rudéral*. BILL, 1980. 85 meas.; 3'15" (3'30"); B'-c♯'; 3. tba (C or B♭), pf (1 or 2 hands)

♩ = 112: C : 20 meas.: 45"
Poco meno: C : ♩ = 104: 17 meas.: 40"
Récitativo: C : 28 meas.: 1'5"
Tempo primo: C : ♩ = 112: 20 meas.: 45"

This piece won the *Prix de Composition de la Confédération Musicale de France* in 1980. Written in e minor, the works follows the ABA pattern, but an optional cut deletes the *"Récitativo"* section. Both the soloist and pianist read from a full score which shows the solo part in both C and B♭ and the piano part. It contains no problems for performance on bass trombone.

†**Kaï, Naohiko**. *Légende*. LED, 1962. 149 meas.; 5'50" (6'35"); F♯' (B')-(a♭'/g♯') b♭'; 8*; extended a piacere section. tba/b trbn/b saxhn, pf

1. A piacere. Andante a piacere: $\frac{1}{4}$, $\frac{3}{4}$, $\frac{4}{4}$: ♩ ≈ 72: 9 meas.: 25"
   Agitato: $\frac{3}{4}$, $\frac{4}{4}$: 9 meas.: 25"
   Tempo I°: $\frac{3}{4}$, $\frac{4}{4}$: 13 meas.: 45"
   Un poco più lento: $\frac{4}{4}$, $\frac{5}{4}$: 5 meas.: 20"
   A piacere = 36 meas.: 1'55"
2. Allegro. Allegro ma non troppo: $\frac{1}{4}$, $\frac{2}{4}$, $\frac{3}{4}$, $\frac{4}{4}$, $\frac{5}{4}$: ♩ ≈ 112: 113 meas.: 3'55"

The opening "Andante a piacere" section is essentially a cadenza with occasional piano responses to the soloist's activity; it should be interpreted with much expression and freedom. Rhythmic precision and pitch accuracy are essential in the "Allegro ma non troppo," because nearly every grouping of four or more sixteenth notes for the soloist is unaccompanied. The piano part contains many clusters and rhythmic punctuations but little else. Overall, this is a very demanding work because of the required concentration and coordination.

Laburda, Jiří (b. 1931). *Sonate*. BILL, 1987. 287 meas.; 10'5" (12'40"); F♯'-f'; 6. tba, pf

I. Allegro moderato: C : 80 meas.: 3'
   Meno mosso: C : 25 meas.: 1'
   Mvt. I = 105 meas.: 4'
II. Larghetto caloroso: C : 45 meas.: 2'30"
III. Allegro assai: $\frac{2}{4}$, $\frac{3}{4}$, C, $\frac{5}{4}$: 137 meas.: 3'35"

While there are many accidentals in the first movement, most of the running passages are scalar. It is in ABAB form, and the "Meno mosso" is related to the lyrical portion of the A section. The final movement has several passages extending into the low register that require good breath control and phrasing. In general, this is a fine intermediate work.

Lancen, S. *Grave*. tba/bar saxhn/b saxhn, pf

Lantier, Pierre [Luis César François] (b. 1910). *Andante et allegro.* LEM, 1964. 228 meas.; 9'10"; (F')A'-a'; 7; cadenza. tba, pf

"à Paul Bernard, Professeur au Conservatoire National Supérieur de Musique de Paris"

I. Andante. Andante sostenuto: $\frac{2}{4}$, $\frac{3}{4}$, C : ♩ = 72: 52 meas.: 2'50"
II. Allegro. (𝅗𝅥 = 108-112) : ¢ : 67 meas.: 2'25"
Poco più vivo: $\frac{6}{4}$, $\frac{9}{4}$, cad. ($\frac{6}{4}$, $\frac{2}{2}$): 70 meas.: 2'35"
a Tempo: ¢ : 23 meas.: 50"
Poco più vivo: ¢ : 16 meas.: 30"
Allegro = 176 meas.: 6'20" (7')

This work is a nice change of pace from other works in this category because of its complex sonorities between the soloist and accompanist. The "Andante" is a very lyrical movement with many flowing sixteenths, quintuplets, and sextuplets that are mostly scalar. It is in ABA form, and the tessitura is mostly in the middle register. The "Allegro" is also in ABA form, but the piano takes the melody on the return, and the soloist enters with a counter melody. A tie was left out of the solo part in meas.3, sys. 4, p. 1, between the two d♯ triplet eighths.

———. *Introduction, romance et allegro.* LEM, 1965. 202 meas.; 5'55"; F♯'-a'; 7; cadenza. b trbn/vc, pf

Introduction. Calme: C : ♩ = 76: 18 meas.: 55"
Romance: Andante: $\frac{3}{4}$: ♩ = 72: 21 meas.: 55"
a Tempo: $\frac{6}{8}$: ♩. = ♩ précédente: 4 meas.: 5"
Meno mosso: $\frac{6}{8}$: ♩. = 66: 17 meas.: 30"
a Tempo: $\frac{3}{4}$: 12 meas.: 30"
Romance = 54 meas.: 2'
Allegro. Allegro: $\frac{2}{2}$: 𝅗𝅥 = 112: 46 meas.: 50"
a Tempo: $\frac{2}{4}$, C : ♩ = 𝅗𝅥 précédente: 13 meas.: 25"
Tempo I°: $\frac{2}{2}$: 16 meas.: 15"
♩ = 𝅗𝅥 précédente: C, cad. (C, $\frac{2}{2}$): 35 meas.: 1'10"
Tempo I°: $\frac{2}{2}$: 20 meas.: 20"
Allegro = 130 meas.: 3'

The "Introduction" has a smooth, flowing melodic line and sets up the "Romance" well. The "Romance" has a very rhythmic melody, but it should be interpreted as smoothly as possible; there are moments when the soloist has more freedom of expression, but agogic accents could be employed in the stricter sections. The "Allegro" is much more lively, yet should retain a connected feel. It is in ABA form, and the movement must be carefully paced in order to sustain the forte f♯' and fortissimo a' at the end with vibrancy. This piece is among the finest works written specifically for bass trombone.

Leclair, Jean-Marie (1697-1764). *Sarabande.* and
Senallié [Senaillé], Jean-Baptiste (1687-1730). *Courante.* Adapted by André Goudenhooft, piano realizations by Augustin Maillard.. BILL, 1989. 6'5" (≈ 5'); G'-f'; 7; trills. b trbn/tba, pf

Sarabande. Lent et expressif: $\frac{3}{4}$: 32 meas. (2R): 3'25"
Courante. Assez vif et souple: $\frac{3}{4}$: ♩ = 138-144: 62 meas. (R): 2'40"

These works have been united into a suite performed "da capo" style. The *Sarabande* is extracted from Leclair's *Violin Sonata No. 3*, and the Courante is extracted from Senallié's *Violin Sonata No. 8*. They are presented in a very playable edition, yet it would present technical and musical challenges for the advanced player. Persons interested in performing this work should probably consult an *Urtext* edition of the original and might consider using a continuo consisting of a viola da gamba or cello and harpsichord instead of a piano.

This edition was prepared by André Goudenhooft, currently bass trombonist with *l'Orchestre National de France*. This adaptation is an extension of Mr. Goudenhooft's use of earlier works in order to develop musical feeling as well as technique.

Leduc, Simon (fl. 18th c.). *Andante*. Adapted by André Goudenhooft, piano realization by Augustin Maillard. BILL, 1986. 3'30" (≈ 4'); B'-b; 6. b trbn, pf

Andante: $\frac{3}{4}$: ♩ = 69-76: 63 meas. (R): 3'30"

No indication is made in the score as to the source of the theme on which this piece was based. Written in a D.S. style ABA form, the solo part has a low tessitura and would work well to improve a nice, fluid sound in the low register. Twenty measures are repeated. Although many breath markings are indicated, the performer will still need to carefully plan additional ones in order to effectively perform the piece.

Lejet, Edith (b. 1941). *Méandres*. BILL, 1985. 82 meas.; 5'20" (5'30"); G'-g♯'; 8; cadenza, feathered beaming, flutter tongue, trills. b saxhn, pf

"À Fernand Lelong, professeur au CNSMP"

♩ = 60: $\frac{4}{4}$: 17 meas.: 1'10"
♩ = 92: $\frac{2}{4}$, $\frac{4}{4}$, $\frac{5}{4}$: 15 meas.: 40"
♩ = 50: $\frac{4}{4}$: 5 meas.: 25"
Più mosso: $\frac{4}{4}$: ♩ = 60: 2 meas.: 10"
a Tempo: $\frac{4}{4}$: ♩ = 50: 2 meas.: 10"
Più mosso: $\frac{3}{4}$, $\frac{4}{4}$, $\frac{5}{4}$: 5 meas.: 15"
♩ = 50: $\frac{3}{4}$, $\frac{4}{4}$, $\frac{5}{4}$: 10 meas.: 45"
Cadence ad libitum: $\frac{4}{4}$, $\frac{5}{4}$: ♩ = 60: 15 meas.: 1'
♩ = 60: $\frac{4}{4}$: 11 meas.: 45"

In addition to the techniques listed above, this work includes many quintuplets, septuplets, and grace notes. This piece is readily playable on a bass trombone with the omission of the trills. The solo part must be transposed.

†**Lemaire** [Sindorff], **Jean** (b. 1931). *Trois [3] exercises de style*. LED, 1971. 222 meas.; 5'50" (≈ 5'45"); E'-b♭'; 8*; trills. b saxhn/tba/b trbn, pf

"à Paul Bernard"

I. Andante: $\frac{3}{8}$, $\frac{5}{8}$: ♪ ≈ 72: 29 meas.: 2' (≈ 2')
II. Allegro: $\frac{4}{4}$: ♩ ≈ 116: 60 meas.: 2'5" (≈ 2')
III. Vivace: $\frac{3}{8}$, $\frac{5}{8}$, $\frac{2}{4}$: ♩ ≈ 126 (♪ constant): 133 meas.: 1'45" (≈ 1'45")

The first movement exploits the smooth, lyrical qualities of the solo instrument. The key to its successful performance lies in relaxing through the many thirty-second-note sextuplets while mentally keeping track of the pulse. The second movement emphasizes a bravura style, and the third takes on a light, bouncy style. The tessitura generally lies higher than most works, and there is very little that requires a valve. With the exception of the last two measures of the first movement (which can be taken up one octave), this piece is entirely playable on a tenor trombone.

Lesaffre, Charles. *En glissant...* [On Sliding...] BILL, 1984. 2'15" (2'); c-(d')e♭'; D. b saxhn/tba/trbn, pf

"À mon frère Directeur de l'école de Musique de Dammarie"

Allegro: $\frac{4}{4}$: ♩ = 72: 40 meas. (2R)

Although the publisher suggests it can also be performed on bass saxhorn and tuba, the title has no meaning unless it is performed on trombone. There are several glissandos in the second half of this two-section piece; the first section is in B♭ and the second is in E♭. Fourteen measures are repeated twice, first with a written repeat and again upon a D.S. Most of the movement is diatonic, and the glissandos are the only interesting material. The piano part is extremely simple.

———. *Petite chanson pour Marion* [Little Song for Marion]. BILL, 1988. 2'20" (2'15"); B♭-(d')f'; D; mute. tba/trbn/bar/trpt/cor, pf

"À ma mère"

Dolce mais sonore [Sweet but resonant]: $\frac{2}{4}$: ♩ = 80: 92 meas.

The epigraph quoting George Bernard Shaw reads: "Happy is the man who can make a living by his hobby!" The composer also includes a table that indicates the specific pedagogical intentions of the piece: slurs, attacks, mute, neighboring alterations of Do, nuances, and a rhythmic progression. There is some pedagogical benefit in this work, but it should probably not be programmed for a public performance. An optional cut omits the more difficult rhythmic section (eight measures) for those soloists who are new to their instrument.

Lodéon, André. *Campagnarde* [Country Woman]. LED, 1964. 80 meas.; 2'10"; c-d'; 1-2*. tba/b saxhn, pf

Modérément animé: $\frac{3}{4}$: 𝅗𝅥. = 58: 36 meas.: 35"
Calme: $\frac{4}{4}$: ♩ ≈ 𝅗𝅥.: 16 meas.: 1'5"
Tempo I°: $\frac{3}{4}$, $\frac{4}{4}$: 28 meas.: 30"

This piece is in three somewhat related sections, modulating from B♭ Major to D Major and back. The outer sections are closely related in style, but the melodic material is only vaguely similar. The overall range is not prohibitive for its performance on tenor trombone. The piano part is more involved than in similar works.

——. *Tuba show*. LED, 1968. 118 meas.; 4' (4'45"); A'-(a')b♭'; 6* [8]; cadenza, complex meters. tba/b saxhn, pf

Allegro moderato: $\frac{3}{8}$, $\frac{2}{4}$, $\frac{3}{4}$, $\frac{4}{4}$: ♩ = 88: 17 meas.: 35"
Poco meno mosso: $\frac{2}{4}$, $\frac{3}{4}$, $\frac{4}{4}$: 7 meas.: 15"
Très souple et sans hâte: $\frac{2}{4}$, $\frac{3}{4}$, $\frac{4}{4}$: 12 meas.: 30"

Tempo giusto: $\frac{3}{8}$, $\frac{4}{4}$: 30 meas.: 45"
Più lento: $\frac{3}{8}$: 8 meas.: 10"
Lento: $\frac{2}{8}$, $\frac{3}{8}$: 19 meas.: 20"
Tempo I°: $\frac{3}{8}$, $\frac{2}{4}$, $\frac{3}{4}$, $\frac{4}{4}$, cad.: 16 meas.: 1'15"
Vivo: $\frac{3}{8}$, $\frac{2}{4}$, $\frac{3}{4}$, $\frac{4}{4}$: 9 meas.: 10"

This piece demands both slurred and detached sixteenth-note passages throughout. As the title might suggest, this piece, in ABA form, contains many flashy technical passages. Because of the technique required, the degree of difficulty has been adjusted to eight for the bass trombonist. This was the contest piece of the *Conservatoires Régionaux de France* in 1968 and governed by the *Ministère des Affaires Culturelles*.

†**Louvier, Alain** (b. 1945). *Cromagnon*. LED, 1973. 56 meas.; 4'30" (4'50"); C♯'-c"; 6*; GB; cadenzas, complex rhythms, extreme dynamics, feathered beaming, flutter tongue, glissandos, *sourdine sèche* [fiber straight mute], trills. b saxhn/tba, cel/pf

"à Monsieur Paul Bernard, aux étudiants du Conservatoire de Paris"

Cadenza: n.m.: 1'
Modéré: $\frac{3}{4}$, $\frac{4}{4}$, cad.: ♩ = 60: 55 meas.: 3'30"

The author's note in the score is translated below:

> The accompaniment is conceived, in principle, for a celeste. For the study of this piece, when a celeste is not available, play the part on the piano one octave higher. Adopt the pedal indications according to the instrument. In the same way, exaggerate the dynamics for the celeste.

Though the tempo remains constant, rhythmic variety is created through the alteration of the subdivision of the basic pulse; this creates some extremely difficult rhythms to interpret. Because of this, coordination between soloist and accompanist will be difficult at times. This work contains a great deal of disjunct motion, and almost the entire range is used frequently. Relatively quick movement of more than three octaves is not uncommon; there is one passage which is one step shy of four octaves. With the exception of some of the trills and one thirty-second-note octave lower passage, this work is entirely playable on bass trombone.

†**Manen, Christian** (b. 1934). *Grave et scherzo, Op. 107*. BILL, 1978. 121 meas.; 6'25"; F'-a'; 8; cadenzas, complex meters, glissandos, unmetered sections. b trbn/tba/b saxhn, pf

"À Paul Bernard, en toute amitié"

Grave: n.m., cad.: ♩ ≈ 52: 21 meas.: 3'
Scherzo: $\frac{5}{8}$, $\frac{6}{8}$, $\frac{7}{8}$, $\frac{3}{4}$: ♩ = 168: 67 meas.: 1'35"
Grave: $\frac{4}{4}$, $\frac{3}{2}$, n.m., cad.: 10 meas.: 1'25"
Scherzo: $\frac{7}{8}$, $\frac{3}{4}$, $\frac{4}{4}$: 18 meas.: 20"
Presto: $\frac{3}{4}$, $\frac{4}{4}$: 5 meas.: 5"

In ABAB form, this piece exploits the interval of the tritone. The cadenzas are essentially the same, except that the second one is a little more extended. The second A and B sections are abbreviated versions of the first, and in the second B section the trombone line changes to ascending tritones rather than descending ones. The tempo of the coda (Presto) can be set at the pianist's discretion. Although the piece suggests it can also be performed on bass saxhorn, there is no transposed part included.

†**Margoni, Alain** (b. 1934). *Après une lecture de Goldoni: Fantaisie dans le style du XVIIIe siècle* [After a Lecture of Goldoni: Fantasy in the Style of the 18th Century]. LED, 1964. 123 meas.; 5'20" (5'30"); G♯'/ A♭'-f♯'; 7*; cadenza, trill. b trbn/tba/b saxhn, pf

"à Paul Bernard, Professeur au Conservatoire National Supérieur de Musique, très cordialement"

Allegretto: C : 40 meas.: 1'25"
Senza rigore: C : 39 meas.: 1'30"
I° Tempo: C, cad.: 44 meas.: 2'25"

This piece contains many scalar and arpeggiated passages. Written in D Major, this ABA-form work is unusual in that the second A section begins like an inversion of the first one in the solo part. The disjunct movement of an octave and a fifth may require some extra attention. This is a fine piece for good college students.

†**Martelli, Henri** (b. 1895). *Dialogue, Op. 100.* ESC, 1966. 207 meas.; 7'30"; B'-f'; 8; cadenza, complex meters, mute. b trbn/tba/ b saxhn, pf

"À Monsieur Paul Bernard, Professeur au Conservatoire National"

Adagio sostentuto: $\frac{3}{4}$, $\frac{5}{4}$: ♩ = 52: 18 meas.: 1'15"
Un poco animando: $\frac{3}{4}$, $\frac{5}{4}$: 36 meas.: 2'10"
Allegro mosso: $\frac{9}{8}$: ♩. = 144-152: 79 meas.: 1'35"
Moderato (alternates with "Allegro mosso" interludes): $\frac{9}{8}$, cad.:
♩. = 100: 31 meas. (8 meas. "Moderato," 23 meas. "Allegro mosso"): 1'30"
Presto: $\frac{12}{16}$: ♪. = 160: 43 meas.: 1'

Like other works by Martelli, this piece is meticulously notated down to virtually every nuance. Because of this, there seems to be very little freedom for expression in the cadenza; it will take much practice to convince the audience that the interpretation is "your own." The muted last note ends the piece rather like an afterthought. The many tempo changes, the meticulous detail, and the extremely demanding piano part make coordination between soloist and accompanist difficult.

†——. *Sonate, Op. 87*. COM, 1956. 101 meas.; 5'25"; G'-a'; 8; cadenza. b trbn, pf

"À Monsieur Paul Bernard, Professeur au Conservatoire National de Paris"

Allegretto: $\frac{9}{8}$: ♩. = 63: 26 meas.: 1'15"
Lento moltissimo: C : ♩ = 42: 15 meas.: 1'25"
Allegro: C, cad.: ♩ = 128: 60 meas.: 2'45"

This work includes many specific indications to be observed by the performer, even in the cadenza. The parts are quite busy, and it is a challenge to concentrate at such a high level throughout. The cadenza will need to be practiced extensively to give the interpretation a more personal touch. Because of the detail included in the solo part and the concentration required to interpret it, this is probably his most difficult work for bass trombone.

This was the Paris Conservatory contest piece for 1956.

†——. *Suite, Op. 83*. ESC, 1954. 245 meas.; 6'50"; G'-a♭'; 7; cadenza. tba/b saxhn/b trbn, pf

"à Monsieur Paul Bernard, Professeur au Conservatoire National de Musique"

Lento: C : ♩ = 48: 28 meas.: 2'20"
Allegro con brio: $\frac{3}{4}$: ♩ = 144: 64 meas.: 1'20"
Lento: $\frac{3}{4}$, C, cad.: ♩ = 48: 54 meas.: 2'
Presto: $\frac{2}{4}$: ♩ = 176: 99 meas.: 1'10"

Virtually every nuance is notated for the soloist, and there is little room for alternate interpretations. This piece is easier than his other works, and the range and endurance required is moderate. The cadenza passes between moderato, lento, and allegro giusto frequently and is difficult to interpret.

Meunier, Gérard. *Anapausis (ΑΝΑΠΑΥΣΙΣ)* [Repose]. BILL, 1987. 177 meas.; 8'35" (9'45"); D'-(g')a♭'; 8; complex meters, feathered beaming, non-standard meter indication, quasi cadenzas. tba, pf

"À mon cher ami, l'incomparable musicien Fernand Lelong, professeur au C.N.S.M. de Paris"

I. Très lent: n.m.: 9 meas.: 1'35"
Mesuré: 4(/4), 5(/4), 6(/4), 8(/4) : 9 meas.: 25"
Mvt. I = 18 meas.: 2'
II. Agité: $\frac{4}{8}$, $\frac{5}{8}$, $\frac{7}{8}$, $\frac{2}{4}$, $\frac{3}{4}$, $\frac{4}{4}$: ♩ = 138: 113 meas.: 2'35"
III. Très lent: $\frac{3}{4}$, $\frac{4}{4}$: ♩ = 46: 59 meas.: 4'

Unlike most sonatas, the order of movements in this piece is slow, fast, slow. The first movement is like an extended cadenza with short interludes by the piano. The second movement is full of constantly-changing complex meters, and a few sixteenth-note passages may be difficult at the indicated tempo. Many of the triplet and quintuplet markings in the score have been left out of the solo part.

——. *Tubabil* [Tuba Prattle]. LEM, 1987. 1'50" (2'); F-d'; D-P*. tba/b saxhn, pf

Modéré: C : ♩ = 108: 50 meas.
This piece is written in c minor, and it is in ABA form. The melodic material is mostly diatonic. Although the range would allow for its performance on tenor trombone, an F valve would facilitate the numerous shifts between C and B♭.

†**Mihalovici, M.** *Serioso.* LED. b saxhn, pf

Moreau, James. *Couleurs en mouvements* [Moving Colors]. LED, 1969. 270 meas.; 6'35" (7'10"); A'-c"; 6* [8]; GB; cadenza, complex meters, triple tonguing. tba/b saxhn, pf

"À ma mère, affectueusement"

Jaune chivré [Copper Yellow].
Cadenza: Allegro deciso: 3/8, 6/8 : ♩. = 116: 9 meas.: 5"
Vif: 2/8, 3/8 : ♩. = 88: 12 meas.: 5"
Moderato: 2/8, 3/8 : ♪ = 104: 4 meas.: 5"
Adagio: 2/8, 3/8, 4/8, 5/8, 6/8 : ♪ = 69: 9 meas.: 25"
Tempo I°: 3/8, 6/8, 2/4 : 12 meas.: 10"
Allegro molto: 2/4 : ♩ = 120: 3 meas.: 5"
(Cadenza = 49 meas.: 55")
Allegro moderato: 2/2 : 𝅗𝅥 = 104: 17 meas.: 20"
♩ = 𝅗𝅥 précédente: 3/8, 4/8, 2/4, 3/4 : 20 meas.: 25"
(Allegro moderato = 37 meas.: 45")
Maestoso: 2/4 : ♩ = 47: 3 meas.: 10"
Vif: 2/8, 3/8, 4/8, 5/8, 2/4 : ♪ = 192: 8 meas.: 10"
Tempo I°: 6/8 : ♩. = 116: 2 meas.: 5"
Più vivo: 2/4 : ♩ = 126: 2 meas.: 5"
Jaune chivré = 101 meas.: 2'10"

Bleu azur [Sky Blue].
Larghetto tranquillo: 2/4, 4/4 : ♩ = 63: 15 meas.: 50"
Meno mosso: 2/4, 3/4, 4/4 : ♩ = 60: 8 meas.: 25"
Tempo I°: 4/4 : ♩ = 63: 6 meas.: 25"
Meno mosso: 3/4, 4/4 : ♩ = 60: 3 meas.: 10"
♪ = 126: 5/8, 7/8, 10/8 : 3 meas.: 10"
Tempo I°: 2/4, 3/4, 4/4 : ♩ = 63: 10 meas.: 30"
Bleu azur = 45 meas.: 2'30"

Rouge flamboyant [Flaming Red].
Prestissimo: 2/8, 3/8, 4/8 : ♪ = 200: 28 meas.: 25"
Meno mosso: 2/8, 3/8 : ♪ = 176: 20 meas.: 20"
Tempo I°: 2/8, 3/8, 4/8, 7/8, 2/4, 3/4, 4/4, 5/4 : ♪ = 200: 40 meas.: 40"
Meno mosso: 2/8, 3/8, 4/8 : ♪ = 176: 10 meas.: 10"
Tempo I°: 2/8, 3/8 : 15 meas.: 10"
Très vif: 2/8, 3/8, 3/4 : ♩. = 96: 9 meas.: 5"
Prestissimo: 2/8 : ♩ = 104: 2 meas.: 5"
Rouge flamboyant = 124 meas.: 1'55"

The writing is quite nice, and it would work well as a "filler" piece on recitals. The second movement has a range of D♯-g♭' and a difficulty of about "four," making it accessible by a number of players. Mistakes include a $\frac{2}{4}$ sign notated as $\frac{2}{8}$ in the 4th meas., 7th sys., p. 1; a flag left off the eighth note in the tempo indication in the 4th meas., 7th sys., p. 4; and a $\frac{3}{8}$ sign notated as a $\frac{3}{4}$ in the 5th meas., 3d sys., p. 5 in the tuba part; and a flag left off the eighth note in the tempo indication at the beginning of the last movement in the bass saxhorn part. This piece is one of the few in this body that is not idiomatic for the bass trombone. There are numerous rapid chromatic and scalar passages in the outer movements that are virtually impossible to execute effectively on the bass trombone; though the second movement is approachable. The piano part has a series of parallel intervals, and the melody is chantlike, consisting of mostly whole steps.

This was the contest piece of the *Conservatoires Régionaux de France* in 1969 and governed by the *Ministère des Affaires Culturelles*.

Murgier, Jacques (b. 1912). *Concertstück* [Contest Piece]. EDMT, 1961. 246 meas.; 8'10"; F'-c♭"; 8; non-standard meter indication, trills. tba/db, pf

Andante con moto: $\frac{2}{4}$, $\frac{3}{4}$, $\frac{4}{4}$, $\frac{5}{4}$: ♩ = 60: 33 meas.: 2'10"
Allegro scherzando: $\frac{5}{8}$: measure = 60: 86 meas.: 1'25"
I° Tempo: $\frac{4}{4}$: ♩ = 60: 4 meas.: 15"
Adagio: $\frac{4}{4}$: ♩ = 46: 16 meas.: 1'25"
Allegro risoluto: $\frac{4}{4}$: ♩ = 138-144: 17 meas.: 30"
Meno mosso: $\frac{4}{4}$, $\frac{5}{4}$: ♩ = 116: 7 meas.: 15"
a Tempo: $\frac{12}{8}$, $\frac{4}{4}$: ♩ = 138-144 (pulse remains constant): 33 meas.: 55"
Meno mosso: $\frac{4}{4}$: 7 meas.: 15"
Più mosso: $\frac{2}{2}$: ♩ = 152: 26 meas.: 40"
Presto: $\frac{3}{8}$, $\frac{8}{8}$, $\frac{3}{4}$: 𝅝 = 48: 17 meas.: 20"

A note from the composer states, "The signs of alteration only affect the notes at their initial height and they do not last longer than signs of alteration fixed 'with caution'" (i.e., accidentals affect only the octave in which they are placed, and they are canceled at the end of each measure). This is a very difficult multi-sectioned work that contains much quick, disjunct melodic material. The tessitura is moderately high, and, when the general lack of rests is considered, this piece demands much endurance.

———. *Dialogue*. SYM. b trbn, perc, pf

Naulais, Jérôme. *Stratos*. LED, 1987. 4'45" (5'); B"(F♯')-d♯'; 7; complex meters, unaccompanied sections. (solo) tba (C or B♭)/b trbn, 4 trbns/hns

Lent: $\frac{3}{16}$, $\frac{5}{16}$, $\frac{6}{16}$, $\frac{7}{16}$, $\frac{9}{16}$, $\frac{2}{8}$, $\frac{3}{8}$, $\frac{4}{8}$, $\frac{4}{4}$, $\frac{5}{4}$: ♩ = 56: 88 meas.: 4'45"

This is a good piece for those who have performed Henri Tomasi's *Être ou ne pas être!* and are looking for something similar to program. Although not explicitly stated, the ensemble could be comprised of a combination of horns and trombones, if need be. The first part goes up to a concert d", and an indication is made in the trombone accompaniment parts for bucket mutes, although not indicated in the score or horn parts. Although the underlying pulse remains constant, variety is created through changes between slow and fast units of division (i.e., $\frac{4}{4}$ changing to $\frac{5}{16}$, etc.).

†**Pascal, Claude** (b. 1921). *Sonate en 6 Minutes 30.* DUR, 1958. 242 meas.; 6'10" (6'25"); E'(F')-b'; 6. tba/b trbn/b saxhn, pf

"à Paul Bernard, Professeur au Conservatoire National Supérieur de Musique de Paris"

I. Animé: $\frac{2}{4}$, $\frac{3}{4}$, $\frac{4}{4}$, $\frac{3}{2}$: 90 meas.: 2'10"
Un peu élargi: $\frac{2}{4}$, $\frac{3}{4}$: ♩ ≈ 120: 6 meas.: 10"
Tempo I°: $\frac{4}{4}$: 2 meas.: 5"
Le double plus lent: $\frac{3}{8}$, $\frac{2}{4}$, $\frac{3}{4}$: 6 meas.: 15"
Tempo I°: $\frac{4}{4}$, $\frac{3}{2}$: 19 meas.: 30"
Mvt. I = 123 meas.: 3'10" (3'10")

II. Lent et calme: $\frac{2}{4}$, $\frac{3}{4}$: ♩ ≈ 56: 19 meas.: 1'
Allant: $\frac{4}{4}$, $\frac{5}{4}$: ♩ = 120: 14 meas.: 30"
Vif: $\frac{2}{4}$, $\frac{6}{8}$: ♩. = 132-138 (pulse remains constant): 43 meas.: 40"
Allant: $\frac{4}{4}$: ♩ = 120: 9 meas.: 20"
Très vif: $\frac{6}{8}$: ♩. = 144-152: 34 meas.: 30"
Mvt. II = 119 meas.: 3' (3'15")

This sonata is one of the finer compositions written for bass trombone. The first movement is in sonata form, and it contains a light, lyrical melody. There are some slurs over leaps of nearly two octaves that are difficult to make speak clearly. The second movement is really two movements in one with an attacca connecting them. The "Lent et calme" is brief, but contains a beautiful melody that requires good breath control. The "Vif" begins the second major section, and there are a few difficult technical passages in the low register. At one point, the soloist is required to play three sustained (E')'s at ***ff***. The piano part is quite difficult. The page layout of the solo part is such that copies are required, unless the solo is memorized. This is a major work for bass trombone.

This was the Paris Conservatory contest piece for 1958.

†**Petit, Pierre** (b. 1922). *Fantaisie.* LED, 1953. 146 meas.; 4'5"; F'-a'; 8*; TB; glissando, trill. tba/b trbn/b saxhn, pf

"à mon cher Maître et ami Paul Bernard"

Modéré: $\frac{6}{8}$: 16 meas.: 20"
Tempo gai: $\frac{6}{8}$: 26 meas.: 30"
Calme bien chanté: C : ♩. = ♩: 73 meas.: 2'40"
Très gai: $\frac{6}{8}$: 31 meas.: 35"

This piece is a good showcase because of its light character, while at the same time it provides a nice challenge for the soloist. This piece uses more tenor clef than most others in the French literature. There are not too many surprises, but this piece demands a technically solid player.

———. *Grave.* LED, 1952. 42 meas.; 3'; A♭'-a'; 3* [4]; TB; unaccompanied section. tba/b trbn/db/b saxhn, pf

"à Paul Bernard"

Lento: C : 15 meas.: 1'
Meno lento: C : 8 meas.: 30"
Un poco più mosso: $\frac{6}{4}$: 14 meas.: 1'10"
Tempo du début (très lent): C : 5 meas.: 20"

This piece makes a good solo for young students. The lowest part of the solo is unaccompanied and will require good breath control. The use of tenor clef should not frighten off younger players, because it only affects five notes. The accompaniment is very simple.

†———. *Thème varié.* LED, 1965. 200 meas.; 7' (7'30"); E'-c"; 7*; quasi cadenza, unaccompanied sections. b saxhn/tba, pf

"à mon cher maître Paul Bernard"

Tema: Modéré: ¢ : 16 meas.: 25" (25")
Var. 1: Pas vite, tendre: C : 16 meas.: 50" (50")
Var. 2: Gai: ¢ : 16 meas.: 25" (25")
Var. 3: Allant, chanté: $\frac{3}{4}$: 32 meas.: 35" (35")
Var. 4: Tranquille: C : 16 meas.: 25" (25")
Var. 5: Volubile: $\frac{6}{8}$: 32 meas.: 30" (30")
Var. 6: Très lent: C : 17 meas.: 1'20" (1'20")
Var. 7: Désinvolte: $\frac{7}{8}$: 20 meas.: 30" (30")
Var. 8: Pas vite: $\frac{6}{4}$: 16 meas.: 1'5" (1'5")
Coda: Quasi cadenza: n.m.: 1 meas.: 30"
Tempo I°: ¢ : 18 meas.: 25"
Coda = 19 meas.: 55" (55")

This piece is a bit different than most theme and variations. The soloist plays nearly all the time, and the accompanist plays only occasionally; only variations 3, 6, and 8 have accompaniment the entire time. In many cases, each performer plays only when the other does not. The high c" comes at the end of variation 8, which requires very sustained playing. The "Tempo I°" in the coda is a return to the original theme, this time with piano in octaves. The piano part is simple. This piece requires a mature performer to maintain continuity and interest.

†———. *"Wagenia."* LED, 1957. 113 meas.; 5'20" (5'30"); A♭'-d'; 7*. b trbn/tba/b saxhn, pf

Grave et lent: C : 61 meas.: 3'40"
Allegro ma non troppo (♩ [3] = 𝅗𝅥): ¢ : 48 meas.: 1'25"
Très lent et solennel: C, $\frac{3}{2}$: 4 meas.: 15"

The "Grave" is in a rather haunting mood, as there is no distinct tonal area, and the interval of a minor second is predominant. It is in ABA form, but on the return the solo is raised one whole step and the accompaniment is lowered by a minor third. The solo part is extremely connected and full voiced at the beginning of each A section, then decrescendos continually thereafter. The "Allegro" is attacca, and the solo and piano parts exchange brief statements. This section begins at *p* and continually gets softer until it reaches *ppp* near the end. The "Très lent et solennel" comes as a surprise at *ff*, with full-voiced chords in the piano; the progression goes from IV to I in F Major, with some non-standard chords in between. Balance must be exact, or the effect will be lost. The idea of unresolved tension until the very end is similar to some effects Richard Wagner (1813-1883) used in his music dramas and operas (e.g., "Introduction" to *Tristan und Isolde* (1857)), and perhaps this piece is a tribute to him through the use of this device.

†**Pichaureau, Claude** (b. 1940). *Seringa: Suite dialyséquence en duo ou trio.* CHO, 1977. $163\frac{1}{2}$ meas.; 10' (10'45"); C♯'-a'; 8; beams extended from note heads, cadenzas, complex meters, flutter tongue, glissandos, half valve, proportional notation, quarter tones, straight mute (fiber), trills, unaccompanied sections. (solo) b trbn, db/pf; or (solo) b trbn, db, pf

"à mon Maître Paul Bernard, amicalement"

Prologue: n.m.: 1 meas.: 10"
Presto: 5/8, 7/8, 2/4, 3/4, 4/4 : ♩ = 130: 18 meas.: 25"
Meno vivo: 3/8, 2/4, 3/4 : ♩ = 90: 4 meas.: 5"
Tempo: 3/8, 6/8, 7/8, 9/8, 3/4, 4/4, 5/4 : ♩ = 130: $24\frac{1}{2}$ meas.: 45"
Meno vivo: 9/8, 3/4, 4/4, n.m.: ♩ = 90: $16\frac{1}{2}$ meas.: 45"
Lento: 3/4, 4/4, 5/4, n.m.: ♩ = 52: 21 meas.: 1'50"
Vivo: 7/16, 2/8, 3/8 : ♪ = 126: 48 meas.: 50"
Tempo 1er Lento: 3/4, 4/4, cad.: ♩ = 52: 6 meas.: 1'15"
Tempo: 9/8, 3/4, 4/4, 5/4, cad.: ♩ = 112: $16\frac{1}{2}$ meas.: 1'
Final: n.m.: pulse = 42: 1 meas.: 2'40"
Epilogue: 3/8, 2/4, 4/4 : ♩ = 90: 7 meas.: 15"

To clarify the instrumentation listing, *Seringa* can be performed either as a duo with bass trombone and double bass, a duo with bass trombone and piano, or as a trio with bass trombone, double bass, and piano. This is an outstanding chamber piece that demands playing on the highest level from all performers. The bass trombone writing is rather disjunct, and the work provides an excellent vehicle for exploration into contemporary effects, chamber music, and a challenge for advanced players. All players must read from the score, so separate parts must be purchased for each player. A conductor is highly recommended. There is an optional cut that omits the "Final" section, thus reducing the length to 7'20". The word *"dialyséquence"* is apparently formed by combining dialysis [from Greek *dialuein: dia-*, apart + *luein*, to loosen] and sequence [from Latin *sequī*, to follow].

This was the Paris Conservatory contest piece for 1977.

†**Planel, Robert** (b. 1908). *Air et final.* LED, 1968. 179 meas.; 6'25" (6'45"); C♭-g'; 7*. b trbn, pf

"À Paul Bernard, Professeur au Conservatoire"

Modéré: 2/4, 4/4 : ♩ = 58: 10 meas.: 40"
Lent et calme: 2/4, 4/4 : ♩ = 54: 17 meas.: 1'15"
Un peu plus animé: 4/4 : ♩ = 69: 9 meas.: 30"

Tempo I°: 6/8, 9/8, 12/8, 2/4, 3/4, 4/4, 5/4 : ♩ = 54 (pulse remains constant): 26 meas.: 1'40"
Animé: 6/8, 2/4 : ♩. = 100 (pulse remains constant): 52 meas.: 1'
Plus calme: 6/8, 9/8, 3/4, 4/4 : ♩ = 92 (pulse remains constant): 27 meas.: 40"
Vif: 6/8 : ♩. = 112: 38 meas.: 40"

The beginning is "quasi récitativo" for the soloist, and is quite free. The first note for the soloist is a low C♭ at a *p* dynamic; good breath control and support is needed to make the note speak fully while maintaining a soft dynamic. The melody in the "Lent et calme" is sort of like a jazz ballad and is one of the most beautiful melodies ever written for bass trombone; there are moments in the accompaniment that are reminiscent of Bozza's *Ballade, Op. 62* (1944) for tenor trombone. This is contrasted by the lively "Animé" section, that requires a much lighter style. The final "Vif" is in the same style, but much quicker. A G♭ valve could come in handy for a few of the trickier passages. This piece is among the most enjoyable to prepare and perform in the entire body of literature for bass trombone.

Porret, Julien (b. 1896). *1re pièce de concours* [First Contest Piece]. BILL, 1963. 96 meas.; 4'55"; G'-d'; 3. b saxhn, pf

Allegretto: 4/4 : ♩ = 84: 48 meas.: 2'15"
Andante: 4/4 : ♩ = 63: 24 meas.: 1'30"
I° Tempo: 4/4 : ♩ = 84: 24 meas.: 1'10"

The main theme in this work contains many dotted-eighth sixteenth rhythms, and tends to make the soloist become tense. Written in an ABA form, this piece would make a good intermediate solo. The solo part must be transposed.

Poutoire, Patrick. *Petit air.* COM. 2*.

Quérat, Marcel. *Allegretto comodo.* COM, 1971. 68 meas.; 2'30"; G-f'; 4; unaccompanied sections. b saxhn/tba, pf

𝅗𝅥 = 54-63: ¢ : 17 meas.: 1'5"
Tempo ♩ = 108-126: 2/4, 3/4 : 26 meas.: 30"
Tempo I°: ¢ : 25 meas.: 55"

This is a lively piece in ABA form, although the return is a fifth higher than the beginning. It seems to be based in g minor, but the numerous chromatic alterations effectively obscure any definite tonal center. The outer sections are smooth and lyrical, and the middle section is jaunty with more dotted-eighth sixteenth rhythms. Although the range would allow for its performance on tenor trombone, an F valve would be useful.

———. *Relation.* COM, 1971. 77 meas.; 1'45"; B♭-d'; 3. tba/b saxhn, pf

Semplice: 3/4 : ♩ = 90: 20 meas.: 40"
Allegro moderato: 2/4 : ♩ = 108: 57 meas.: 1'5"

The "Semplice" is in g minor and contains lyrical melodic material that is repeated. The "Allegro moderato" is in two parts, the second of which is an inversion of the first; the underlying tonality is A♭ Major. This is a good work suitable for younger trombonists.

Rougeron, Philippe. *Valse nostalgie*. BILL, 1979. 1'35"; C(E)-c'; 2. tba/trbn, pf

Moderato: $\frac{3}{4}$: 64 meas. (R): 1'35"

Endurance could become a problem for very young players. Eleven measures are repeated.

Rougnon. *Prière*. LED. saxhn, pf

——. *Sicilienne*. LED. saxhn, pf

——. *Valse lente*. LED. insts in B♭, pf

†**Rueff, Jeanine** (b. 1922). *Concertstück* [Contest Piece]. LED, 1960. 270 meas.; 6'55" (6'45"); A♭'-a'; 8*; TB; complex meters. b saxhn/ tba/b trbn, pf

"à Paul Bernard, Professeur au Conservatoire National Supérieur de Musique de Paris"

Allegro deciso: $\frac{3}{8}$, $\frac{5}{8}$, $\frac{2}{4}$, $\frac{3}{4}$: ♩ = 120: 56 meas.: 1'
Poco meno mosso: $\frac{3}{8}$ + $\frac{5}{8}$ + $\frac{6}{8}$, $\frac{3}{8}$, $\frac{2}{4}$: 68 meas.: 1'35"
Andante: $\frac{2}{4}$, $\frac{3}{4}$, $\frac{4}{4}$, $\frac{5}{4}$, $\frac{6}{4}$: ♩ = 80: 34 meas.: 2'5"
Allegro deciso: $\frac{3}{8}$, $\frac{5}{8}$, $\frac{2}{4}$, $\frac{3}{4}$: ♩ = 120: 60 meas.: 1'5"
Poco meno mosso: $\frac{3}{8}$ + $\frac{5}{8}$ + $\frac{6}{8}$: 39 meas.: 55"
Vivo: $\frac{3}{8}$ + $\frac{5}{8}$ + $\frac{6}{8}$, $\frac{2}{4}$: 13 meas.: 15"

This piece is in an ABCAB form, and each A section is in a small "aba" form of its own. The second A begins a fifth lower than the original and later switches to a fourth higher. The B sections are somewhat enchanting in that the smooth solo line above the constantly changing meter is rather hypnotic. There are some low sixteenth-note passages that require good breath control. The second B begins a fourth higher than the original and later switches to a fifth lower. The C section is very lyrical, and, since the piano part mainly has quarter and half notes, much leeway can be taken to enhance its expressive qualities. Care must be taken to prevent the opening from sounding too heavy. The time signature in the 1st meas., 1st sys., p.4 of the tuba part should read $\frac{2}{4}$ (vice $\frac{3}{4}$). This is one of the finer solos from this body of literature.

Sciortino, Patrice. *Laes*. SYM. b trbn, strg trio

Séguin, Pierre. *Cortège* [Procession]. Collection Rougeron. LED, 1984. 30 meas.; 1'55" (1'50"); D(G)-f'; P1-2*. tba/b saxhn, pf

Larghetto: C : ♩ = 60: 12 meas.: 50"
Più mosso: C : 12 meas.: 40"
Tempo I°: C : 6 meas.: 25"

This piece is written in two parts with a codetta based on the first. It is good for developing a smooth, lyrical tone in and out of the valve range and for maintaining continuity of sound throughout the range of the piece. It is in d minor, and there are no difficulties for the bass trombonist. There are optional notes that would allow its performance on tenor trombone, and the overall range may be too large for the intended performers.

——. *Rupture*. Collection Rougeron. LED, 1987. P2-E1*. tba (C or B♭)/b saxhn (C or B♭)/bn/trbn, pf

——. *Tubavardage* [Tuba Chatter]. Collection Rougeron. LED, 1987. 1'40" (≈ 1'40"); C(G)-e♭'; D1-2*. tba (C or B♭)/b saxhn (C or B♭)/bn/trbn, pf

"à mon ancien Professeur Mr. Henri Dupart"

Moderato: C : ♩ ≈ 108: 45 meas.

This piece is in c minor, and it is written in ABA form. The return has a slight variation on the original theme. The only note below the bass clef staff is the C at the end of the piece; optional notes allow its performance on tenor trombone as well, although there are several shifts between A and B♮. The range of this piece seems ambitious for the intended performers.

Semler-Collery, Jules. *Barcarolle et chanson bachique* [Barcarolle and Drinking Song]. LED, 1953. 134 meas.; 3'40"; B♭'-g♭'; 5*; unaccompanied sections. Recordings: 14, 17, 47. tba/db/b saxhn/b trbn, pf

"à Paul Bernard"

I. Barcarolle. Mouvement de barcarolle: $\frac{3}{8}$, $\frac{6}{8}$: ♩. = 46: 46 meas.: 1'55"

II. Chanson bachique. Gai et spirituel: $\frac{2}{4}$: ♩ = 108: 19 meas.: 20"
Tempo un poco meno vivo: $\frac{2}{4}$: 8 meas.: 10"
Tempo I: $\frac{2}{4}$: 4 meas.: 5"
Tempo II: $\frac{2}{4}$: 8 meas.: 10"
Tempo I: $\frac{2}{4}$: 31 meas.: 40"
Tempo II: $\frac{2}{4}$: 8 meas.: 10"
Tempo I: $\frac{2}{4}$: 6 meas.: 5"
Tempo vivo: $\frac{2}{4}$: 4 meas.: 5"
Mvt. II = 88 meas.: 1'45"

The first movement is one of the more tuneful melodies to be found from this body of literature. It is very lyrical, and only one passage descends into the low register. The term "barcarolle" refers to a Venetian gondolier's song, with a rhythm suggestive of rowing. While the origin of the "Drinking Song" melody is unknown, it is quite lively and spirited. This movement demands a light touch. In general, most sixteenth-note passages and low passages are unaccompanied. Because of the range, this piece can easily be played on a tenor trombone; it remains one of the more popular euphonium solos.

†——. *Cantabile et divertissement.* ESC, 1963. 178 meas.; 7'5" (≈ 7'); B♭'(E♭)-g♭'; 9; cadenza. b saxhn/tba/b trbn/cb (saxhn)/db, pf

"À Paul Bernard, Professeur au Conservatoire National Supérieur de Musique de Paris"

a. Cantabile. Andantino con molto expressione: C, $\frac{5}{4}$: ♩ ≈ 50: 13 meas.: 1'5"
   Tempo un poco più vivo: C : 13 meas.: 55"
   Tempo I: C : 3 meas.: 15"
   Tempo II: $\frac{2}{4}$, C : 10 meas.: 40"
   Tempo I: C, $\frac{5}{4}$: 16 meas.: 1'20"
   Cantabile = 55 meas.: 4'15"

b. Divertissement. Allegretto: $\frac{2}{4}$: ♩ à partir de 104 [from 104]: $\frac{2}{4}$, cad.: 110 meas.: 2'35"
   Tempo con brio: $\frac{2}{4}$: 13 meas.: 15"
   Divertissement = 123 meas.: 2'50"

The "Cantabile" is a florid, lyrical melody that will need careful practice to produce a smooth, connected sound throughout. Because the accompaniment is chiefly supportive, some latitude can be taken with the tempo to enhance the melody's expressive qualities. It is in ABA form. The "Divertissement" is in ABAB form and begins in c minor. The melody is arpeggiated, and it demands a light playing style. This first section ends in E♭ Major. The B section begins in B Major, and the character of the solo becomes more lyrical using many slurred triplets. The second half of the B section uses an inversion of the melody in G Major. The A theme returns after the cadenza, though only one statement is heard. The B section jumps in, this time in c minor, and after only one statement, it is interrupted by a fast-paced coda in C Major. The accompaniment is rather easy. Because of the ossias indicated for the double bass, this piece could be played on a tenor trombone.

†——. *Deux [2] pièces brèves.* ESC, 1973. 89 meas.; 3'45" (≈ 5'); F'(B♭')-f♯'; 7; cadenza. b trbn/tba, pf

"Bien amicalement à Paul Bernard, Professeur au Conservatoire National Supérieur de Musique de Paris"

a. Andantino cantabile. $\frac{2}{4}$, C : ♩ = 60: 32 meas.: 2'
b. Allegretto con spirito. $\frac{2}{4}$: ♩ = 96: 18 meas.: 25"
   Un peu moins vite: $\frac{2}{4}$: 6 meas.: 10"
   Tempo I: $\frac{2}{4}$, cad.: 13 meas.: 45"
   Tempo II: $\frac{2}{4}$: 20 meas.: 25"
   Allegretto = 57 meas.: 1'45"

The first movement is in F Major and contains more disjunct motion than in his other works. There is much dynamic contrast, and phrasing should be planned in advance. The second movement passes between two themes of different styles. Most of this movement is in the bass clef staff. A rallentando was left out of the solo part beginning on the last eighth note, 7th meas. of "E," 2d mvt. This work is quite accessible.

†———. *Saxhornia.* LED, 1959. 149 meas.; 5'25" (≈ 6'); F'-a♭'; 7*; unaccompanied sections. b saxhn/tba/b trbn, pf

"à Paul Bernard, Professeur au Conservatoire de Musique de Paris"

a. Cantus recitativo. Calme et expressif: 2/4, 3/4, C : 20 meas.: 1'
   Tempo calme: 12/8, C : 4 meas.: 20"
   Tempo calmato: 12/8, C : 7 meas.: 30"
   Con moto: 3/4 : 4 meas.: 10"
   Tempo calmato: 12/8, 3/4, C : 8 meas.: 35"
   Tempo I: 3/4, C : 12 meas.: 35"
   Cantus recitativo = 55 meas.: 3'10"

b. Tarantella. Mouvement de Tarantelle: 6/8 : 44 meas.: 40"
   Tempo meno mosso: 6/8 : 16 meas.: 15"
   Tempo I°: 6/8 : 54 meas.: 50"
   Meno vivo: 6/8 : 8 meas.: 10"
   Tempo I°: 6/8 : 16 meas.: 20"
   Tarantella = 94 meas.: 2'15"

The theme in the first movement is quite beautiful and covers a wide range. There is more playing in the low register here than in his other works. The numerous unaccompanied sections allow much freedom for interpretation. The "Tarantella" is quite bold and brilliant. Careful attention must be made of the dynamic contrasts and accented passages. The tessitura generally lies in the bass clef staff. There are numerous minor mistakes in the solo parts with the most important one being a "Tempo I" indication omitted from the tuba part in the 1st meas., 3d sys. from the end of the "Cantus recitativo"; the others are too numerous to list. Compare the parts carefully.

†———. *Tubanova: Solo de concours.* ESC, 1967. 139 meas.; 5'45" (6'15"); A♭'(E♭)-g'; 8; cadenzas, trills. tba/b saxhn/b trbn/cb (saxhn)/db, pf

"À Paul Bernard, Professeur au Conservatoire National Supérieur de Musique de Paris, en toute amitié"

1. Andantino espressivo. 2/4, C, cads.: ♩ = 56: 48 meas.: 4'
2. Allegretto spiritoso. 2/4, C : ♩ = 112: 91 meas: 1'45"

The melodic material in the first movement is quite florid and expressive. There are many accidentals, and two brief cadenzas are very well written. The second movement should be played in a light and spirited manner. Because of the ossias intended for double bass, this piece can be played on a tenor trombone.

Senallié [Senaillé], Jean-Baptiste (1687-1730). *Courante.* See **Leclair**.

Tomasi, Henri [-Frédien] (1901-1971). *Danse sacrée* [Ritual Dance]: No. 3 des "Cinc danses profanes et sacrées." LED, 1960. 2'25" (3'); G-a♭'; 5*; GB. Recording: 55. tba/trbn/b saxhn, pf/ch orch

See entry in Chapter 3.

†——. *Être ou ne pas être!: Monologue d'Hamlet* [To Be or Not to Be!: Hamlet's Monologue]. LED, 1963. 67 meas.; 4'25" (≈ 6'10"); B♭'-d'; 7*; complex meters, mute (optional) [trbn version only], unaccompanied sections. Recordings: 10, 23, 26, 31. b trbn/ tba, pf; solo b trbn/tba, 3 trbns

(Piano version): "À Paul Bernard, Professeur au Conservatoire National Supérieur de Musique, très cordialement"

(Trombone version): "Au Quatuor de Trombones de l'Orchestre National de la R.T.F. Messieurs M. Suzan, G. Destanque, C. Verdier, H. Arqué"

Lento: 2/4, 3/4, 4/4 : ♩ = 52: 15 meas.: 1'
Lento: 2/4, 3/4, 4/4, 5/4 : ♩ = 54: 14 meas.: 1'
Tempo I°: 2/4, 3/4, 4/4 : ♩ = 52: 9 meas.: 30"
Agitato: 3/4, 4/4 : ♩ = 80: 4 meas.: 10"
♩ = 54: 4/4 : 2 meas.: 10"
Più mosso: 5/8, 3/4 : 4 meas.: 10"
Tempo I°: 4/4 : ♩ = 52/54: 6 meas.: 30"
♩ = 80: 3/4 : 2 meas.: 5"
Tempo I°: 3/4, 4/4 : ♩ = 52: 7 meas.: 30"
Lento: 2/4, 4/4 : ♩ = 46/44: 4 meas.: 20"

As the annotation might suggest, there is much tempo fluctuation; ensemble is more of a problem with the trombone version, and a conductor is highly recommended. The work is rather somber with many abrupt style changes. Good breath control is required for the sustained low-register passages. Numerous errors exist in both editions; it would be best to compare both of them side by side. Although not indicated, effective lower octave displacements can be made of the 5th meas. of "2," the 6th meas. of "4," and the 2d meas. of "11." The trombone version requires two mutes for the accompaniment: a *Sourd. ord.* and *Sourd. Robinson.* A metal and fiber straight mute work well, respectively. Most of the mute changes are very fast. The range of the Trombone 1 part goes to c", and all trombone accompaniment parts use both tenor and bass clefs. An optional cut eliminates only five measures. This is one of the most outstanding compositions and, understandably, one of the most frequently performed works for the bass trombone.

Toulon, Jacques. *Hymne, cadence et danse.* Piano accompaniment by Jacqueline Vernier. LED, 1983. 100 meas.; 3' (≈ 2'40"); B♭'-e'; 4*; cadenza. b trbn, pf

Noble et soutenu: 3/4 : ♩ = 92: 20 meas.: 40"
Un peu plus lent: 2/4, 3/4, 4/4 : 11 meas.: 25"
a Tempo: 3/4, cad.: 11 meas.: 50"
Tempo di Valse: 3/4 : 𝅗𝅥. = 69: 33 meas.: 30"
Tempo più lento: 3/4 : 13 meas.: 25"
Tempo plus rapide: 3/4 : 12 meas.: 10"

Although the main theme of this piece resembles the first several notes and rhythms of the "Star Spangled Banner," it is a clever piece and is quite good for younger players who have just switched to bass trombone. There are a variety of style changes, and a brief cadenza suitable for players who have not been exposed to many.

——. *Trois [3] caricatures*. MAR, 1989. 105 meas.; 2'10" (2'10"); G'-b♭'; E*[5]. tba/(b) saxhn

I. Dinosaurus. Pesante: ₵ : 𝅗𝅥 = 66: 47 meas.: 1'25" (1'20")
II. Valse. Tempo de Valse: $\frac{3}{4}$: 𝅗𝅥. = 76: 45 meas.: 35" (40")
III. Presto. Très rapide: $\frac{3}{4}$: ♩ = 126: 13 meas.: 10" (10")

These pieces are melodically based, and they make use of traditional harmony and structure. The extremes of range are approached only once each, but the publisher's degree of difficulty still seems exceptionally low.

†**Tournier, Franz**. *Récit et rondo*. RID, 1969. 256 meas.; 8'55"; F'-b♭'; cadenza, complex meters, trill, unaccompanied sections. tba/b saxhn, pf

Récit. Récit: $\frac{5}{8}$, $\frac{6}{8}$, $\frac{7}{8}$, $\frac{2}{4}$, $\frac{3}{4}$: ♩ ≈ 60: 65 meas.: 2'25"
Rondo. Presto: $\frac{5}{4}$: ♩ ≈ 144: 191 meas.: 7'15" (6'30")

The "Récit" contains several unaccompanied passages that should be interpreted freely. There are a number of slurs greater than an octave, with ninths and tenths being used the most. In the "Rondo," there is much exchange between dotted eighth-sixteenth and triplet rhythms. The solo and piano share equal roles, and any feeling of tonality is obscured by the numerous tone clusters. Endurance may become a problem because of a general lack of rests.

This was the Paris Conservatory contest piece for 1969.

Tremblot de la Croix, Francine. *Le Tombeau de Goya* [Goya's Tomb]. LED, 1982. tba/trbn/b saxhn, pf

See entry in Chapter 3.

Uga, Piérre. *Promenade*. BILL, 1978. 52 meas.; 2'45"; C-e'; 5. t trbn/b trbn/tba/b saxhn, pf

Andantino: $\frac{2}{4}$, **C** : ♩ = 66: 21 meas.: 1'15"
Allegretto: **C** : ♩ = 100: 22 meas.: 55"
a Tempo: **C** : 9 meas.: 35"

This work focuses on smooth, lyrical playing throughout. The return of the main theme is abbreviated followed by a brief codetta in this ABA-form work. Although primarily intended for tenor trombone, the score includes optional parts for tuba, bass trombone, and bass saxhorn. The tenor trombone range is F-a' and uses both tenor and bass clefs; this version would also be suitable for bass trombone.

†**Villette, Pierre**. *Fantaisie concertante*. LED, 1962. 100 meas.; 4'30" (≈ 5'30"); G'-a♭'; 8*; TB; cadenza, complex meters, mute. b trbn/tba/t trbn/b saxhn, orch/pf

"à Monsieur Paul Bernard, Professeur au Conservatoire National Supérieur de Musique de Paris"

Andante (quasi adagio): $\frac{3}{4}$, $\frac{4}{4}$: ♩ = 58-60: 13 meas.: 50"
Un peu plus allant (andante): $\frac{4}{4}$: ♩ = 63: 5 meas.: 20"
Tempo I°: $\frac{2}{4}$, $\frac{3}{4}$, $\frac{4}{4}$, cad.: 18 meas.: 1'5"
Plus lent (adagio): $\frac{2}{4}$, $\frac{4}{4}$: 7 meas.: 25"
Vivace: $\frac{3}{8}$, $\frac{5}{8}$, $\frac{2}{4}$, $\frac{4}{4}$, ¢ : ♩ = 126: 31 meas.: 50"
Andante (quasi adagio): $\frac{4}{4}$: ♩ = 58-60: 6 meas.: 25"
Tempo vivace: $\frac{4}{4}$: ♩ = 126-132: 20 meas.: 35"

This multi-section work is divided into two parts—one slow and the other fast. The first section displays the lyrical talents of the soloist in the high register. This is later contrasted with several low passages that require good breath control and careful phrasing. The fast section is spirited, and requires a light touch. Although this piece is of very high quality, it is apparently one of the lesser known solos in this repertoire. There are numerous ossias indicated, but they seem to be primarily for the tenor trombone version. The range for the tenor trombone is E-c". This work has all the elements of an outstanding French conservatory piece, and it even has an orchestral accompaniment. The chamber orchestra parts are available on rental from the publisher. The instrumentation includes: fl, ob, cl, bn, hn, trpt, perc, hp, strgs.

†**Weber, Alain** (b. 1930). *Soliloque.* LED, 1969. 100 meas.; 6'10" (6'45"); G'-a♯'; 7-8*; flutter tongue, quasi cadenza, trill, unaccompanied sections, unmetered sections. b trbn/tba/b saxhn, pf

"À Monsieur Paul Bernard, Professeur au Conservatoire National Supérieur de Musique"

Lent: n.m.: ♩ ≈ 42: 8 meas.: 2'20"
Allegro: n.m.: ♩ ≈ 66: 7 meas.: 1'10"
Librement (quasi cadenza): n.m.: 1 meas.: 45"
Vif: $\frac{2}{8}$, $\frac{3}{8}$, $\frac{4}{8}$: ♪ = 144-152: 84 meas.: 1'55"

The difficulty in this piece comes from the extended unmetered section, where much room is left for interpretation. This piece demands a mature performer. The coordination should not be a problem, since the solo part has been very meticulously supplied with piano cues. A mistake in the bass trombone/tuba part shows the unit of pulse at the "Vif" being a quarter; it should be changed to an eighth. Tenor clef is used for only five notes.

Weber, Carl Maria von (1786-1826). *Un adagio.* Adapted by André Goudenhooft, piano realization by Augustin Maillard. BILL, 1986. (2'); G'-e; 5. b trbn/tba, pf

Adagio: C : ♩ = 54: 33 meas.: 2'25"

This edition exploits the low range of the solo instrument almost exclusively. The tessitura is very low, and breath control at the indicated tempo will be a problem for most players. There is one mistake in the solo part: the B♭' in the 1st meas., 4th sys. should be a B♮'.

†**Werner, Jean-Jacques** (b. 1935). *Libre-episode* [Free Episode]. EDMT, 1979. 54 meas.; ≈ 5'; F'-a♭'; 7; beams extended from note heads, cadenza, flutter tongue, a piacere sections, unmetered sections. b saxhn/b trbn/tba/db, pf/org

"Pour Monsieur Paul Bernard"

♩. ≈ 96: 6/8, n.m., cad.: 22 meas.: 2'20"

♩ ≈ 54: 4/4, n.m.: 5 meas.: 25"

♩. ≈ 60: 9/8, n.m.: 5 meas.: 20"

♩ ≈ 54: 2/4, 3/4, 4/4, n.m.: 11 meas.: 1'15"

♩. ≈ 60: 9/8, 12/8, 3/4 : 3 meas.: 10"

♩. ≈ 96: 6/8, n.m.: 8 meas.: 30"

The extended unmetered sections require a mature soloist to unify the piece. There are many changes in style and tempo, and the piano basically responds to the soloist's activity. Because of this, the organ would probably provide a better accompaniment. This piece is worth exploring because of the modern techniques used and the relatively few pieces of this type that have an organ accompaniment.

†**Zbar, Michel** (b. 1942). *Jeu 3*. LED, 1972. 81 meas.; (≈ 4'40"); E♭'-b'; 8*; TB; beams extended from note heads, feathered beaming, flutter tongue, glissandos, plunger, proportional notation, timed events, unaccompanied sections, variable slide vibrato (wide to narrow). b trbn/t-b trbn, pf

This piece uses brackets to indicate in seconds the length of a given measure. An adequate technique must be developed for following the plunger indications; a separate staff below the traditional staff indicates the degree to which the plunger should be open or closed. For the most part, the piano plays clusters against the the trombone solo. B♮' appears frequently, and it may require the retuning of the F-valve to "E" for tenor trombonists.

The title seems to refer to the organ stop *Jeu de tierce*, that indicates the pitches of the cornet stop in the classical French organ; this is the most important voice in French organs.

6
Bass Trombone, Tuba, and Bass Saxhorn: Pedagogical Materials

Because of the nature of this section, durations of exercises will not be included, and any special techniques discussed or used will be detailed in the "General Comments" portion of each annotation. For studies only, an overall range and degree of difficulty will be indicated. The total number of pages will be reflected at the end of the "Descriptive Information."

Bach, Johann Sebastian (1685-1750). *Suites pour violoncelle seul.* Edited for bass trombone by Jean-Claude Barbez. LED, 1982. C-g', 8*, 28 pp.

These suites include the complete set of movements from the first three original suites, most of the fourth suite, and two movements from the fifth. The original order of the suites (Prelude, Allemande, Courante, Sarabande, Other [Menuet or Bourée], and Gigue) has been altered for no apparent reason; the reason for the omission of portions of the fourth and fifth suites and all of the sixth is also unclear. The order of movements in each suite is as follows:

Suite	Order of Movements
I	P S A C MI MII G
II	P S A C MI MII G
III	P C S A BI BII G + S [from Suite V]
IV	P A C S B[I] + G [from Suite V]

The editorial markings assume a knowledge of the editor's book *Technique du trombone basse double noix*, where "o" indicates use of the F valve, "x" means both valves, and "+ " means a shortened slide position. This edition assumes the use of a dependent tuning system, since no indication is given for an independent use of the second valve. The editor also suggests that these suites can be played by two performers, alternating phrases at the breath marks.

It is not known whether this edition was influenced by the Lafosse edition for tenor trombone (LED, 1946), but it is extremely coincidental that the Lafosse edition also contains only four suites. All movements in the Barbez edition are in the Lafosse; however, the Lafosse also contains the "Gigue" from Suite IV and the "Courante" from Suite VI. Many of the dynamic indications are similar in both editions, but the articulations and phrasings are usually different.

Barbez, Jean-Claude. *Technique du trombone basse double noix, si♭-fa-(♭)mi ou si♭-fa-ré* [Technique of the Double-Valve Bass Trombone in B♭-F-(♭)E or B♭-F-D]. LED, 1981. F×'/G'-a', 4-7*, 47 pp.

This book is divided into two parts, both emphasizing the use of a bass trombone with a dependent valve system. The first section discusses the use of each valve in its various tunings; exercises for each tuning (F, (♭)E, and D) are each from eight to ten pages in length. All slide positions are shown relative to the tenor trombone slide positions with an awkward but useable notation system. There are several useful charts, and a page each is devoted to other dependent tunings (B♭-F-E♭ and B♭-F-D♭) and independent tunings (B♭-F-G-E♭ and B♭-F-G♭-D). The second part is a set of thirty scale exercises in all keys, major and minor. Many exercises include instructions, and tenor clef is occasionally used. Double-valve positions are not indicated because of the various tuning systems, but an "x" shows when they are to be used.

Bernard, Paul. *Méthode complète pour trombone basse, tuba, saxhorns basses et contrebasse.* LED, 1960. 136 pp.

This useful method provides text in French, English, German, and Italian, and studies all the particular difficulties of the bass trombone, five- and six-valve bass tubas, and four-valve bass and contrabass tubas. Notable sections include a brief history of these instruments, a ten-page section discussing the bass trombone, and drawings of all the tubas (with fingering charts). A section discussing nuances, taste, expression, and style (pp. 97-98) is valuable. There are ten studies taken directly from J. S. Bach's *Suites for Violoncello*, but perhaps most useful are the twelve modern studies (mislabeled *"Dix [10] études modernes")*. Their composers include Robert Clérisse, Jules Semler-Collery, Marcel Bitsch, Pierre Max Dubois, Robert Bariller, Jean-Michel Defaÿ, François Julien Brun, Roger Boutry, José Berghmans, Jeanine Rueff, Henri Tomasi, and Jacques Castérède, many of which have composed contest solos for these instruments as well. These studies are all fine examples of contemporary writing (as of 1960) for these instruments. Each generally contains one or more examples of disjunct melodies, complex meters, large dynamic contrasts, and/or large range. The overall range for these studies is G'-c", and the degree of difficulty is between six and eight.

———, ed. *Études et exercises.*

Douze [12] pièces mélodiques: Extraites de la collection de vocalises-études publiées sous la direction de A. L. Hettich. LED, 1947. F♯-f♯', 4-6*, 16 pp.

This is an assorted collection of melodious studies from many different composers including Claude Delvincourt (2), Gabriel Fauré, Florent Schmitt, G. Lefebvre, Guy Ropartz, Louis Vierne, P. L. Hillemacher, Pierre de Bréville, Henri Busser, Henri Fevrier, and Alfred Bruneau.

There is one in treble clef, and it should be read as a transposed part in B♭. These studies are a nice change of pace from the Bordogni vocalises, yet they serve an important role in developing a smooth, singing style of playing. There are some occasional trills that are manageable on bass trombone, and about half of the studies have some mixed meter; one study places the meter changes above the staff rather than in it. Most of them are in sharp keys, and many accidentals are used. Because of their range, these studies could also be used by tenor trombonists who have recently acquired an instrument with an F attachment.

Quarante [40] études d'après J. Forestier. LED, 1948. F♯'-c', 6* [6-7], 17 pp.

As the range suggests, all of these exercises have a low or very low tessitura. They are all technical in nature, and they provide excellent material for working in and out of the valve register of the bass trombone from both ends. Most of the exercises are only a few lines in length. Many of the ornaments are not feasible. They cover nearly every key, and they are not very idiomatic for the bass trombone, which is why the degree of difficulty has been adjusted.

———, ed. *Traits difficiles tirés d'œuvres symphoniques et dramatiques pour tuba et trombone basse* [Difficult Brilliant Passages Extracted from Symphonic and Dramatic Works]. LED, 1951. 8 pp.

There are two anthologies each containing two parts, but only parts three and four (the second anthology) contain excerpts for bass trombone. In general, these excerpts are intended for individual practice instead of section work. There are numerous excerpts from French composers which are not found in any other source.

Bitsch, Marcel. *Quatorze [14] études de rhythme pour trombone basse ou tuba adaptées des «15 études de rhythme» pour trombone.* Edited by Anthony Greiner. LED, 1956 and 1988. F'-c", 8*, 29 pp.

"To John D. Hill, Professor of Trombone, The University of Iowa"

These studies are not merely octave transpositions of the original set. They include extra material to enable octave shifts, while retaining the rhythmic integrity of the original studies; the vertical spacing has been increased to allow each study to occupy two pages instead of just one like the original. Tenor clef is used only in the first study. The articulations and tempos that Gabriel Masson had placed in the original set were retained by Mr. Greiner. Only the fifteenth study was omitted from this edition, though one may question why. In the third study, the rhythm on the 1st beat, 3d meas., 7th sys., p. 6 should be dotted-eighth, eighth, sixteenth (vice dotted-eighth, sixteenth, eighth). It is quite useful to study both the tenor and bass trombone versions simultaneously. These are among the most challenging studies specifically intended for bass trombone available.

Charlier, Théo. *Trente-deux études de perfectionnement pour trombone in si bémol [B♭] à 4 pistons ou tuba.* [32 Finishing Studies]. LEM, 1946. C-d", 5-8, 55 pp.

"Au Maître Léon Jongen, Directeur du Conservatoire Royal de Bruxelles"

Although all the instructions are in French, it is relatively easy to determine what is expected from each study. An indication on page 5 suggests that bass trombonists should read the studies down one octave, but this may prove impractical in some places. Perhaps another transposition, such as reading the part in tenor clef down one octave, would be more appropriate. Each study emphasizes a particular facet of performance technique; the study for trills and ornaments (no. 17) may prove itself impossible. These studies are apparently written for valved trombones, but they work well as advanced studies on slide trombones.

Chevaillier, Claude. *Étude du trombone basse*. CHO, 1982. B♭"-d", 3-7, 65 pp.

"dédié à Jean-Luc Chevaillier, Trombone Basse"

Although the forward is written in French, English, and German, all other comments are in French. These studies are intended for a bass trombone tuned to B♭/F/G♭/D, and the composer has developed a special code to indicate each tuning system: O = no valve, V = F valve, ▼= G♭ valve, and V̳= D valve. These indications are combined with a slide position (e.g., "5,V" for "5th position, F valve") and are only used in the first 11 exercises. The first twenty exercises are for "setting the sound" and for developing facility with the valves; many have more than one version to allow for different keys. There are two pages of chromatic scales, and a short scale study in every major and melodic minor key. These are followed by seven studies of various styles (overall range: C'-a') assumed to be composed by the author; they focus on equal quality of sound in and out of the lowest range of the instrument.

The author also transcribed and adapted thirteen of the *15 Vocalises, Op. 12* of Giuseppe Concone. The tessitura of these exercises is quite low, and the overall range is G'-b♭'. The solo line is two octaves lower than the "soprano/mezzo-soprano" edition for voice. It would be beneficial to consult the vocal editions for a different view on phrasings and expression markings. These vocalises would work well with the vocal accompaniments and could be programmed on recitals. In vocalise no. 3, the key signature (E♭ Major) has been included only on the first staff.

Perhaps the greatest value in this collection is the set of *Dix [10] études de concert* by Jacques Murgier. These are among the most superior modern studies composed specifically for bass trombone. In a variety of styles, these studies contain many large intervals, tenor and bass clef changes, difficult rhythms, complex meters, wide dynamic contrasts, glissandos, use of mute, use of flutter tongue, and awkward technical passages. Meters are indicated by a numeral over the actual note receiving the pulse. The overall range of these studies is E'-b'/c♭".

The entire volume has been written in extremely neat manuscript, but occasionally sixteenth- and thirty-second-note beams appear to run together. In general, the layout of the studies could have been done better, and the awkward page turns could have been prevented. Nevertheless, this is one of the best collections of studies available for bass trombone.

Clodomir, Pierre François. *Méthode complète pour tous les saxhorns, nouvelle édition entièrement revue et corrigée et augmentée par M. Job.* LED, 1947. f♯-b♭"; 1-7; Vol 1., 60 pp.; Vol. 2, 62 pp.

This method covers all basics of playing a valved brass instrument. M. Job has "entirely reviewed and corrected and augmented" this celebrated method. It is written in treble clef as it is primarily intended for cornet and other treble clef brass. The exercises contained in this method are quite useful as supplementary material or when learning to transpose from treble clef (either down one octave or a major ninth). This method presents some excellent duets and concert etudes. The *Méthode complète* is also published in one single volume.

——. *Méthode élémentaire pour saxhorn basse à 3 pistons.* LED.

Couillaud, Henri. *Traits difficiles tirés d'œuvres symphoniques et dramatiques pour trombone* [Difficult Brilliant Passages Extracted from Symphonic and Dramatic Works]. LED, 1943. 8 pp.

Although it includes mostly major works, this collection also presents excerpts from lesser-known composers. Four excerpts are intended for section practice. Excerpts include:

Pierné, Gabriel	*Images: Divertissement sur un thème pastoral* (trbn 1 solo)
Pierné, Gabriel	*Impressions de Music-Hall*
Ravel, Maurice	*Bolero* (trbn 1 solo)
Rossini, Gioacchino	*Guillaume Tell (Overture)*
Saint-Saëns, Camille	*Danse macabre* (trbn 1 solo)
Schmitt, Florent	*Oriane et le Prince d'Amour*
Stravinsky, Igor	*Pulcinella*
Tomasi, Henri	*La Rosière du Village*
Wagner, Richard	*Lohengrin* (trbn 1 only)
Wagner, Richard	*L'or du Rhin* (trbn 1 only)

Cummings, Barton, ed. *Dix-sept études de virtuoiste pour tuba, trombone basse, saxhorns basse et contrebasse d'après Maxime-Alphonse* [17 Studies in Virtuosity]. LED, 1984. F'-e', 6-7*, 21 pp.

These studies help develop technical virtuosity in the low range of the instrument. There are a number of various styles and techniques required, and study no. 16 is a "Théme et variations." These are excellent studies for working into the middle-low register both from above and from below.

——, ed. *Trente [30] études pour tuba, trombone basse, saxhorns basse et contrebasse d'après Maxime-Alphonse.* LED, 1978. C'-b, 4-6*, 12 pp.

These studies are anywhere from three lines to a full page in length and primarily help develop technical facility in the low range of the instrument. By the range stipulation above, one can tell that some of these studies have an extremely low tessitura. Two studies include the low C', and both are at the dynamic *p* and either arrive or leave the note by a slur.

Defaye, Jean-Michel. *Six études pour tuba.* LED, 1990. B'-f', 5-6, 13 pp.

Each study is exactly two pages in length, and the title of each describes what particular facet of technique is to be emphasized: (1) intonation, (2) rhythm, (3) détaché, (4) intervals, (5) legato, and (6) velocity. Study no. 1 contains a proportionally notated section, study no. 3 is unmetered and unmeasured, and there is occasional use of feathered beaming. These are excellent intermediate studies.

Delgiudice, Michel. *Douze [12] études rhythmiques et mélodiques pour trombone-basse, saxhorn-basse et tuba.* ESC, 1954. F'-c", 5-9, 25 pp.

Each study is two pages in length, and most cover nearly the entire range of the instrument. These are both technically and musically challenging studies, and they belong in the small category of the finest studies for low brass. Nearly every technical facet of performance is covered in this set. Paul Bernard includes brief annotations of each study (in French) at the beginning, and they are translated below:

No. 1. Work this etude very slowly, then as quickly as possible, finally at the indicated tempo. For bass trombone, attention to the accuracy of the e-naturals and b-naturals at the first position [Mr. Bernard probably meant the second position e♮ and the F-valve second position E♮ and B♮].

No. 2. Without dragging, very sustained. 16th and 17th measures [quarter note pickup counts as first measure], watch the accuracy of the D♯ (grave). 54th and 55th measures, mentally count (1,2,3,4—1,2,3—1,2) (1,2,3,4—1,2,3,4—1,2,3).

No. 3. Watch the articulations. Example 1st measure, give the same importance to the g and b as to the f and a  not emphasizing the first note by accent to the detriment of the second  .

No. 4. Same remark goes for Etude No. 1, attention to the accuracy of the e-naturals, b-naturals, and d-sharps.

No. 5. Do not accent the first note of each beat to the detriment of the other notes. This remark is valid for all slurs.

No. 6. Do not use vibrato (as in jazz) particularly for the bass trombone, that is not the purpose of this etude. Give the notes their intrinsic value, and above all keep the tempo steady. Use and even abuse indeed the metronome; the performer will be astonished and surprised (agreeably or disagreeably) with the results of this comparison.

No. 7. The tessitura of this etude being rather extended (in range), attention should be given to the intonation and to the homogeneity of the sound. Accuracy of the b-naturals and e-naturals for the bass trombone, C♯ (grave) for the bass saxhorn and tuba. Do not drag.

No. 8. Play very slowly in order to arrive at the indicated tempo.

No. 9. Carefully sustain the values in each phrase. Do not interrupt the air column.

No. 10. Do not stress the first note of each slur.

No. 11. Play this chromatic etude very slowly to start. Repeat every two or four measures in order to not make a marshmallow of this exercise (i.e., to prevent making it sound mushy).

No. 12. Interpret each cadenza liberally, without rhythmic constraint. The performer's personality ought to free itself and grow stronger at this time. Always keep in mind the following observation for the $\frac{9}{16}$ and the $\frac{7}{8}$: do not stress the first note of a slur to the detriment of the other notes.

Dondeyne, Désiré. *Douze déchiffrages: Degré supérieur pour trombone, tuba, basson, violoncelle* [12 Sightreading Exercises: Advanced Level]. BILL, 1981. (C♯)E-a', 7-9, 12 pp.

A positive step in providing material for sight reading, this book contains some of the most challenging studies of this kind. A great part of the challenge is interpreting the manuscript. For example, the accidentals are sometimes blurred and tend to obscure the notated music. Expression markings can also be difficult to read at-a-glance. But this is all a part of the overall test. Tenor clef is used only in Nos. 8 and 10 and only for two or three measures each. As one may assume, mixed meters occur frequently.

Douay, Jean. *à propos du...trombone: Pédagogie fondamentale sur l'enseignement du trombone* [On the Subject of the...Trombone: Fundamental Pedagogy on Teaching Trombone]. BILL, n.d. 135 pp.

The discussions of the bass and contrabass trombones are more detailed than in Lafosse, and the discussion of the Paris Conservatory gives keen insight on the way the French prepare for a career in music. For more information, see entry in Chapter 4.

Dubois, Pierre Max. *Douze soli en forme d'études pour tuba* [12 Soli Forming Studies]. LED, 1961. E'-a', 7-8*, 16 pp.

Most of the studies in this collection are about one page long, except the first three which are two pages long. They cover a wide variety of styles, and nearly every study covers the entire range of the instrument; these are good characteristic examples of French conservatory writing.

Goudenhooft, André. *Aperçu du trombone-basse double noix* [Survey of the Double-Valve Bass Trombone].

Vol. 1. BILL, 1980. E♭'-a', 1-5, 34 pp.

There are forty-two exercises in this volume, most of which are written on a double staff so they can be played in "duet" style; though many are only octave transpositions, which provide excellent intonation practice, there are a number of good duets for tenor and bass trombone. Two duets are written for two bass trombones (nos. 36 and 39). The author provides useful one- or two-line comments throughout, and he describes the purpose of this volume below:

Since the manufacture of the bass trombone may evolve, the only reason for these exercises is to give the musician a working knowledge permitting him to overcome the difficulties met in the lower register of the repertoire.

Tenor clef is used, but it is primarily used in the tenor trombone parts in this book.

Vol. 2. BILL, 1980. G'-a', 4-6, 29 pp.

This is a continuation of the first volume and includes exercises nos. 43-67. The author's statement as to its purpose follows [the translation was taken from the text]:

The object of this second booklet is to study thoroughly the technique, so, it has to be the most careful to reach a perfect synchronism of the tongue, the valve and the slide.

The skilled instrumentalist must take care not to neglect the musical feeling on behalf of technique only.

It includes thirteen exercises of his own and transcriptions and adaptations of the works of François Duval, Arcangelo Corelli, J. S. Bach (from his *Suites for Violoncello*), Jean-Baptiste Lully, and Friedrich Dotzauer (from his *Studies for Violoncello*). Tenor clef is used more frequently than in Volume 1, and there are only a few comments by the author.

Vol. 3. BILL, 1988. C'-c", 7-8, 42 pp.

Written in two parts, this volume contains thirty arpeggios and variations in the first part and eight various studies in the second. The exercises in part one involve a major and minor arpeggio and a brief scale study for every possible key signature. These are perhaps the most imaginative scale studies available for bass trombone, and they incorporate many modern techniques such as clef changes, complex meters, complex rhythms, extreme ranges, multiphonics, multiple tonguing, and proportional notation. The second part is a set of eight studies (different ones than in Volume 2) by Friedrich Dotzauer (from his *Studies for Violoncello*) and J. S. Bach transcribed for bass trombone; they range from two to five pages in length. These studies use a fair amount of tenor clef.

——. *Vingt-quatre [24] études techniques.* BILL, 1985. C'-a', 5-8, 30 pp.

These are among the lowest technical exercises specifically written for bass trombone available. Many quick register shifts are included, and some attention is given to slurring in and out of the extreme pedal register. There is a moderate amount of tenor clef, and a special marking (an encircled double sharp) is frequently attached to note stems in the place of a note head as an optional place to breathe.

——. *Trente-deux [32] études pour le trombone basse ou le tuba basse.* BILL, 1992. C'(E')-(a♭')c", 7-9, TB, 36 meas.

This book is one of the most outstanding contributions to the study literature for low brass instruments. Virtually every facet of technique is addressed in terms of range, technique, style, and endurance. Most of the etudes cover a range of two and one-half to three octaves with two etudes coming a third shy of four full octaves. Melodic leaps of an octave or more are not uncommon, with several leaps being greater than two octaves and one of two octaves and a perfect fourth (G'-d'). These etudes are written from four flats to five sharps, and there are numerous facets of one's playing that are kept occupied at all times.

Ornaments exist in the form of trills, turns, and mordents, with the composer's suggested execution occasionally given for the latter two. There are only two etudes which include tenor clef: No. 8 (1 meas.) and No. 29 (3 meas.). This is worth mentioning, because the publisher has created a visually awkward passage by adding smaller notes a fourth below with an indication for the tuba to read them in bass clef. Throughout the book there are numerous ossia 8vb passages for the tuba; the highest written note for which the tuba is required to play is an a♭'. The composer suggests various articulations and executions of etude No. 12 below the staff. He uses multiphonics twice (etudes Nos. 4 and 9) for the final chord of the etude—both are at the interval of a major tenth.

This is a superior book which should be in the libraries of all serious professionals and advanced students.

——, ed. *Quinze [15] études complementaires d'après différents auteurs anciens.* BILL, 1983. E'-g♯'/a♭', 4-8, 31 pp.

The book begins with twenty-four two-line scale exercises, one for each chromatic scale degree in major and minor, ranging from four flats to seven sharps. These seem to be an extension of his philosophy that one should not neglect musicality for technique; technique should merely be an extension of one's musicality. These studies are transcribed and adapted from the works of Carl Maria von Weber, Luigi Cherubini, Frédéric Chopin, George Frideric Handel, J. S. Bach, François Joseph Gossec, Friedrich Dotzauer, Marcel Grandjany, Mazas, and Tommaso Albinoni. The first study is also available with a piano realization (see von Weber's *Un adagio* in Chapter 5). The general tessitura is quite low, and some of the extended passages require carefully-planned phrasing and good breath control. There are no comments from the editor, but his markings are generally very fine, and their meanings are usually obvious.

Kreutzer, Rodolphe (1766-1831). *Vingt [20] études*. Edited by Claude Chevaillier. ARP, 1984. F'-g'; 7-9; 37 pp.

(original) "à Monsieur le Comte de Bondy"

Adapted from Kreutzer's *40 études pour violon* (1812), these studies are understandably not very idiomatic for the bass trombone. All studies have been transposed down by either an octave or by multiple octaves. Although the overall range is large, the tessitura is generally very low. The editor gives examples of different articulations and rhythms for many of the exercises, and most of the parts are clean enough so that the performer can further add his own indications. Only these studies from the original forty seem to be of significant use to the bass trombonist, since many of the rest involve double stops or other impractical effects. These studies have been extracted from the original in the sequence displayed below:

Chevaillier	Kreutzer
1	1
2	2
3	3
4	4
5	6
6	7
7	8
8	9
9	12
10	14
11	15
12	18
13	19
14	20
15	22
16	24
17	25
18	26
19	28
20	29

Lafosse, André. *Méthode complète de trombone à coulisse*. LED, 1921 and 1946.

The current edition is published in three volumes. This series is primarily intended for tenor trombone, but these are beneficial for the bass trombonist as a general guide for trombone technique. There is a six-page appendix on the bass trombone, including a brief discussion of the instrument (with only one valve) and a study that includes a variety of styles with a range from F♯'-d'. The earlier edition of this method included over fifty pages of difficult trombone excerpts and over ten more useful studies, but unfortunately these are no longer available. For more information, see entry in Chapter 4.

———. *Traité du pédagogie du trombone à coulisse* [Treatise on Teaching the Slide Trombone]. LED, 1955.

This is a useful guide on teaching trombone, and includes topics of general and specific interest to trombonists. There is a brief history of the instrument that is followed by twenty-five "chapters," each discussing a particular facet of trombone playing and how it is taught. There is one chapter of four paragraphs on the bass trombone (following the chapter on jazz). Many of the items of discussion are cross-referenced to his *Méthode complète* to provide further elaboration on a specific topic. For more information, see entry in Chapter 4.

———. *Vade mecum du tromboniste.* LED, 1956.

Since the Latin *vade mecum* means "go with me," this book is intended to be a guidebook for trombonists. In three parts, the first spells out chords and mostly minor and chromatic scales. The second part is a set of thirty exercises on all major and minor keys with arpeggios. The final part is a series of twenty-five studies, each covering the specific style indicated at the beginning; the last four are arranged from Franz Schubert, Giuseppe Tartini, Antonio Vivaldi, and J. S. Bach. Though it is mostly useful for tenor trombonists, the range of these studies lies generally within the feasible range of the bass trombone. The overall range of the studies in Part III is E-d", and they are primarily in tenor clef; they would make excellent studies for reading tenor clef down one octave. For more information, see entry in Chapter 4.

Lelong, F. *Spécial souplesse et gammes pour saxhorn basse B♭ et tubas ténor et basse (pour tous les degrés)* [Special Flexibilities and Scales]. LED. 2 vols.

———. *Traité des gammes d'après G. Balay.* LED. 2 vols.

Pichaureau, Claude, and **Gérard Pichaureau**. *Vingt [20] études atonales pour trombone ténor, simple ou complet.* LED, 1972. A'-d", 4-8*, 16 pp.

These studies provide a fine introduction into contemporary music. Although written for tenor trombone, many of these exercises extend into the valve register, and several include low (B')'s. Some of the techniques covered include clef changes, complex meters, large interval shifts, mutes, proportional notation, and quarter tones. The constant shifting and/or lack of tonality provides excellent intonation training as well. Although the range above identifies the overall notated range, there are also indications for highest and lowest notes possible.

Pichaureau, Gérard. *Spécial legato: Vingt-quatre [24] études pour le trombone ténor (simple et complet).* LED, 1978. B♭'-d"; 4-6*; 22 pp.

The composer describes this book's intended purpose in the preface:

> The aim of this book is to keep the player "in form" through the suppleness of lip, of tongue and of arm. It is directed to trombonists already in possession of the technical fundamentals of "LEGATO."

These *24 Studies* are not arranged in a progressive order of difficulty; they can be used in any order that suits the requirement and wish of the player. There is a wide variety of keys and meters in these studies, there are many large slurred intervals, and tenor clef is used as frequently as bass clef. There are occasional indications for tenor trombone to play an octave higher, taking the range up to e♭".

———. *Trente études dans tous les tons pour trombone basse, transcrites et adaptées des "30 études pour trombone"* [30 Studies in Every Key for Bass Trombone, Transcribed and Adapted from the "30 Studies for Trombone"]. Edited by Jean-Claude Barbez. LED, 1963 and 1988. D'-a♯'/b♭'; 8*, 30 pp.

This edition makes many of these useful exercises accessible by bass trombonists. Several studies make use of quotes from the symphonic literature. The techniques required include complex meters, double and triple tonguing, glissandos, inverted mordents, trills, and turns. Many of the tempos have been adjusted slightly in both directions, and there is a limited use of tenor clef. The first twenty-eight exercises have been transposed down a perfect fifth, and the last two down a doubly diminished octave. The sequence of studies has been altered from the original and is displayed below:

Barbez	Pichaureau
1	17
2	18
3	15
4	16
5	1
6	2
7	3
8	4
9	5
10	6
11	7
12	8
13	9
14	10
15	11
16	12
17	19
18	20
19	21
20	22
21	23
22	24
23	25
24	26
25	27
26	28
27	29
28	30
29	13
30	14

Poullot. *Préambule, initiation aux saxhorns basse et contrebasse si♭ et tuba en ut "français" à six pistons*. 1-5*. 3 vols.

Rieunier, Françoise. *Vingt-deux déchiffrages rythmiques instrumentaux pour tous les instruments* [22 Rhythmic Instrumental Sight-reading Exercises for All Instruments]. LED, 1972. 7-9, 15 pp.

See entry in Chapter 4.

Rys, Gilbert. *Cinquante [50] études de perfectionnement pour tuba basse en fa, tuba contrebasse en si♭ ou ut, et tuba en ut "français"* [50 Finishing Studies]. LED, 1983. A"-g', 7*, 25 pp.

Each of these studies is one-half page in length, and nearly every facet of style and technique is addressed. They range from six flats to four sharps, and all would work well on bass trombone. Much facility will be needed for the extremely low passages, and several passages are quite awkward.

——. *Cinquante [50] études faciles pour tuba basse en fa, tuba contrebasse en si♭ ou ut, et tuba en ut "français"* [50 Easy Studies]. LED, 1983. E'(F♯')-a, 2-4*, 33 pp.

Each study is between one-half to one page in length and covers a wide range of styles. Because the tessitura is generally below the bass clef staff and the degree of difficulty is low, these studies would be appropriate for bass trombonists who switch from tenor either in high school or early in college. A good control of the airstream is required, and some of the phrases will be taxing if played correctly. The print is not always perfectly clear, but all the notes are legible.

——. *Cinquante [50] études progressives pour basse si♭ ou tuba ut*. MAR, 1981. D-e', 2-4, 16 pp.

Each of these studies is from three to five lines in length, and the tessitura is generally in the bass clef staff. These well-marked pieces cover a variety of styles, articulations, and dynamic contrasts. François Poullot, a colleague of Mr. Rys, gives the following endorsement in the cover of the volume:

> Done very rarely, these "50 études progressives" are written for young tubists by an eminent specialist.
>
> We congratulate Monsieur Gilbert Rys for his initiative; this work fortunately comes to complete the literature destined for the first cycle of studies for the instrument.

The quality of these studies is on the highest level; each is musically rewarding and has material to maintain a young player's interest. The musical benefit of these studies is worthy of attention.

Senon, Gilles. *Kaléïdoscope: Trente-deux petits textes en tout genre* [Kaleidoscope: 32 Short Themes in Every Style]. 3 vols. BILL, 1984.

Toulon, Jacques. *Basiques pour le trombone complet ou basse fa et mi* [Basics for Tenor-Bass Trombone or Bass Trombone in F and E].

Basique I: Initiation [Introduction]. LED, 1976. G'-g♯'/a♭', 3-4*, 28 pp.

There are seventeen exercises in this volume (some with written-out variations, others with suggested variations), and each is prefaced with a brief comment addressing its purpose. The slide positions are indicated with Roman numerals when the valve is engaged, and the standard positions are indicated by Arabic numerals. Each study is clearly marked with the specific valve to be used, and subsequent changes are also clearly marked; most exercises are designed for only one specific valve or tuning. There are many scales and arpeggios, and tenor clef is used moderately. Although intended for instruments tuned in F and E, this method contains studies usable with all configurations of the bass trombone.

Basique II: Technique générale. LED, 1978. B'-b', 4-5*, 14 pp.

The second volume contains twelve studies that focus on developing control of articulations with a secondary goal of improving intonation. Like the first volume, this one contains brief comments addressing each study's intended purpose. Tenor clef is used more than in the first volume.

Basique III: Les tonalités. LED, 1978. A'-c", 5-7*, 18 pp.

There are nineteen studies in this volume, and, either through variation or modulation, nearly every major and minor key is addressed. Tessitura is generally in the bass clef staff but gets higher throughout the book. Tenor clef is used about half the time. These studies are good for intonation practice.

Basique IV: Style et nuances [Style and Dynamics]. LED, 1978. F♯'-a', 6-7*, 13 pp.

Although only ten studies are included, virtually every facet of style is addressed. There are many gradual and sudden dynamic changes, and the many tricky rhythmic patterns are excellent for developing precision. Tessitura is generally low, and valve positions are seldom indicated. Tenor clef is used very sparingly. Many of the patterns in each study are sequential. There is a comment only for the first study, and most of the studies have only a tempo indication at the beginning. These studies are markedly more advanced than those in the previous volumes.

———. *Dix études pour le trombone basse fa et ré d'apres «Être ou ne pas être!» d'Henri Tomasi pour trombone basse ou tuba et trois trombones ou pour trombone basse ou tuba et piano* [10 Studies for Bass Trombone in F and D after "To Be or Not To Be!" by Henri Tomasi]. LED, 1980. B♭"-a', 5-7*, 29 pp.

These studies are designed for developing facility in and out of the valve range of the bass trombone. The composer uses a rather busy system to indicate slide positions: the open positions are indicated with Arabic numerals, and the F and D valve positions are indicated by Roman numerals plus the letter for the specific valve (e.g., third position, D valve = III D). A series of eight preliminary exercises discusses this system in detail, and the first two studies use them regularly; they are not used in subsequent studies. Performance techniques covered include intervals, articulation, broad sound, light sound, legato, staccato, very sustained sound, extreme contrasts, and wide leaps. These all lead to the final study on style that combines all these techniques in a contemporary setting.

Vieulou, E. *Études charactéristiques pour basse à 4, 5, et 6 pistons.* GRAS, 1939; LED, 1988. F'-c", GTB, 7-9, 32 pp.

There are eighty studies in nearly every possible key in this collection. They change between bass, tenor, and treble clefs frequently; the treble clef should be read down one octave. One confusing indication in the GRAS edition suggests the range goes up to a"', which is above the range of most trumpet players! These studies are very technical in nature, and many are not idiomatic for bass trombone. They are useful in shifting quickly between extreme ranges and for quick clef changes.

Appendix A
Publishers' Codes and Addresses

All publishers found in this book are listed here. Those which do not have a code are believed to be out of business. The listing is alphabetical by code; if no code is given, a dash (——) is used as a placeholder and the publisher's name is alphabetized.

AM	Amphion Éditions Musicales 5, rue Jean Ferrand 75006 Paris, France
——	Éditions Andrieu
ARP	International Music Diffusion Arpèges 24, rue Etex 75018 Paris, France
AS	Associated Music Publishers (c/o LEO)
BARO	M. Baron Company PO Box 149 South Road Oyster Bay, NY 11771 (USA)
BEL	CCP/Belwin, Inc. 15800 NW 48th Avenue Hialeah, FL 33014 (USA)
——	Big Hill Music Press
BILL	Gérard Billaudot, Éditeur 14, rue de l'Échiquier 75010 Paris, France
——	Le Chant du Monde
CHO	Éditions Choudens 38, rue Jean Mermoz 75008 Paris, France
COM	Éditions Marcel Combre (formerly Éditions Philippo) 24, boulevard Poissonnière 75009 Paris, France
——	Cundy-Bettoney Company, Inc. (many works still available through FISC)
DEL	Georges Delrieu & Cie. Nice, France

DUR	Éditions Durand & Cie. 21, rue Vernet 75008 Paris, France
—	Éditions Musicales Andrieu Frères
EDFR	Éditions Françaises de Musique 12, rue Magellan 75008 Paris, France
EDMT	Éditions Musicales Transatlantiques 14, avenue Hoche 75008 Paris, France
—	Éditions Philippo (see COM)
ELKH	Henri Elkan Music Publisher PO Box 7720 FDR Station New York, NY 10150 (USA)
ESC	Éditions Max Eschig 48, rue de Rome 75008 Paris, France
—	Evette et Schaeffer
FISC	Carl Fischer, Inc. 62 Cooper Square New York, NY 10003 (USA)
GERV	Gervan Édition Musicale 352, avenue de la Couronne Brussels, Belgium
—	Girod
GRAS	Éditions Gras 36, rue Pape Carpentier LaFlèche, France
HEU	Éditions Heugel (formerly Heugel et Cie.) 2 bis, rue Vivienne Paris, France
HIN	Hinrichsen Edition 10-12 Baches Street London N1 6DN, England
INT	International Music Company 5 West 37th Street New York, NY 10016
JOB	Société des Éditions Jobert 44, rue de Colisse Paris, France
KING	Robert King Music Sales, Inc. 140 Main Street North Easton, MA 02356 (USA) (KING is the U.S. agent for LED)
KJOS	Neil A. Kjos Music Company 4382 Jutland Drive San Diego, CA 92117 (USA)

LED	Alphonse Leduc Éditions Musicales 175, rue Saint-Honoré 75040 Paris, France
LEM	Henri Lemoine & Cie. 17, rue Pigalle 75009 Paris, France
LEO	Hal Leonard Publishing Corporation 7777 West Bluemont Road PO Box 13819 and 960 East Main Street Milwaukee, WI 53213 (USA) Winona, MN 55987 (USA)
LF	Lino Florenzo 121, rue Barthelemy Delespaul 59000 Lille, France
—	René Margeritat
MAR	Éditions Robert Martin 106, grande-rue de la Coupée 71009 Mâcon Cédex, France
MAU	J. Maurer Éditions Musicales 7, avenue du Verseau Woluwe St. Lambert Brussels 1200, Belgium
MET	Éditions Metropolis Van Ertbornstraße 5 2000, Antwerpen, Belgium
—	Millereau
MOLE	Uitgave Molenaar, N. V. Wormerveer, Holland
—	Auguste O'Kelley
PH	Philharmusica Corporation 234 Fifth Avenue, 3d floor New York, NY 10001 (USA)
PR	Theodore Presser Company Presser Place Bryn Mawr, PA 19010 (USA) (PR is the U.S. agent for BILL)
PROA	Pro Art Publications (c/o BEL)
REIF	ITC/Editions Marc Reift/Macrophon Schwäntenmos 15 CH-8126 Zumikon bei Zurich, Switzerland
RICI	G. Ricordi & C. Milano, Italy
RICP	Éditions Ricordi 3, rue Roquepine Paris, France
RID	Éditions Rideau Rouge 24, rue de Longchamp 75016 Paris, France

RUB	Rubank, Inc. PO Box 69000A 16215 NW 15th Avenue Miami, FL 33169 (USA)
SAL	Éditions Salabert 22, rue Chauchat 75009 Paris, France
SCHF	Schott Frères 300, rue Saint-Jean Brussels, Belgium
SCHG	G. Schirmer, Inc. (distributed by LEO)
SCHL	Schott & Co., Ltd. 48, Great Marlborough Street London, England
SEL	Éditions Selmer 18, rue la Fontaine au Roi 75011 Paris, France
—	Société Éditions Musicales Internationales
SOUT	Southern Music Company P.O. Box 329 San Antonio, TX 78292 (USA)
SYM	Symphony Land 24, rue Utrillo 93370 Montfermeil, France
UE	Universal Edition Vienna, Austria
WAR	Warner Bros. Music 265 Secaucus Road Secaucus, NJ 07094 (USA)

Appendix B
Discography

Recordings are an essential tool for the student to fully learn and comprehend musical works. The interpretations found on these albums are intended to guide the soloist toward a musical performance. The musicianship on these albums provides useful examples of performing techniques, such as phrasing, articulation, intonation, and style, that can serve as excellent role models. Since this discography is only concerned with the works discussed in the previous sections of this text, the complete contents of each album will not be listed. The works are listed in alphabetical order by title; the number preceding each recording is cross-referenced to Chapters 3 and 5. The data pertinent to this discography include (with examples):

Album Title
Le Trombone Français

Primary Performer
Ronald Barron, trombone

Other Personnel
Fredrik Wanger, piano

Manufacturer's Name
Boston Brass

Issue Number and Mono/Stereo/Quadrophonic
BB 1001, stereo

Composer
Roger Boutry

Compositon Title
Cappricio

This data will appear in the format shown below (all works cited):

60. Le Trombone Français

Ronald Barron, trombone
Fredrik Wanger, piano

Boston Brass BB 1001, stereo

José Berghmans. *La Femme à Barbe*, No. 4 of the *Tableaux Forains*
Roger Boutry. *Capriccio.*
Jean-Michel Defaÿ. *Deux Danses.*
Alexandre Guilmant. *Morceau Symphonique, Op. 88.*
Joseph Guy Ropartz. *Pièce en mi bémol mineur.*
Camille Saint-Saëns. *Cavatine, Op. 144.*
Carlos Salzédo. *Pièce Concertante, Op. 27.*

1. The Art of Trombone

   Carsten Svanberg, trombone
   Valeria Zanini, piano

   Danica Records DLP 8071

   Camille Saint-Saëns. *Cavatine, Op. 144.*
   Jules Semler-Collery. *Fantaisie Lyrique.*

2. The Art of Trombonist Mikio Wada

   Mikio Wada, trombone
   Nobuyuki Hirose, piano
   Kuniko Wada, organ

   Pro Arte Musicae PAM-CD-PT 1005

   Eugène Bozza. *Ballade.*
   Alexandre Guilmant—Klemens Schnorr. *Morceau Symphonique, Op. 88.* [trombone and organ]

3. Boboissimo! The Best of Roger Bobo

   Roger Bobo, tuba

   Crystal Records CD125, stereo
   [re-issue of S125 and most of S392]

   Joseph Edouard Barat. *Introduction et Danse.*

4. The Brass Amuse Themselves

   Musical Heritage Society MHS 3753, stereo
   (rerelease of ERATO STU 70959, stereo)

   Georges Barboteu, horn
   Marcel Lagorce, trumpet
   Bernard Jeannoutot, trumpet
   Camille Verdier, trombone
   Elie Reynaud, tuba

   Georges Barboteu. *Divertissement.*

5. The Burlesque Trombone

   Christian Lindberg, trombone
   Roland Pöntinen, piano

   BIS LP-318 and CD-318

   Jacques Castérède. *Sonatine.*
   Jean-Michel Defaye. *Deux Danses.*
   Henri Dutilleux. *Choral, Cadence et Fugato.*

6. Christopher Torgé—Trombone

   Christopher Torgé, trombone
   Hans Fagius, organ

   BIS LP-138, stereo

   Richard de Guide. *Suite: "Les Caractères du Trombone."*

7. College Band Directors National Association—Fifteenth National Conference—1969

   Raymond G. Young, euphonium
   The University of Southern Mississippi Symphonic Band
   Alan Drake, conductor

   J. Ed. Barat—Joe Berryman. *Pièce in Mi Bémol.*

8. Concertos pour Trombone

   Branimir Slokar, trombone
   Orchestre de Chambre de Lausanne
   Jean-Marie Auberson, conductor

   Claves D 8407 (digital - DMM)

   Frank Martin. *Ballade.*
   Henri Tomasi. *Concerto.*

9. Concertos, Volume II

   Armin Rosin, trombone
   Wiener Kammerorchester
   Philippe Entremont, director

   Telefunken 6.42532AW, stereo

   Christian Gouinguene. *Concerto.*

10. Concert Works and Orchestral Excerpts from Wagner, Berlioz, Mahler and More!

    The Chicago Symphony Trombone and Tuba Sections
    Jay Friedman, solo trombone, tenor tuba
    James Gilbertsen, assistant first trombone
    Frank Crisafulli, second trombone
    Edward Kleinhammer, bass trombone
    Arnold Jacobs, tuba

    Educational Brass Recordongs EBR 1000, stereo

    Henri Tomasi. *Être ou ne pas être!: Monologue d'Hamlet.* (Arnold Jacobs, soloist)

11. Contrasts

    Stanley Clark, trombone
    Avis Romm, piano

    EBS 6023 DDD

    Eugène Bozza. *Ballade.*
    Jacques Castérède. *Sonatine.*
    Frank Martin. *Ballade.*

12. (no title)

    Davis Shuman, trombone
    Leonid Hambro, piano

    Golden Crest Records Recital Series RE 7011, stereo

    Frank Martin. *Ballade* (1940).

13. Dennis Smith, The Virtuoso Trombonist

Dennis Snith, trombone

T. and A. Recordings

Eugène Bozza. *Ballade.*

14. Donald Knaub—bass trombone, Barry Snyder—piano

Golden Crest Records Recital Series RE 7040, stereo

Jules Semler-Collery. *Barcarolle et Chanson Bachique.*

15. Donald Knaub—bass trombone, Barry Snyder—piano

Golden Crest Records Recital Series RE 7070, stereo

Jean-Michel Defaye. *Deux Danses* (adapted for bass trombone by Donald Knaub).

16. Euphonium Recital

Raymond G. Young, euphonium
Mrs. Raymond Young, piano

Raymond G. Young—personally released recording
Century 17647 (?), stereo

J. Ed. Barat. *Introduction et Danse.*
J. Ed. Barat. *Andante et Scherzo [Andante et Allegro?].*
Paul V. de la Nux. *Solo de Concours.*
Joseph Guy Ropartz. *Andante and Allegro.*

17. Euphonium Solos

Fred M. Dart, euphonium
Gertrude Kuehefuhs, piano

OMEA Contest List Recordings
Coronet Recording Company COR 1054
(SR4M-7275/7276), mono

Alexandre Guilmant. *Morceau Symphonique, Op. 88.*
Jules Semler-Collery. *Barcarolle et Chanson Bachique.*

18. Euphonium Solos

Paul Droste, euphonium
Anne Droste, piano

Coronet LPS 3026, stereo

Jacques Castérède. *Fantaisie Concertante.*

19. Fantastic

Armin Bachmann, bass trombone
Wolfgang Wagenhauser, piano

Macrophon CD 892 CD-DDD

Eugène Bozza. *Prélude et Allegro.*

20. Festliche Musik für Trompete, Posaune, Orgel

    Sebastian Krol, trombone
    Ludger Lohmann, organ

    Audite FSM 63404, stereo (1981)

    Roger Boutry. *Choral varié.*

21. First Four Encores, Volume I

    Henry Charles Smith, trombone
    Philadelphia Orchestra
    Eugene Ormandy, conductor

    Alexandre Guilmant. *Morceau Symphonique, Op. 88.*

22. Frank Martin

    Armin Rosin, trombone
    Chamber Orchestra of Lausanne
    Frank Martin, conductor

    Ballade for Trombone and Orchestra (1940).

23. Graduate Trombone Quartet

    University [of Illinois] Brass Recordings, Vol. 1

    G. David Peters, tenor trombone
    Larry Dwyer, tenor trombone
    Neale Bartee, tenor trombone
    Robert L. Kidd III, bass trombone

    Henri Tomasi. *Être ou ne pas être!: Monologue d'Hamlet.*

24. Jean Douay, Trombone et Orgue

    Jean Douay, trombone
    Chalo Saint-Mars, orgue

    Corelia CC78030, stereo

    Christian Gouinguene. *Concerto.*
    Giles Senon. *Prière.*

25. John Kitzman, Trombone

    John Kitzman, trombone
    Janice Kay Hodges, piano

    Crystal Records S386, stereo

    Jean-Michel Defaye. *Deux Danses.*

26. Leningrad Trombone Quartet

    Alexej Evtushenko, bass trombone
    Melodia CM 04239-40

    Henri Tomasi. *Être ou ne pas être!: Monologue d'Hamlet.*

27. Leonard Falcone and His Baritone

    Leonard Falcone, euphonium
    Joseph Evans, piano

Golden Crest Records Recital Series RE 7001, mono

Alexandre Guilmant. *Morceau Symphonique, Op. 88.*

28. Leonard Falcone, Baritone, Volume III

Leonard Falcone, euphonium
Joseph Evans, piano

Goldcn Crest Records Recital Serles RE 7036, stereo

J. Ed. Barat. *Andante et Allegro.*
Eugène Cools. *Allegro de Concert.*
Paul V. de la Nux. *Solo de Concours.*

29. A Little Trombone Music

John Swallow, trombone
Gunther Schuller, conductor

G. M. Recordings G.M. 2009

Darius Milhaud. *Concertino d'Hiver.*

30. The Lyric Trombone

Richard L. Cryder, trombone
Jane Cryder, piano

Richard L. Cryder—Lawrence, Kansas/
Potsdam, New York LT 1001, stereo

J. Ed. Barat. *Andante et Allegro.*
Alexandre Guilmant. *Morceau Symphonique, Op. 88.*
Florentin Morel. *Pièce en fa mineur.*
Samuel Rousseau. *Pièce Concertante.*

31. Michigan State University Trombone Quartet

stereo cassette tape recording

Curtis Olson, bass trombone

Henri Tomasi. *Être ou ne pas être!: Monologue d'Hamlet.*

32. Midwest National Band and Orchestra Clinic—1972

Michel Peterson, trombone
Elbow Lake-Wendell High School Band, Elbow Lake, MN
Justin Swenson, comments
James D. Ployhar, Justin Swenson, Theodore W. Thorson, guest conductors
Gordon Peterson, conductor

Silver Crest Records MID-72-9, stereo/quadrophonic

A. Guilmant—W. Shephard. *Morceau Symphonique, Op. 88.*

33. Miles Anderson Plays His Slide Trombone Again

Miles Anderson, trombone
Uriko Baley, piano
Los Angeles Trombone Ensemble

Crystal Records S385, stereo

Jacques Castérède. *Sonatine* (1958).
Charles Chaynes. *Impulsions* (1971).
Jean-Michel Defaye. *Deux Danses* (1954).
Carlos Salzédo. *Pièce Concertante* (1958).

34. Milhaud—The Four Seasons

Maurice Suzan, trombone
Ensemble of the Concerts Lamaureux
Darius Milhaud, conductor

Epic LC 3666, mono
Epic BC 1069, stereo
Philips 6504-111, stereo

Darius Milhaud. *Concertino d'Hiver.*

35. Music at SFA

J. Mark Thompson, bass trombone
Jan McDaniel, piano

Stephen F. Austin State University SFA 1002 (CD), stereo

Jacques Castérède. *Sonatine.* [tuba] (1st and 2d mvts.)

36. Music Educators National Conference—1970 Convention

Earle L. Louder, euphonium
Holmes High School Band

Crest Records 70MENC6

Alexandre Guilmant. *Morceau Symphonique, Op. 88.*

37. Music for Trombone and Piano

Carl Christensen, trombone
Robert Nelson, piano

Coronet LPS 3111

Camille Saint-Saëns. *Cavatine, Op. 144.*

38. Music for Trombone and Piano—Music Minus One—Laureate Series Contest Solos—Advanced Level

Keith Brown, trombone
Harriet Wingreen, piano

Music Minus One MMO 8055, stereo

Alexandre Guilmant. *Morceau Symphonique, Op. 88.*
Julien Porret. *Esquisse No. 1.*
Julien Porret. *Esquisse No. 2.*

39. Music for Trombone and Piano—Music Minus One—Laureate Series Contest Solos—Advanced Level

Keith Brown, trombone
Harriet Wingreen, piano

Music Minus One MMO 8057, stereo

B. Croce-Spinelli. *Solo de Concours.*

40. Music for Trombone and Piano—Music Minus One—Laureate Series
Contest Solos—Advanced Level

Jay Friedman, trombone
Harriet Wingreen, piano

Music Minus One MMO 8058, stereo

Paul V. de la Nux. *Solo de Concours.*
Samuel Rousseau. *Pièce Concertante.*

41. Music for Trombone and Piano—Music Minus One—Laureate Series
Contest Solos—Advanced Level

Per Brevig, trombone
Judith Olson, piano

Music Minus One MMO 8059, stereo

J. Ed. Barat. *Andante et Allegro.*

42. Ralph Sauer Plays Music for Trombone by Milhaud, Persichetti, Bassett and Pergolesi.

Ralph Sauer, trombone
Alan de Veritch, viola
Paul Pitman, piano

Crystal Records S381, stereo

Darius Milhaud. *Concertino d'Hiver.*

43. Raymond G. Young, Baritone Horn

Raymond G. Young, euphonium
Tom Fraschillo, piano

Golden Crest Records Recital Series RE 7025, stereo

J. Ed. Barat. *Andante et Allegro.*
Florentin Morel. *Pièce en fa mineur.*

44. Recital

Alain Trudel, trombone
Guy Few, piano

Société Nouvelle D'Enregistrement SNE-563-CD

Henri Dutilleux. *Choral, Cadence et Fugato.*

45. A Recital for Trombone

Robert Gillespie, trombone
Judith Olson, piano

MACE MCS 9112, stereo

Jacques Castérède. *Sonatine.*

46. Recital Music for Trombone

Richard Fote, trombone
Brian Dykstra, piano
Gail Davis Fote, piano

Mark Educational Recordings, Inc./
Mark Custom Records MRS 28250, stereo

J. Ed. Barat. *Andante et Allegro.*
Alexandre Guilmant. *Morceau Symphonique, Op. 88.*

47. Recital Music for Tuba

Mark Educational Recordings MRS 28437, stereo

Peter Popiel, tuba

Jules Semler-Collery. *Barcarolle et Chanson Bachique.*

48. Roger Behrend, Euphonium

Roger Behrend, euphonium
Richard A. Donn, piano

Coronet Recording Company COR-400-0

J. Ed. Barat. *Morceau de Concours.*

49. Roger Bobo and Tuba

Crystal Records S125, stereo

Joseph Edouard Barat. *Introduction et Danse.*

50. The Romantic Trombone

Christian Lindberg, trombone
Roland Pöntinen, piano

Grammofon AB BIS LP-298 and CD-298

Philippe Gaubert. *Morceau Symphonique.*
Joseph Guy Ropartz. *Pièce en mi bèmol mineur.*
Camille Saint-Saëns. *Cavatine, Op. 144.*
Sigismond Stojowski. *Fantaisie, Op. 27.*

51. Romantic Trombone Concertos

Christian Lindberg, trombone
Bamberger Symphoniker
Leif Segerstam, conductor

BIS LP-378 and CD-378

Alexandre Guilmant. *Morceau Symphonique, Op. 88.*

52. Slide Area

Joseph Alessi, trombone
Jonathan Feldman, piano

Jean-Michel Defaye. *Deux Danses.*

53. Solo Pro Series—Contest Music for Trombone

Thomas Ashworth, trombone
Theodor Lichtmann, piano

Summit Records DCD 105 cassette

Paul V. de la Nux. *Concertpiece.*

54. Spotlight on Brass

Josef Orosz, tenor trombone
Notes by R. D. Darrell
Illustrated booklet by R. D. Darrell
Produced by Ward Botsford

(This album also contains demonstrations of other brass instruments such as alto and bass trombones, baritone horn, euphonium, serpent, cornett, horn, trumpet, cornet, and tuba.)

Vox DL 300, mono

Anonymous—Paul Delisse. *Tyrolean Air.*

55. Spotlight on Winds and Brass

Josef Orosz, tenor trombone

Notes by R. D. Darrell
Illustrated booklet by R. D. Darrell
Produced by Ward Botsford

(This album also contains a simllar demonstration of historical and recent wind instruments and other brass instruments.)

Vox PLS 2, mono

Anonymous—Paul Delisse. *Tyrolean Air.*

56. Stewart Sounds

M. Dee Stewart, trombone, bass trombone, euphonium
Diane Birr, piano

Houston Publishing CD 2

Jacques Castérède. *Fantaisie Concertante.* [bass trombone]
Henri Tomasi. *Danse Sacrée.* [euphonium]

57. Trombone and Organ

Abbie Conant, trombone
Klemens Schnorr, organ

Audite 368.410 CD-DDD, 68.410 LP, and 268.410 cassette

Alexandre Guilmant—Klemens Schnorr. *Morceau Symphonique, Op. 88.*

58. Trombone and Piano

Gilles Milliere, trombone
Camille Merlin, piano

NUM 48012 (France)

Claude Arrieu. *Mouvements.*
Eugène Bigot. *Impromptu.*
Henri Dutilleux. *Choral, Cadence et Fugato.*
Odette Gartenlaub. *Improvisation pour Trombone.*
Alexandre Guilmant. *Pièce de Concert.*
Samuel Rousseau. *Pièce Concertante.*

59. Le Trombone Contemporaine

Benny Sluchin, trombone
Pierre-Laurent Aimard, piano

ADDA 581087

Henri Dutilleux. *Choral, Cadence et Fugato.*

60. Le Trombone Français

Ronald Barron, trombone
Fredrik Wanger, piano

Boston Brass BB 1001, stereo

José Berghmans. *La Femme à Barbe*, No. 4 of the *Tableaux Forains*
Roger Boutry. *Capriccio.*
Jean-Michel Defaÿ. *Deux Danses.*
Alexandre Guilmant. *Morceau Symphonique, Op. 88.*
Joseph Guy Ropartz. *Pièce en mi bémol mineur.*
Camille Saint-Saëns. *Cavatine, Op. 144.*
Carlos Salzédo. *Pièce Concertante, Op. 27.*

61. Trombone Odyssey—20th Century Landmarks for Tormbone and Orchestra

Christian Lindberg, trombone
Swedish Radio Symphony
Leif Segerstam, conductor

BIS CD-538

Frank Martin. *Ballade.*

62. Trombone—Organ and Piano

Carsten Svanberg, trombone
Birgit Marcussen, organ

EMI (Electric and Musical Industries) Parlophone MOAK 37, stereo

Jules Demersseman. *Cavatine, Op. 47.*
Alexandre Guilmant. *Morceau Symphonique, Op. 88.*

63. Trombone Solos

Alan Raph, bass trombone
R. Byron Griest, piano

Coronet Recording Company COR 1407 (W4RS-3107/3108), stereo

Eugène Bigot. *Impromptu* for [Tenor] Trombone and Piano.

64. Trombone Solos

William Shepherd, trombone
Lima (OH) Symphony Orchestra
J. Firszt, conductor

Coronet Recording Company COR 3001, stereo

Eugène Bozza. *Ballade, Op. 62.*
Carlos Salzédo—Anonymous. *Pièce Concertante, Op. 27* (arrangement for orchestra).

65. The Trombone, Volume I (Demonstrating Selmer Trombones)

Gabriel Masson, trombone
Serge Baudo, piano
Jean-Michel Defaÿ, piano

London LS 989, mono

Serge Baudo. *Petite Suite pour Trombone.*
Jean-Michel Defaÿ. *Deux Danses.*

66. Tuba Tracks

Gene Pokorny, tuba

Summit Records DCD 129

Jacques Castérède. *Sonatine* (2d mvt.).

67. The Versatile Trombonist

Robert Reifsnyder, trombone and euphonium
Karl Paulnack, piano and harpsichord

Five Oaks Recordings KM 14385

Henri Dutilleux. *Choral, Cadence et Fugato.*
Jacques Castérède. *Fantaisie Concertante.*

68. Victor Venglovskii, Trombone

Victor Venglovskii, trombone
T. Venglovskaia, piano

Melodia CM 01921-22 (USSR)

Henri Dutilleux. *Choral, Cadence et Fugato.*
Eugène Bozza. *Ballade, Op. 62.*
Marcel Poot. *Impromptu.*

69. (no title)

Victor Venglovsky, trombone
Leningrad Chamber Orchestra
Lazar Gozman, conductor

Westminster Gold WGS 8336, stereo

Darius Milhaud. *Concertino d'Hiver.*

70. Virtuose Kammermusik

Armin Rosin, trombone
David Levine, piano

Telefunken 6.42828 AP, stereo

Camille Saint-Saëns. *Cavatine, Op. 144.*
Sigismond Stojowski. *Fantaisie, Op. 27.*

71. The Virtuoso Trombone

Christian Lindberg, trombone
Roland Pöntinen, piano

Grammofon AB BIS LP-258 and CD-258
Musical Heritage Society MHS 7330Z (cassette, MHC 9330A)

Frank Martin. *Ballade.*

72. The Virtuoso Trombonist

Dennis Smith, trombone
Western Washington State College Wind Ensemble
William Cole, conductor

Pandora Records PAN 2001, stereo

Eugène Bozza—E. L. Barrow. *Ballade, Op. 62* (trans. for band).

73. The Winter Trombone

Christian Lindberg, trombone
New Stockholm Chamber Orchestra
Okko Kamu, conductor

BIS CD-348

Darius Milhaud. *Concertino d'Hiver.*

Appendix C

Listing of Solos by Title

This listing is provided to serve as an aid to those who only know the title of a particular work but do not know the composer's name. The chapter in which the complete citation is given is listed at the right. Works identified with a double dagger (‡) have large ensemble accompaniments available.

TITLE	COMPOSER	CH
Abuto	Delgiudice, Michel	5
Acclamation concertino	Bleuse, Marc	3
Un adagio	Weber, C. M.—Goudenhooft	5
Aerème	Tournier, Franz	3
Air de pharaon dans "Moïse"	Rossini, Gioacchino—Signard	3
Air du saqueboutier	Gouinguene, Christian	3
Air et final	Planel, Robert	5
Air noble	Robert, Jacques	3
À la manière de Bach	Defaye, Jean-Michel	3
Ali-baba	Delgiudice, Michel	5
Allegretto comodo	Quérat, Marcel	5
Allegro	Weber, Alain	3
Allegro de concert, Op. 81	Cools, Eugène	3
Allegro et finale	Bozza, Eugène	5
À Longchamp, Op. 117	Dorsselaer, Willy van	3
Ambiances	Senon, Gilles	3
Anapausis (ΑΝΑΠΑΥΣΙΣ)	Meunier, Gérard	5
Andante	Cohen, Jules	3
Andante	Dhaene	3
Andante	Leduc, Simon—Goudenhooft	5
Andante dans un style classique	Bessonet, Georges	3
Andante et allegro	Barat, Joseph Edouard	3
Andante et allegro	Barraine, Elsa	5
Andante et allegro	Lantier, Pierre	5
Andante et allegro	Mignion, René	3
Andante et allegro	Ropartz, J. Guy	3
L'antre de Polypheme	Delgiudice, Michel	5
Après une lecture de Goldoni	Margoni, Alain	5
Aria	Coriolis, Emmanuel de	3
Aria	Gallois-Montbrun, Raymond	3
Aria	Vallier, Jacques	3
Aria, scherzo et finale	Aubain, Jean Marie	3
Au temps de la cour	Brouquières, Jean	5
Automne	Damase, Jean-Michel	5
Avenue Washington	Sichler, J.	3
‡Ballade, Op. 62	Bozza, Eugène	3

TITLE	COMPOSER	CH
Ballade	Destanque and Larguèze	3
Ballade	Maillard, A.	3
‡Ballade	Martin, Frank	3
Ballet pour un kangourou	Fiche, Michel	3
Barcarolle et chanson bachique	Semler-Collery, Jules	5
Bassutecy	Amellér, André	5
Batifol	Amellér, André	5
Belle province: Hauterive	Amellér, André	5
Belle province: Rivière du loup	Amellér, André	3
Blues, reflets et cabriolets	Senon, Gilles	3
Bourrée	Damase, Jean-Michel	5
Bras d'acier	Amellér, André	3
Bravaccio	Fayeulle, Roger	5
Burlesque	Rivière, Jean-Pierre	3
Campagnarde	Lodéon, André	5
Cantabile et caprice	Dondeyne, Désiré	3
Cantabile et divertissement	Semler-Collery, Jules	5
Cantabile et minuetto	Mignion, René	3
Cantabile et scherzando, Op. 51	Büsser, Henri	3
Cantabile et scherzetto	Gaubert, Philippe	3
Cantilène et baladine	Senon, Gilles	3
Canzone	Bon, André	3
Capriccio	Bonneau, Paul	3
Capriccio	Boutry, Roger	3
Capriccioso brilliant, Op. 22	Mendelssohn, Felix—Delisse	3
Caprice médiéval	Barat, Joseph Edouard	3
Capricorne	Sendrez, M.	3
Carillon et bourdon	Bigot, Eugène	5
Cavatine, Op. 47	Demersseman, Jules	3
Cavatine, Op. 144	Saint-Saëns, Camille	3
Ce que chantait l'æde	Depelsenaire, Jean-Marie	3
Chanson d'août	Séguin, Pierre	3
Chanson d'autrefois	Bouny, Jean-Pierre	3
Chanson de Blondel	Joubert, Claude-Henry	3
Des chansons dans la coulisse	Desportes, Yvonne	3
Chant d'amour	Clérisse, Robert	5
Chant et danse	Bondon, Jacques	3
Chevauchée	Senon, Gilles	3
Chiens de paille	Barraine, Elsa	5
Choral, cadence et fugato	Dutilleux, Henri	3
Choral, canon I et II	Reichel, Bernard	3
Choral varié	Boutry, Roger	3
Choral varié	Denisov, Edison	3
Choral varié	Lamy, Fernand	3
Ciaccona	Bozza, Eugène	3
Cinc concerti "minute"	Pichaureau, Claude	3
Cinc études (w/pf acc)	Dondeyne, Désiré	5
Cinc "pièces courtes"	Dondeyne, Désiré	5
Cocktail	Lys, Marc	3
Collection enfants—Décidé	Toulon, Jacques	3
Collection enfants—Enfant de chœur	Toulon, Jacques	3

TITLE	COMPOSER	CH
Collection enfants—Gai	Toulon, Jacques	3
Collection enfants—Rêveur	Toulon, Jacques	3
Collection enfants—Triste	Toulon, Jacques	3
Comme un air d'opera	Bessonet, Georges	3
Comme un souvenir	Roizenblatt, A.	3
Complainte	Gabaye, Pierre	3
‡Concertino	Berghmans, José	3
‡Concertino	Bozza, Eugène	5
Concertino	Daucé, Edouard	5
Concertino	Leclercq, Edgard	3
‡Concertino	Rasse, François	3
‡Concertino	Spisak, Michel	3
‡Concertino d'hiver	Milhaud, Darius	3
Concertino No. 7	Porret, Julien	3
Concertino No. 8	Porret, Julien	3
Concertino No. 10	Porret, Julien	3
Concertino No. 23	Porret, Julien	3
Concertino No. 24	Porret, Julien	3
Concertino, Op. 6	Muller, J. P.	3
Concerto	Boutry, Roger	3
‡Concerto	Defaye, Jean-Michel	3
Concerto	Defossez, René	3
Concerto	Delerue, Georges	3
Concerto	Gotkovsky, Ida	3
Concerto	Gouinguene, Christian	3
‡Concerto	Tomasi, Henri	3
‡Concerto	Weber, Alain	3
‡Concerto dit "l'Irrespecteux"	Dubois, Pierre Max	3
Concerto en fa mineur	Handel, G. F.—Lafosse	3
Concerto "Gli elementi"	Constant, Marius	3
Concerto in si-bémol	Vivaldi, Antonio—Thilde	3
Concerto minute, Op. 4	Muller, J. P.	3
Concertstück	Murgier, Jacques	5
Concertstück	Rueff, Jeanine	5
Confidence	Séguin, Pierre	3
Contacts	Zbar, Michel	3
Conte d'hiver	Arrieu, Claude	3
Contest Piece	Gédalge, André	3
Cordelineété	Meyer, Jean-Michel	3
Cornemuse	Dubois, Pierre Max	5
Cortège	Beaucamp, Albert	5
Cortège	Bigot, Eugène	5
Cortège	Dubois, Pierre Max	3
Cortège	Séguin, Pierre	5
Cortège et danse	Charles, Claude	5
Couleurs en mouvements	Moreau, James	5
Coulissiana	Dautremer, Marcel	3
Courante	Senallié [Senaillé]—Goudenhooft	5
Crépuscule	Pares, Gabriel	3
Cromagnon	Louvier, Alain	5
Danse de l'éléphant	Delgiudice, Michel	5

TITLE	COMPOSER	CH
‡La danse du Herisson	Dubois, Pierre Max	3
Danse sacrée	Tomasi, Henri	3
Danse villageoise	Beethoven—Goudenhooft	5
Deux ans déjà trombone	Galliègue and Naulais	3
Deux danses	Defaye, Jean-Michel	3
Deux danses	Defaye, Jean-Michel—Knaub	5
Deux interludes	Vachey, Henri	3
Deux marches	Dubois, Pierre Max	3
Deux mouvements contrastés	Devos, Gérard	5
Deux pièces	Gabitchvadzé	3
Deux pièces brèves	Semler-Collery, Jules	5
Dialogue	Durand-Audard, Pierre	5
Dialogue	Murgier, Jacques	5
Dialogue II	Clostre, Andrienne	3
Dialogue du captian et du coucou	Joubert, C. H.	3
Dialogue, Op. 100	Martelli, Henri	5
Diptyque: "Aux statues de Bomarzo"	Boizard, Gilles	5
‡Divertimento	Dondeyne, Désiré	5
Divertissement	Barboteu, Georges	5
Divertissement	Douay and Gouinguene	3
Dix petits textes	Delgiudice, Michel	5
Doubles sur un choral	Duclos, René	3
12 [douze] transcriptions	Delisse, Paul, ed.	3
Ébauche	Dachez, Christian	3
Élégie	Hugon, Georges	3
Élégie I	Lucie, Robert	3
Élégie I	Robert, L.	3
Élégie II	Robert, L.	3
Élégie et burlesque, Op. 32, No. 1	Tisné, Antoine	3
En allant	Toulon and Brouquières	3
En coulisse	Dubois, Pierre Max	3
En glissant...	Lesaffre, Charles	5
En quatre actes	Bosseur, J. Y.	3
L'enterrement de Saint-Jean	Bariller, Robert	5
En vacances	Fiche and Pichaureau	3
Ergies (à Paraitre)	Sciortino, Patrice	3
Eria	Creuze, Roland	5
Essai	Breuil, Helene	3
Essai	Gartenlaub, Odette	5
Essai I	Galliègue, Marcel	3
Essai II	Galliègue, Marcel	3
Essai III	Galliègue, Marcel	3
Essai IV	Galliègue, Marcel	3
Étrange ballad	Dachez	3
Étreinte	Séguin, Pierre	3
Être ou ne pas être!	Tomasi, Henri	5
Étude de concert, Op. 79	Büsser, Henri	3
Étude de concert	Poot, Marcel	3
Étude polyphonique	Reutter, Hermann	3
L'exploit de la coulisse	Desportes, Yvonne	3
Exponentielles	Bernaud, Alain	3

TITLE	COMPOSER	CH
Fanfare, andante et allegro	Franck, Maurice	3
Fantaisie	Dubois, Pierre Max	5
Fantaisie	Maillard, A.	3
Fantaisie	Petit, Pierre	5
Fantaisie	Stojowski, Sigismond	3
Fantaisie	Tamba, Akira	3
Fantaisie	Vallier, Jacques	3
‡Fantaisie concertante	Bonneau, Paul	3
Fantaisie concertante	Castérède, Jacques	5
‡Fantaisie concertante	Villette, Pierre	5
Fantaisie in B♭	Desportes, Yvonne	3
Fantaisie lyrique	Semler-Collery, Jules	3
Fantasia	Boutry, Roger	3
‡La femme à barbe	Berghmans, José	3
Fête à l'abbaye de Theleme	Margoni, Alain	3
Funambules	Depelsenaire, Jean-Marie	5
Gargantua apprend la sacqueboute	Margoni, Alain	3
Le grand duc	Dorsselaer, Willy van	3
Grand solo	Chrétien, Hedwige	3
Grave	Lancen, S.	5
Grave	Petit, Pierre	5
Grave et cantilène	Legron, Léon	3
Grave et scherzo, Op. 107	Manen, Christian	5
La guerre picrocholine	Margoni, Alain	3
Hans de Schnokeloch	Bariller, Robert	5
La Harangue de Janotus	Ancelin, Pierre	3
Hialmar	Loucheur, Raymond	3
Histoire de trombone	Dubois, Pierre Max	3
Histories de tuba, Vols. 1-4	Dubois, Pierre Max	5
Hommage à Bach	Bozza, Eugène	3
Hommage à V. F. Verrimst	Goudenhooft, André	5
Humoresque	Bernaud, Alain	5
Humoresque, Op. 89	Dewanger, Anton	3
Hydre à cinq têtes	Louvier, Alain	3
Hymne, cadence et danse	Toulon, Jacques	5
Hypnose	Tillet, Louis	3
Idylle	Clérisse, Robert	3
Ignéscence	Tillet, Louis	3
‡Impromptu	Bigot, Eugène	3
Impromptu	Bitsch, Marcel	5
Impromptu	Clergue, Jean	3
Impromptu	Depelsenaire, Jean-Marie	3
Impromptu	Massis, Amable	3
Impromptu	Poot, Marcel	3
Improvisation	Landowski, Marcel	3
Improvisation en forme de canon	Pascal, Claude	3
Improvisation pour Trombone	Gartenlaub, Odette	3
Impulsions	Chaynes, Charles	3
Intermezzo	Bitsch, Marcel	5
Intermezzo	Challan, Henri	5
Introduction et allegro	Hugon, Georges	3

TITLE	COMPOSER	CH
Introduction et allegro	Perrin, Jean	3
Introduction et allegro martial	Dorsselaer, Willy van	3
Introduction et danse	Barat, Joseph Edouard	5
Introduction et polonaise, Op. 30	Demersseman, Jules	3
Introduction et rigaudon	Faillenot, Maurice	5
Introduction et sérénade	Barat, Joseph Edouard	5
Introduction et toccata	Carles, Marc	5
Introduction, romance et allegro	Lantier, Pierre	5
Irish-Cante	Amellér, André	5
Je voulais vous dire	Boudry, G.	3
Jericho	Dorsselaer, Willy van	3
Jeu 3	Zbar, Michel	5
Jeux chromatiques	Depelsenaire, Jean-Marie	5
Kryptos: Étude	Amellér, André	5
Labyrinthes	Marie, Jean-Marie	3
Laes	Sciortino, Patrice	5
Lamento	Barraine, Elsa	3
Largo et toccata	Houdy, Pierick	3
Légende	Beugniot, Jean-Pierre	5
Légende, Op. 64	Délcroix, Léon	3
Légende	Gallet, Jean	3
Légende	Kaï, Naohiko	5
Légende	Niverd, Lucien	3
Légende	Tournemire, Charles	3
Légende celtique	Fievet, Paul	3
Légende nervienne	Depelsenaire, Jean-Marie	3
Libre-episode	Werner, Jean-Jacques	5
Lied	Gotkovsky, Ida	5
Logos	Amellér, André	5
Maestoso et scherzando	Niverd, Raymond	3
Marche et danse	Toulon and Brouquières	3
Marine	Clérisse, Robert	5
Marine	Pichaureau, Claude	3
Marine	Séguin, Pierre	3
Méandres	Lejet, Edith	5
Méditation	Brown, Charles	3
Mélodica	Dachez	3
Mélodie	Senon, Gilles	3
Menuet d'automne	Dubois, Pierre Max	3
Menuet éclaté	Damase, Jean-Michel	5
Menuet pour un ours	Lancen, Serge	3
Morceau de concours	Bachelet, Alfred	3
Morceau de concours	Barat, Joseph Edouard	5
Morceau de concours I	Defaye, Jean-Michel	5
Morceau de concours II	Defaye, Jean-Michel	5
Morceau de concours III	Defaye, Jean-Michel	5
Morceau de concours	Missa, Edmond Jean Louis	3
Morceau symphonique	Gaubert, Philippe	3
‡Morceau symphonique, Op. 88	Guilmant, Alexandre	3
Mouvement	Defaye, Jean-Michel	3
Mouvement	Henry, Jean-Claude	5

TITLE	COMPOSER	CH
Mouvements	Arrieu, Claude	3
Musique	Lejet, Edith	3
New Orleans	Bozza, Eugène	5
Nocturne	Chopin, Frédéric—Delisse	3
Océane et parodie	Senon, Gilles	3
Ohio	Amellér, André	3
Olivet	Amellér, André	3
L'Olympienne	Roche, G.	3
Ostinato	Gouinguene, Christian	3
Ostinato	Reutter, Hermann	3
Les ours	Domrœse, Wilhelm	3
Parcours	Durand, Pierre	3
Par les chemins	Brouquières, Jean	3
Pastorale héroïque	Pascal, Claude	3
Petit air	Poutoire, Patrick	5
Un petit air dans le vent	Desportes, Yvonne	3
Le petit baobab	Delgiudice, Michel	5
Petit chanson pour Marion	Lesaffre, Charles	5
Petite suite	Baudo, Serge	3
Petites inventions	Maurat, Edmond	3
Petit interlude	Dalbavie, Marc-André	5
Le petit mammouth	Delgiudice, Michel	5
Phantasy, Op. 42	Weiner, Stanley	3
Pharaon des mers	Coiteux, F.	3
Phoebus variations, Op. 87	Büsser, Henri	3
‡Piccolo suite	Dubois, Pierre Max	5
Pièce brève	Boutry, Roger	5
Pièce brève	Cals, Michel	5
Pièce concertante	Rousseau, Samuel-Alexandre	3
‡Pièce concertante, Op. 27	Salzédo, Carlos	3
Pièce de concert	Lepetit, Pierre	3
Pièce en fa	Rougeron, Philippe	3
Pièce en fa majeur (Mozart)	Pucci, Alain	3
Pièce en fa mineur	Morel, Florentin	3
Pièce en mi bémol	Barat, Joseph Edouard	3
Pièce en mi bémol, Op. 33	Büsser, Henri	3
‡Pièce en mi bémol mineur	Ropartz, J. Guy	3
Pièce en ré mineur (Haendel)	Pucci, Alain	3
Pièce en si bémol majeur (Brahms)	Pucci, Alain	3
Pièce lyrique	Clérisse, Robert	5
Pièce No. 1	Toulon, Jacques	3
Pièces classiques	Douay, Jean	3
Pièces classiques	Sciortino, Patrice, ed.	3
Plain-chant et allegretto	Désenclos, Alfred	3
Plaisance	Constant, F.	3
Poeme	Clérisse, Robert	3
Pour la promotion	Dorsselaer, Willy van	3
Pour le trombone élémentaire	Dubois, Pierre Max	3
Pour le trombone moyen	Dubois, Pierre Max	3
Pour le trombone préparatoire	Dubois, Pierre Max	3
Pour rire et pleurer	Holstein, J. P.	3

TITLE	COMPOSER	CH
Poursuite	Dachez	3
Prélude	Sendrez, M.	3
Prélude, arioso et rondo	Franck, Maurice	5
Prélude et allegro	Bozza, Eugène	5
Prélude et allegro	Charpentier, Jacques	5
Prélude et cadence	Barboteu, Georges	5
Prélude et danse	Depelsenaire, Jean-Marie	3
Prélude et divertissement	Clérisse, Robert	3
1re [Première] pièce de concours	Porret, Julien	5
Prière	Clérisse, Robert	3
Prière	Rougnon	5
Prière	Senon, Gilles	3
Primo concertino	Nicolas, M.	3
Promenade	Uga, Piérre	5
Quartre piècettes	Coriolis, Emmanuel de	3
Quartre récréations	Coriolis, Emmanuel de	3
Quelques chants, 4 vols.	Galliègue and Dupin	3
Récitatif et petit allegro	Bessonet, Georges	3
Récitatif, lied et final	Brown, Charles	5
Récitative	Toulon and Brouquières	3
Récit et rondo	Tournier, Franz	5
Récit pour un débutant	Lemaire, Jean	3
Relation	Quérat, Marcel	5
Relax	Baudrier, Emile	3
Réminiscences de Navarre	Barat, Joseph Edouard	5
Résonances	Dachez	3
Le rêve de Jeanne d'Arc	Bleger, Marcel	3
Rêverie et ballade	Mignion, René	3
Rhapsodie	Rivière, Jean-Pierre	3
Rhapsodie	Rueff, Jeanine	3
Rhizome	Nicolas, M.	3
Ricercare	Bitsch, Marcel	3
Rite	Gartenlaub, Odette	3
Le Roi Renaud, varitations	Berthelot, René	3
Romance	Clérisse, Robert	5
Romance en ré mineur	Destanque, Guy	3
Romance	Gotkovsky, Ida	3
Romance	Toulon and Brouquières	3
"Romantic flash"	Barboteu, Georges	5
Rudéral	Joubert, Claude Henry	5
Rupture	Séguin, Pierre	5
Sa majesté le trombone	Duclos, René	3
Sarabande	Gagnebin, Henri	3
Sarabande	Leclair, J.-M.—Goudenhooft	5
Saxhornia	Semler-Collery, Jules	5
Sérénade et ballade mosellanes	Mignion, René	3
Sérénité	Delgiudice, Michel	3
Seringa: Suite dialyséquence	Pichaureau, Claude	5
Serioso	Mihalovici, M.	5
Sicilienne	Bach, J. S.—Rougeron	5
Sicilienne	Rougnon	5

TITLE	COMPOSER	CH
Silences	Rieunier, Jean-Paul	3
Si trombone m'était conté	Dubois, Pierre Max	5
Six esquisses	Porret, Julien	3
Six petites pièces de style	Niverd, Lucien	3
Soliloque	Weber, Alain	5
Solo de concert	Dubois, Théodore	3
‡Solo de concert No. 2	Vidal, Paul	3
Solo de concours	Croce-Spinelli, B.	3
Solo de concours	Nux, Paul V. de la	3
Solo de concours	Wurmser, Lucien	3
Solo de concours en b mineur	Mazellier, Jules	3
Solo de concours No. 15	Porret, Julien	3
Solo de concours No. 16	Porret, Julien	3
Solo de concours No. 29	Porret, Julien	3
Solo de concours No. 30	Porret, Julien	3
Solo de concours No. 31	Porret, Julien	3
Solo de concours No. 32	Porret, Julien	3
Solo de trombone	Pfeiffer, Georges-Jean	3
Sonate	Laburda, Jiří	5
Sonate	Pascal, Claude	3
Sonate concertante	Capdeville, Pierre	3
Sonate en 6 minutes 30	Pascal, Claude	5
Sonate en fa majeur	Albinoni, T.—Goudenhooft	5
Sonate en ré majeur	Albinoni, T.—Goudenhooft	5
Sonate, Op. 5, No. 7	Corelli, A.—Chevaillier	5
Sonate, Op. 87	Martelli, Henri	5
Sonatine (tba/b saxhn)	Castérède, Jacques	5
Sonatine (t trbn)	Castérède, Jacques	3
Sonatine impromptu	Dubois, Pierre Max	3
Sonatine in C	Dondeyne, Désiré	5
Un souffle profond	Desportes, Yvonne	5
Souvenir de Calais	Liagre, Dartagnan	3
‡Spécial	Gabaye, Pierre	3
Stratos	Naulais, Jérôme	5
Suite	Dubois, Pierre Max	3
Suite	Gotkovsky, Ida	5
Suite brève dans le goût classique	Désenclos, Alfred	5
Suite: "Les caractères du trombone"	Guide, Richard de	3
Suite marine	Defaye, Jean-Michel	5
Suite, Op. 83	Martelli, Henri	5
Tendres mélodies	Wurmser, Lucien	3
Thème de concours	Clérisse, Robert	3
Thème et variations	Aubain, Jean	5
Thème et variations	Douay and Gouinguene	3
Thème varié	Bozza, Eugène	5
Thème varié	Casinière, Yves de la	3
Thème varié	Petit, Pierre	5
Le Tombeau de Goya	Tremblot de la Croix, Francine	3
Tournevalse	Durand [-Audard], Pierre	5
Trés sympa trombone	Galliègue and Naulais	3
Triade	Holstein, Jean Paul	5

TITLE	COMPOSER	CH
Trio extrait du deuxieme quatuor	Haydn, Joseph—Delisse	3
Trio, Op. 20	Beethoven—Delisse	3
Trois caricatures	Toulon, Jacques	5
Trois duos	Jolas, Betsy	5
Trois essais	Bozza, Eugène	3
Trois exercises de style	Lemaire, Jean	5
Trois pièces de style	Lafosse, André, ed.	3
Trombonaria	Brouquières, Jean	3
Trombone blues	Sichler, J.	3
Trombone circus	Gouinguene, Christian	3
Trombonera	Boutry, Roger	3
Trombonica	Dachez	3
Trombonite	Delbecq, Laurent	3
Tuba-I	Cecconi, Monic	5
Tuba-abut	Ameller, André	5
Tubabil	Meunier, Gérard	5
Tubabillage	Gabaye, Pierre	5
Tubacchanale	Boutry, Roger	5
Tuba-concert, Op. 69	Ameller, André	5
Tubanova: Solo de concours	Semler-Collery, Jules	5
Tubaria	Brouquières, Jean	5
‡Tubaroque	Boutry, Roger	5
Tuba show	Lodéon, André	5
Tubavardage	Séguin, Pierre	5
Tubissimo	Dondeyne, Désiré	5
Tyrolean Air	Anonymous—Paul Delisse	3
Utah	Ameller, André	3
Valse lente	Rougnon	5
Valse nobile	Clérisse, Robert	5
Valse nostalgie	Rougeron, Philippe	5
Variations	Bigot, Eugène	3
Variétés	Bertholon, L.	3
Le vieux berger raconte	Depelsenaire, Jean-Marie	3
Voce nobile	Clérisse, Robert	5
Volupté	Devogel, J.	3
"Wagenia"	Petit, Pierre	5

Bibliography

Almanach Illustré Chronologique, Historique, Critique et Anecdotique de la Musique, par un Musicien. Paris: A. Ikelmer et C. E., 1866.

Anderson, Paul G., and Larry Bruce Campbell, compilers. *Brass Music Guide: Solo and Study Material in Print.* 1985 edition. Music Guide Series, no. 4. Northfield, IL: The Instrumentalist Company, 1984.

Apel, Willi. *Harvard Dictionary of Music.* 2d ed., revised and enlarged. Cambridge, MA: The Belknap Press of Harvard University Press, 1977.

Arling, Harry J. *Trombone Chamber Music: An Annotated Bibliography.* 2d ed. Brass Research Series, ed. Stephen L. Glover, no. 8. Nashville: The Brass Press, 1983.

Avey, Dennis Hugh, ed. *Brass Players Guide.* North Easton, MA: Robert King Music Sales, Inc., 1993.

Bahr, Edward R. *Trombone/Euphonium Discography.* Stevens Point, WI: Index House, 1988.

Baines, Anthony. *Brass Instruments: Their History and Development.* New York: Charles Scribner's Sons, 1981.

Bate, Philip. "Saxhorn." In *The New Grove Dictionary of Musical Instruments*, ed. Stanley Sadie. New York: Grove's Dictionaries of Music, 1984.

———. *The Trumpet and Trombone: An Outline of Their History, Development and Construction.* 2d ed. Instruments of the Orchestra series. New York: W. W. Norton, 1978.

Bellaman, Joseph C. *Brass Facts: An Outline of Their History, Development and Construction.* 2d ed. New York: W. W. Norton, 1972.

———. *A Survey of Modern Brass Teaching Philosophies of Today's Leading Brass Specialists...* San Antonio, TX: Southern Music Company, 1976.

Bevan, Clifford. "Tuba." In *The New Grove Dictionary of Musical Instruments*, ed. Stanley Sadie. New York: Grove's Dictionaries of Music, 1984.

———. *The Tuba Family.* London: Faber and Faber, Ltd., 1978.

Bibliographie musicale française. Année 1-47 (Nos. 1-192); 1875-January 1920. Scarsdale, NY: Annemarie Schnase, 1968.

Borrel, Eugène. *L'Interpretation de la musique française (de Lully à la Révolution).* New York: AMS Press, 1978.

Bowman, Brian. "New Materials—Euphonium." *T.U.B.A. Journal* 4, no. 3 (Spring/Summer 1977): 8.

Brandon, Stephen Paul. "The French Tuba." *Woodwind World—Brass and Percussion* 15, no. 5 (1976): 38.

Brass Anthology: A Collection of Brass Articles Published in "The Instrumentalist" Magazine from 1946-1986. Anthology Series, no. 3. Evanston, IL: Instrumentalist Company, 1987.

Brevig, Per Andreas. "Avant-garde Techniques in Solo Trombone Music: Problems of Notation and Execution." Ph.D diss., Julliard School, 1971.

Brousse, Joseph. "Le tuba." In *Encyclopédie de la musique et dictionnaire de conservatoire.* 2d pt., vol. 3 (1927). Paris: Delagrave, 1913-1931.

Brown, Leon F. *Handbook of Selected Literature for the Study of Trombone at the University-College Level.* Denton, TX: Leon F. Brown, 1972.

———. "Materials for Tuba." *The Instrumentalist* 10 (November 1955): 37-40.

Bruneau, Alfred. *...la musique française: Rapport sur la musique en France de XIIIe au XXe siècle.* Paris: E. Fasquelle, 1901.

Bull, Storm. *Index to Biographies of Contemporary Composers, Vol. III.* Metuchen, NJ: Scarecrow Press, 1987.

Call, G. K. "Music for Euphonium." *Sounding Brass & the Conductor* 9, no. 3 (1980): 30-31.

Candé, Roland de. *La musique: Histoire, dictionnaire, discographie.* Paris: Éditions du Seuil, 1969.

Carse, Adam. *Musical Wind Instruments.* New York: Da Capo Press, 1965.

Christie, J. M. "Music for Bass Trombone." *The Instrumentalist* 15 (March 1961): 44-45.

Comettant, Jean Pierre Oscar. *La musique, les musiciens et les instruments de musique chez les differents peuples du monde...* Paris: Michel Lévy Frères, 1869.

Le conservatoire national de musique et de déclamation. Paris: Conservatoire National de Musique et de Déclamation, 1930.

Culbertson, Melvin. Interview by J. Mark Thompson, 11 November 1991. Telephone conversation from Iowa City, Iowa to Leognan, France.

Cummings, David M., and Dennis K. McIntire, consultant eds. *International Who's Who in Music and Musicians' Dictionary.* 12th ed. (1990/91). Cambridge, England: Melrose Press, Ltd., 1990.

The Dictionary of Composers. Edited by Charles Osborne. London: The Bodley Head, 1977.

Dictionnaire des musiciens français. Paris: Seghers, 1961.

Douay, Jean. *à propos du...trombone: Pédagogie fondamentale sur l'enseignement du trombone.* Paris: Gérard Billaudot, 1989.

DuFour, Auguste. *Les musiciens la musique et les instruments de musique en savoie, du XIIIe au XIXe siècle.* Genève:Minkoff Reprints, 1972.

Everett, Thomas G. *Annotated Guide to Bass Trombone Literature.* 3d ed. Brass Research Series, ed. Stephen L. Glover, no. 6. Nashville: The Brass Press, 1985.

———. "Solo Literature for the Bass Trombone." *The Instrumentalist* 26 (December 1971): 43-47.

Fasman, Mark J. *Brass Bibliography: Sources on the History, Literature, Pedagogy, Performance, and Acoustics of Brass Instruments.* Bloomington, IN: Indiana University Press, 1990.

Fétis, François. *Biographie universelle des musiciens et bibliographie générale de la musique.* 2d ed. Paris: Firmin Didot Fréres, 1866-70.

Flandril, G. P. A. L. "Le trombone." In *Encyclopédie de lamusique et dictionnaire de conservatoire.* 2d pt., vol. 3 (1927). Paris: Delagrave, 1913-1931.

Flor, Gloria J., ed. "Brass Workshop: The Saxhorn—Past and Present [Heritage Americana Cornet-Saxhorn Brass Band]." *The School Musician* 54 (May 1983): 26-29.

Galpin, Francis W. *A Textbook of European Musical Instruments: Their Origin, History and Character.* New York: J. DeGraff, 1956.

George, Stanley P. "An Annotated Bibliography of Trombone Methods and Study Materials." D.A. diss., University of Northern Colorado, 1982.

Gifford, Robert Marvin, Jr. "A Comprehensive Performance Project in Trombone Literature with an Essay Consisting of a Survey of the Use of the Trombone in Chamber Music with Mixed Instrumentation Composed since 1956." D.M.A. diss., The University of Iowa, 1978.

Gotthold, J. "Reflections sur le trombone basse." *Brass Bulletin—International Brass Chronicle* no. 39 (1982): 49-51.

Gregory, Robin. *The Trombone: The Instrument and Its Music.* New York: Praeger Publishers, Inc., 1973.

Griffiths, John R. *The Low Brass Guide.* Hackensack, NJ: Jerona Music Corporation, 1980.

Hughes, J. E. "An Annotated Listing of Studies for the Bass Trombone." *The Instrumentalist* 36 (August 1981): 54-57.

Kagarice, Vern. *Annotated Guide to Trombone Solos with Band and Orchestra.* Lebanon, IN: Studio P/R, Inc., 1974.

Kagarice, Vern, Leon Brown, Karl Hinterbichler, Milton Stevens, Robert Tennyson, and Irvin Wagner. *Solos for the Student Trombonist.* International Trombone Association Series, no. 8. Nashville: The Brass Press, 1979.

Kleinhammer, Edward. *The Art of Trombone Playing.* Evanston, IL: Summy-Birchard Company, 1963.

Koerselman, Herbert L. "A Comprehensive Performance Project in Trumpet Literature with an Annotated Bibliography of Brass Study Materials Which Deal with Performance Problems Encountered in Contemporary Music." D.M.A. diss., The University of Iowa, 1976.

Lelong, Fernand, and Robert Coutet. "Le tuba en France." *Brass Bulletin—International Brass Chronicle*, no. 13 (1976): 26-35.

Lemke, Jeffrey Jon. "French Tenor Trombone Solo Literature and Pedagogy since 1836." D.M.A. diss., The University of Arizona, 1983.

Lester, Raymond David. "The Emergence of the Bass Trombone in Recent Music Literature." M.A. thesis, California State University (Long Beach), 1981.

Liagra, D. "Le tuba." *Musique & Radio* 47 (1957): 213-14.

Louder, Earle, and David R. Corbin, Jr. *Euphonium Music Guide.* Evanston, IL: The Instrumentalist Company, 1978.

Maldonado, Luis. "Solo Music Literature for Junior High and High School Euphonium and Tuba Performers." *T.U.B.A. Journal* 14, no. 4 (May 1987): 39-41.

Miller, Robert Melvin. "The Concerto and Related Works for Low Brass: A Catalogue of Compositions from c. 1700 to the Present." Ph.D. diss., Washington University, 1974.

Morris, R. Winston. "A Basic Repertoire and Studies for the Serious Tubist." *The Instrumentalist* 27 (February 1973): 33-34.

———. *Tuba Music Guide.* Evanston, IL: The Instrumentalist Company, 1973.

"Music for Bass Trombone." *Sounding Brass & the Conductor* 8, no. 4 (1979): 153.

——. *Sounding Brass & the Conductor* 9, no.2 (1980): 31-32.

Musique de chambre et d'ensemble [Chamber and Ensemble Music Catalog]. Paris: Alphonse Leduc, 1984.

Musique pour trombone [Thematic Catalog for Low Brass Instruments]. 3d ed. Paris: Alphonse Leduc, n.d.

Orchestre [Orchestral Music Catalog]. Paris: Alphonse Leduc, 1974.

Partitions de poche [Orchestral Miniature Scores Catalog]. Paris: Alphonse Leduc, 1981.

Pierre, Constant. *Le conservatoire national de musique et de déclamation: Documents historiques et administratifs recueillis ou reconstitués.* Paris: Imprimerie National, 1900.

Randel, Don Michael. *The New Harvard Dictionary of Music.* Rev. ed. of *Harvard Dictionary of Music*, 2d ed., ed. Willi Apel. Cambridge, MA: The Belknap Press of Harvard University Press, 1986.

Rasmussen, Mary H. *A Teacher's Guide to the Literature of Brass Instruments.* Durham, NH: Appleyard Publications, 1968.

Richardson, William Wells. "Annual Review of Solos and Studies: Trombone and Euphonium." *The Instrumentalist* 37 (January 1983): 52-55.

——. "Annual Review of Solos and Studies: Trombone and Euphonium." *The Instrumentalist* 39 (February 1985): 77-79.

——. "Trombone and Baritone Solos and Study Materials." *The Instrumentalist* 32 (February 1978): 60-61.

——. "Trombone [Annual Review of Solos and Studies]." *The Instrumentalist* 35 (December 1980): 34-36.

——. "Trombone/Baritone [Recent Publications]." *The Instrumentalist* 36 (December 1981): 66-68.

Rodin, J. "Bass Trombone—Perspective." *The School Musician* 47 (May 1976): 20.

Senff, Thomas E. "An Annotated Bibliography of the Unaccompanied Solo Repertoire for Trombone." D.M.A. diss., University of Illinois (Urbana-Champaign), 1976.

Slonimsky, Nicolas, ed. *Baker's Biographical Dictionary of Musicians.* New York: Schirmer Books, 1978.

Stuart, David H. *Songs for Slides: A Course of Study for Trombone.* Ames, IA: Psyclone Music, 1985.

Thompson, John Mark. "An Annotated Bibliography of French Literature for Bass Trombone, Tuba, and Bass Saxhorn Including Solos and Pedagogical Materials." D.M.A. diss., The University of Iowa, 1991.

Trombone, tuba, saxhorns [catalog]. Paris: Alphonse Leduc, 1989.

Tuersot, A. "Le trombone basse." *Musique & Radio* 52 (1961): 291.

Vaillant, Joseph. "The Evolution of the Tuba in France." *T.U.B.A. Journal* 5, no. 3 (Spring/Summer 1978): 17-19.

Weckerlin, J. B. *Bibliothèque du conservatoire national de musique et de déclamation.* Paris: Librairie de Firmin-Didot et Cie., 1885.

Wick, Denis. *Trombone Technique.* Revised ed. London: Oxford University Press, 1980.

Winter, Denis, and David Werden. *Euphonium Music Guide.* 2d ed. New London, CT: Whaling Music Publishers, 1983.

J. MARK THOMPSON is Assistant Professor of Trombone and Low Brass at Stephen F. Austin State University. Formerly Principal Bass Trombone with the Civic Orchestra of Chicago, Dr. Thompson presently performs in that capacity with the Bear Lake Music Festival and the Rapides Symphony Orchestra. A charter life member of the International Trombone Association, he has served on its Publications and Literature Committee since 1989, and his writings have appeared in the *ITA Journal*.

JEFFREY JON LEMKE is Assistant Director of Bands at McNeese State University, where he teaches courses in Music Education and Marching Band Techniques. He is Second Trombone with the Lake Charles Symphony and the Rapides Symphony Orchestra and is active as a guest conductor of concert, marching, and jazz bands throughout the United States.